The Charge of the Heavy Brigade

The Charge of the Heavy Brigade

Scarlett's 300 in the Crimea

M. J. Trow

Pen & Sword
MILITARY

AN IMPRINT OF PEN & SWORD BOOKS LTD.
YORKSHIRE – PHILADELPHIA

First published in Great Britain in 2021 by
Pen & Sword Military
An imprint of
Pen & Sword Books Ltd
Yorkshire - Philadelphia

Copyright © M.J. Trow, 2021

ISBN 978 1 39909 300 2

Printed and bound in England
By CPI (UK) Ltd., Croydon

Pen & Sword Books Ltd. incorporates the Imprints of Pen & Sword Archaeology,
Atlas, Aviation, Battleground, Discovery, Family History, History, Maritime,
Military, Naval, Politics, Railways, Select, Transport, True Crime, Fiction,
Frontline Books, Leo Cooper, Praetorian Press, Seaforth Publishing, Wharncliffe
and White Owl.

For a complete list of Pen & Sword titles please contact

PEN & SWORD BOOKS LIMITED
47 Church Street, Barnsley, South Yorkshire, S70 2AS, England
E-mail: enquiries@pen-and-sword.co.uk
Website: www.pen-and-sword.co.uk

or

PEN AND SWORD BOOKS
1950 Lawrence Rd, Havertown, PA 19083, USA
E-mail: uspen-and-sword@casematepublishers.com
Website: www.penandswordbooks.com

MIX
Paper from
responsible sources
FSC® C013604

Contents

Acknowledgements

My sincere thanks to all who have contributed to the making of this book: my commissioning editor Heather Williams and her team at Pen and Sword; Gaynor Haliday for her excellent proofreading and editorial skills; various individuals and institutions who have given me permission to use images; and, most of all, as always, to my wife Carol, my constant companion of a mile.

Author's Note

At various points in this book, sums of money are mentioned and instead of inserting the value of it today, which is difficult to do and not always accurate in the context, I decided to fill in a little background detail here, so that the amounts are shown relative to the likely financial position of the person involved.

In the mid-1850s, an agricultural labourer earned 10s a week; they are usually quoted as the lowest earners, mainly because they worked such long hours and had to find their own food and living from this wage. Others earned less, but had 'all found', such as servants in big houses who had literally no outgoings from their smaller wage. Compared with agricultural labourers, navvies were the best paid, sometimes earning as much as £2 a week – on the other hand, though, their work was dangerous and their living conditions atrocious. An infantry soldier in this period would earn 1s a day, a cavalryman 1s 6d; they had to pay for meals, but only a token amount. They also had other expenses, outlined later.

Food, at a basic level, was affordable even on the lowest wage, with the ubiquitous 'penny loaf' getting larger or smaller depending on harvests and with beer at 1d for two pints, it was not hard to get drunk. Ironically, milk was a little more expensive. A suit of clothes – not something everyone would have aspired to – would cost £2 or thereabouts. Rent of a small house – the typical worker's cottage – was around 1s 6d a week and for anyone able to consider buying, a small house outside of London would cost £150, a larger family home £500 or even more if it was in a desirable area.

Purchases of commission mentioned in this book are more difficult to 'cost' as, obviously, the person making such a purchase would not be on a wage at all but would have family money. It would depend, therefore, what the size of the family estate might be, where in the family hierarchy the purchaser stood and a number of other factors. However, when a horse costs more than a house, it does put that into perspective. When the winter came in the Crimea and personal belongings such as gloves sold for an ordinary soldier's monthly pay, when a compulsory round of drinks equalled three days' pay, it is easy to see that, despite much lower prices, life was not necessarily any more affordable then than now.

Maps

The Seat of War 1854–6

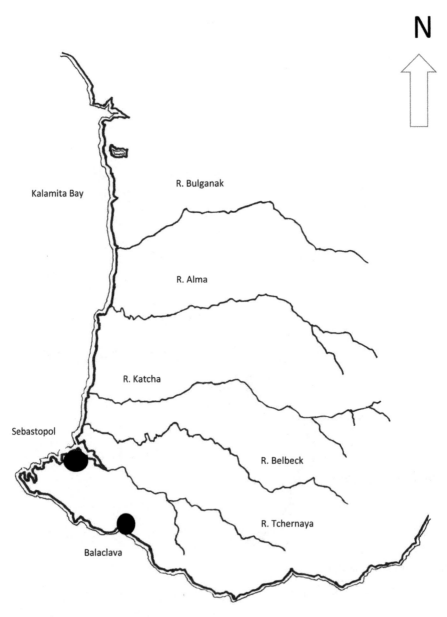

War Zone, South West Crimea

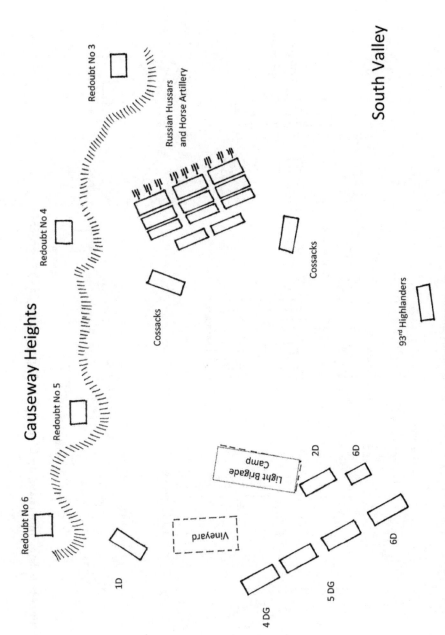

Battle of Balaclava, second phase; the Charge of the Heavy Brigade, 25 October 1854

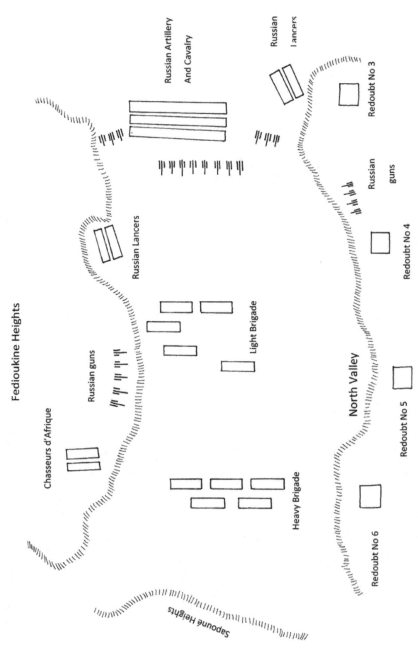

Battle of Balaclava, third phase, the Charge of the Light Brigade, 25 October 1854

Prologue
The Lost Brigade

'Lost are the gallant three hundred of Scarlett's Brigade!'
Alfred, Lord Tennyson, 1882

In the summer that I left school, the most expensive film ever made opened at the Odeon, Leicester Square. It was called *The Charge of the Light Brigade*, a Woodfall/United Artists production and immediately became my favourite historical movie, which it remains to this day. The story sees the cavalry action at Balaclava in October 1854 through the prism of one of the ten regiments involved – Lord Cardigan's 11th Hussars.

The film had its origin with Cecil Woodham-Smith's *The Reason Why*, published to great acclaim in 1957. This was one of those books that capture the imagination of a generation, but Mrs Woodham-Smith's central argument – that the Light Brigade was lost because of an ongoing feud between brothers-in-law Cardigan and Lucan, commanding the Light Brigade and the Cavalry Division respectively – was plain wrong. An examination of the events of 25 October 1854 shows that this irascible pair actually behaved perfectly civilly to each other; the causes of the Light Brigade disaster are much more complex.

The film's plot line follows Captain Louis Nolan (David Hemmings) as he joins the 11th Hussars from India. In fact, the real Nolan served in the 15th Hussars and in the Crimea was one of General Airey's staff officers. He quickly falls foul of the commanding officer, Lord Cardigan (played brilliantly by Trevor Howard) and the real tensions that existed among the officers of the 11th are played out before the unit is ordered to 'sharpen' for the Crimea.

We have the glaring contrast between the social classes in mid-nineteenth-century England. The officers with their sumptuously dressed wives dance at Lady Scarlett's ball, while the randy old generals swap smutty remarks about them. The Other Ranks are shown as scruffy labourers, enlisting because of the lure of the 'queen's shilling'. They do not know their left from their right, they cannot ride and they are hosed down from the barracks pump before being given their uniforms. They live in the squalor of an upstairs room of the stables, with the stench of horse urine seeping through the floor, but at least it is a better life than that of a farm labourer straight out of the 'hungry forties'.

My personal gripe about the 1968 film – and the point of this section of this book – is the disappearance of the Heavy Brigade. For the record, there were three phases of the battle of Balaclava which will be discussed in detail later. First was the stand of the Highlanders under General Colin Campbell, which came to be known as the 'thin red line'. Second was the focus of this book, the charge of the Heavy Cavalry Brigade. And the third was the charge of the Light Brigade. Whereas the first two were successful – and brilliant examples of British guts and knowhow – the third was a pointless disaster. In the film, the Heavy Brigade is hinted at throughout because the lavish officers' ball takes place at Lady Scarlett's town house in London. Her husband, James Yorke Scarlett (Leo Britt), who led the Brigade at Balaclava, appears later with a cluster of senior officers at the War Office. Nobody quite knows what is going on or even exactly where the Crimea is, least of all Scarlett, who grumbles 'Sebastopol? I don't want any damned Sebastopol', presumably because he is hoping to march on Moscow or St Petersburg. The next time we see him, he is at the head of his Heavies (incorrectly dressed in dark blue, as opposed to scarlet, uniforms) annoyed because the cavalry was not used at the battle of the Alma on 20 September 1854. In fact, they were not even in the Crimea at the time.

The irony is that Tony Richardson *did* film the charge of the Heavy Brigade (see plate section) but it ended up on the cutting room floor.

Richardson himself admitted, in his autobiography *Long Distance Runner: a Memoir* (1992) that he was a 'fanatical cutter'.

We have to accept that cinema audiences get less sophisticated the further back in time we go. The plot of the 1936 Errol Flynn version is pure Hollywood. As C.A. Lejeune wrote, 'This scene [the charge] may be villainous history, but it is magnificent cinema.' But where is the Heavy Brigade? Again, nowhere. Scarlett is not in the cast list; neither do we even see his men formed up on the battlefield. There is, ironically, one reference to the Brigade and it is accurate. The Heavies, says an order from Lord Raglan, the commander-in-chief, will support the Lights – such an order was, indeed, given. But in all the dash and fire before the Light Brigade sets off on its fatal charge, the moment is lost.

One of the men who briefly owned the rights to Mrs Woodham-Smith's *The Reason Why* was British film producer Michael Balcon. He had produced an earlier version still (in 1928) for the Gainsborough Studios, called *Balaclava*, one of the last of the silent era's films. It ran for an impressive one hour and twelve minutes. Because of its timing, there was a closer link with reality than any later movie; Edwin Hughes, of the 13th Light Dragoons, had died in the previous year, the last survivor of the Light Brigade. The named cast was small, with Oxford graduate J. Fisher White as Lord Raglan and Harold Huth, who had himself reached the rank of major in the First World War, as Nolan. The story line took us far beyond the remit of the army, however. Lord Palmerston, the prime minister who took control of the chaos in 1855, is there, as is Queen Victoria and Prince Albert. The lead was taken by Cyril McLaglen, younger brother of the much better known Victor, later a stalwart of John Wayne cavalry westerns.

The Americans had an earlier crack at Balaclava in 1912, while several members of both cavalry brigades were still alive. J. Searle Dawley directed for the Edison Studios and the film still survives as an eleven-minuter (originally sixteen minutes) with accompanying piano-led music score. The cards flashed up onto the screen are the stanzas of Tennyson's epic poem, which also appeared over the charge itself in the 1936 version. The whole thing, except for the opening scene, was filmed in Wyoming. The nearby cavalry base at Fort D.A. Russell provided 800 troopers and their mounts – more than the actual Light Brigade – at a time before the American army became mechanised.

The most moving tribute, however, came from T. Harrison Roberts, a Fleet Street journalist who set up a fund with the aid of the Balaclava Commemoration Society for survivors of the Light Brigade charge. The last recipient of the Roberts fund died in September 1920 and the fund died with him. He was extraordinarily kind to the 1912 filmmakers when he wrote, 'The faithful portraits of the leaders – Raglan, Cardigan and Nolan ... and the completeness of the whole presentment renders this to me the most marvellous motion-picture I have ever seen.'

But the 1912 film had no reference to the Heavy Brigade; neither did the otherwise generous and philanthropic Mr Roberts include them in his fundraising.

Nearly seventy years before that first film, Alfred Tennyson, the Poet Laureate, wrote his immortal *The Charge of the Light Brigade*. George Orwell, in *The Lion and the Unicorn* in 1940, wrote:

> English literature ... is full of battle poems, but it is worth noticing that the ones that have won themselves a kind of popularity are always tales of disasters and retreats ... The most stirring battle-poem in English is about a brigade of cavalry which charged in the wrong direction.

> Half a league, half a league,
> Half a league onward,
> All in the valley of Death
> Rode the six hundred.
> 'Forward, the Light Brigade!
> Charge for the guns!' he said:

Into the valley of Death
Rode the six hundred.

****

When can their glory fade?
O the wild charge they made!
All the world wonder'd.
Honour the charge they made!
Honour the Light Brigade,
Noble six hundred!

These epic stanzas, with their repetitive phrases and hypnotic rhythm, hinting at some appalling mistake overcome by the everlasting glory of Cardigan's '600', captured the imagination of the world and do so even today, even after far worse military blunders have happened and casualty rates have soared. Tennyson was at Farringford, his home in the Isle of Wight, when he read *The Times*' report of the charge, as described by William Russell, the war correspondent. The new telegraph system in the Crimea had yet to be completed, so it was weeks before Britain heard the news. *The Times*' article appeared in mid-November and Tennyson wrote the lines on 2 December.

To be fair to Russell, in his despatches he described the action of the Heavy Brigade in as much detail as that of the Lights, but nobody rushed into print with a poem about that until 1882, when a much older Tennyson was persuaded by a friend to write a sort of sequel (or should it be prequel?) to the Light Brigade poem. The moment had gone; the poet's fire had faded and *The Charge of the Heavy Brigade* is not a patch on the earlier effort.

The charge of the gallant three hundred, the Heavy Brigade!
Down the hill, down the hill, thousands of Russians,
Thousands of horsemen, drew to the valley—and stay'd;
For Scarlett and Scarlett's three hundred were riding by

When the points of the Russian lances arose in the sky;
And he call'd, 'Left wheel into line!' and they wheel'd and obey'd.
Then he look'd at the host that had halted he knew not why,
And he turn'd half round, and he bade his trumpeter sound
To the charge, and he rode on ahead, as he waved his blade
To the gallant three hundred whose glory will never die–
'Follow,' and up the hill, up the hill, up the hill,
Follow'd the Heavy Brigade.

The trumpet, the gallop, the charge, and the might of the fight!
Thousands of horsemen had gather'd there on the height,
With a wing push'd out to the left and a wing to the right,
And who shall escape if they close? but he dash'd up alone
Thro' the great gray slope of men,
Sway'd his sabre, and held his own
Like an Englishman there and then.
All in a moment follow'd with force
Three that were next in their fiery course,
Wedged themselves in between horse and horse,
Fought for their lives in the narrow gap they had made–
Four amid thousands! and up the hill, up the hill,
Gallopt the gallant three hundred, the Heavy Brigade.

Fell like a cannon-shot,
Burst like a thunderbolt,
Crash'd like a hurricane,
Broke thro' the mass from below,
Drove thro' the midst of the foe,
Plunged up and down, to and fro,
Rode flashing blow upon blow,
Brave Inniskillens and Greys
Whirling their sabres in circles of light!
And some of us, all in amaze,

Who were held for a while from the fight,
And were only standing at gaze,
When the dark-muffled Russian crowd
Folded its wings from the left and the right,
And roll'd them around like a cloud,–
O, mad for the charge and the battle were we,
When our own good redcoats sank from sight,
Like drops of blood in a dark-gray sea,
And we turn'd to each other, whispering, all dismay'd,
'Lost are the gallant three hundred of Scarlett's Brigade!'

'Lost one and all' were the words
Mutter'd in our dismay;
But they rode like victors and lords
Thro' the forest of lances and swords
In the heart of the Russian hordes,
They rode, or they stood at bay–
Struck with the sword-hand and slew,
Down with the bridle-hand drew
The foe from the saddle and threw
Underfoot there in the fray–
Ranged like a storm or stood like a rock
In the wave of a stormy day;
Till suddenly shock upon shock
Stagger'd the mass from without,
Drove it in wild disarray,
For our men gallopt up with a cheer and a shout,
And the foeman surged, and waver'd, and reel'd
Up the hill, up the hill, up the hill, out of the field,
And over the brow and away.

Glory to each and to all, and the charge that they made!
Glory to all the three hundred, and all the Brigade!

To sum up the 'loss' of the Heavy Brigade: we have the physical removal of them from the 1968 film; the single verbal mention in the 1936 version; the complete avoidance in 1912. In poetry, they only receive a belated second billing after the Tennysonian masterpiece of 1854. And all this must be seen in the context of an engagement which was not only breathlessly daring, but actually (unlike the Light Brigade) successful.

This book seeks to redress a woeful imbalance. In 1896, Rudyard Kipling, outraged at the way old soldiers were routinely neglected by the government, wrote movingly of the survivors of Balaclava – 'Our children's children are lisping "to honour the Light Brigade".'

But no one has really honoured the Heavy Brigade.

Until now.

Chapter 1

The War That Would Not Boil

O n the roof of the church of the Holy Sepulchre in Jerusalem stands a little wooden ladder. It was put there over 150 years ago and cannot be moved for the same reason that the great powers went to war in the Crimea. The Holy Sepulchre, actually the Church of the Resurrection, was built by the Roman emperor Constantine in the fourth century, on what was believed to be the site of the original tomb of Christ on the slopes of the hill at Calvary. The circular building called the Anastasia was destroyed by the Seljuk Turks in 1009 and was rebuilt by Christian crusaders from the west – in a sense the spiritual forebears of the Cavalry Division sent to the 'seat of war' in 1854. The current restored version is shared by the Coptic church, the Armenians and the Syrians, as well as the Catholic Church based in Rome. All of them today claim either the notorious ladder or the ledge on which it stands, meaning that no one can move it.

'Protection of the holy places' was the official cause of the Crimean War. By the middle of the nineteenth century, Christ had been hijacked and thoroughly westernised by Europeans. The disciple James had, according to legend, centuries before, morphed into Santiago, who had sailed to Spain in a stone boat. The Virgin Mary had been sighted at various shrines throughout France. Joseph of Arimathea was Christ's uncle and had brought his nephew with him to England, where he had planted a thorn bush at Glastonbury. Umpteen Victorian paintings of the New Testament portray Jesus as a blue-eyed, auburn-haired Englishman; he was probably the product of a minor public school!

Despite this centuries-old willingness to claim Christianity as a local, European idea, there were other, more practical considerations involved. The powers that be in the 1850s could claim a spiritual cause célèbre, the tired old chestnut of the just war, but everyone knew that the real reason for the Crimean War was naked politics.

From 1793, the armies of Revolutionary France, and all they stood for, had torn Europe apart. The French did their best to annihilate the *ancien régime* which had stood for a thousand years. The French monarchy was overthrown. The Catholic calendar, with its saints' days, its Christmas and its Easter, was torn up and replaced with a Republican version based largely on the weather, so that August, the hottest month, became Thermidor. The aristocracy fled in the face of quasi-legal tribunals and the threat of the guillotine, taking to any country that would have them, tales of terror. The most terrifying aspect of the post-Revolutionary period was the astonishing success of the reformed French army; when that army came to be led by arguably the finest general of his – and several other – generations, the *ancien régime* looked doomed.

Fast forward to 1815. After umpteen coalitions and a great deal of blood and expense, Napoleon was finally defeated at Waterloo and the Congress of Vienna was set up to restore some kind of *ancien régime* sanity to a shell-shocked Europe. Perhaps inevitably, the pendulum of realpolitik swung too far back. The winners at Vienna – Britain, Austro-Hungary, Prussia and Russia – imposed a rigidity on politics to ensure that another Napoleon could never rise. They also, because that is the nature of war-winners, grabbed as much territory as they could.

The problem was that the French Revolution had unleashed ideologies that did not fit into the outdated eighteenth-century concepts of imperial government. Liberalism and nationalism were uneasy bedfellows, but they found common ground in opposing the old tyrants of the *ancien régime* who were, miraculously after 1815, still there. The tsar still lorded it over 'all the Russias' in a despotic, semi-Medieval state where serfdom and abject poverty were the norms. The emperor of Austria-Hungary still attempted to hold together a leaking ship that extended from Vienna to the wild, lawless states of the Balkans. The Sultan, in his legendary city of the Golden Horn, Constantinople, still ruled a vast empire that straddled Europe and Asia with a government so incompetent that Turkey was known as 'the sick man of Europe'.

In these domains, democracy was a joke. The people were yoked to centuries of tradition, yet, surely and steadily, they were demanding change. Having upset the whole apple cart in 1789, the French found that they had a taste for revolution, taking to the streets again in 1830 and yet again in 1848. In Russia, a cohort of young Guardsmen in the tsar's own entourage, became the Decembrists in 1825, demanding an upper- and middle-class government to replace the tsar's autocracy. The Year of Revolutions, 1848, saw armed riots occurring everywhere, from Paris, through Vienna, to Berlin and St Petersburg.

Britain, of course, was different! Here, the 'revolution' of 1848 focused on the Chartists, working men who wanted a six-point charter granting, in effect, power to the people. But the supposed 5 million-signature petition demanding change that was given to parliament in that year, contained fewer than 2 million names; and among these were 'Victoria Rex', 'Pugnose', 'Big Ears' and no less than four versions of the signature of that arch anti-reformer, the Duke of Wellington. When a mass demonstration drew up on Kennington Common in South London, the police outnumbered the protesters.

This was because Britain's path towards imperialism was taking an altogether different direction. By the mid-century, Britain already had the largest empire in the world and that was to grow still further fifty years later. But that empire was entirely overseas. Having lost the American colonies in the War of Independence, Britain concentrated on Canada, Australia, New Zealand and, above all, India, which became, in the cliché of the time, the jewel in the imperial crown. The 'scramble for Africa' would come later. Today, among the chattering classes, British imperialism is a dirty word, ignoring the civilising effect of British control on societies that routinely advocated slavery, female genital mutilation and widow-burning. At the same time, Britain advocated liberty and democracy, being alone among the great powers (other than France) with a truly democratic parliamentary system, albeit a limited one before 1928, when women, as well as men, were given the vote.

Given that the British empire was so far-flung and did not involve the Middle East at that time, squabbles over who controlled the holy places were seen as largely irrelevant. What did concern Britain – and this turned into a phobia by 1854 – was the threat of the Russian bear.

By western European standards, Russia was hopelessly backward. The tiny Medieval kingdom of Muscovy had grown vast by the nineteenth century, largely as the result of the westernisation programme of Tsar Peter the Great and the menacing expansionism of his successors. The growth of industrialisation, world trade, shipping, the railways and advances in medicine and public health, had largely passed Russia by. It would not abolish the Medieval concept of serfdom until after the Crimean War, in 1861, and even then the condition of the peasantry remained economically appalling. Even as late as 1900, the death rate in Russia from disease and starvation was terrifying. Eighty-three per cent of the adult British population was literate, as compared with 28 per cent in Russia. The tsar's empire was the only one in Europe not to have a constitution or a truly national parliament.

What Russia *could* do – and did with vehemence under Nicholas I – was to act as the policeman of Europe and punish would-be offenders. He sent in the army to crush a Polish rebellion in 1830; another in Romania in 1848; a third in Hungary a year later. Basing its power on its rigid autocracy and the rather dubious claim that it had defeated Napoleon in 1812–13, Nicholas's Russia threw its weight around and threatened expansion to the south, which brought it into a headlong clash with the Ottoman empire of the Turks. There was nothing new in this. Catherine the Great had annexed the Crimea in 1783. Alexander I had taken Bessarabia in 1812 and Nicholas himself the Danube delta in 1829. One man who watched his army do it because he commanded a cavalry squadron there, was George Bingham, an officer in the 17th Lancers, who, by the time of the Crimea, was Lord Lucan, commanding the Cavalry Division.

The problem, clear to everybody in the corridors of power, was the 'sick man of Europe'. The 'sublime porte', as the Sultan's government was called, was anything but. The greatest military power on earth in the fifteenth and sixteenth centuries was now a pale imitation of its former self. The porte was trying to hold together a vast territory of Muslims and Christians, ethnic groups from Magyars to Anatolians – and it was not doing very well.

The Congress of Vienna had made much of the balance of power, a political concept of which the rather smug British approved. No one country must be allowed to dominate another, but in the case of Russia and Turkey, this is exactly what was happening. Most British people had no knowledge of Russia at all – it might just as well have been on the far side of the moon. There was, as yet, no link between British and Russian royal families and even though the two countries had been allies against Napoleon, there had never been an occasion for their armies to appear on the same battlefield. Among senior politicians and cabinet ministers at Whitehall, virtually the only one who spoke Russian was the 'terrible Milord', Palmerston; and that skill was considered bizarre.

The prime minister who so badly handled the beginning of the Crimean War was George Hamilton Gordon, the 4th Earl of Aberdeen. Educated, as most politicians were, at a public school (Harrow) and Cambridge University, he had danced gavottes and slogged through mountains of paperwork at the Congress of Vienna as British ambassador to Austria. He sat in the arch-reactionary Tory government of the Duke of Wellington at the end of the 1820s and became Foreign Secretary, a post he took up again under Robert Peel in 1841. A skilled diplomat, Aberdeen did a great deal to establish a working relationship with the old enemy, France, and handled the Oregon Treaty of 1846 which established the 49th Parallel as the frontier between the United States and British Canada. With Peel's fall, effectively over the contentious Corn Laws in that year, Aberdeen became the recognised leader of the party. A free trader and highly experienced, he became prime minister in December 1852.

Whether Aberdeen was actually a pacifist is debatable, but his natural diplomatic tendencies led him to see the Turko-Russian stand-off in the light of arbitration. As happened so often in the nineteenth century, 'our man' on the spot had different ideas. Stratford Canning, 1st Viscount de Redcliffe, had a diplomatic 'history' with Russia. In 1833, when he was given the post of ambassador to St Petersburg, Nicholas refused to meet him. Canning's attitude was decidedly anti-Russia by 1842 when he got the Constantinople post and the 'great Elchi' as the Turks called him, resisted Nicholas's offer to protect Orthodox Christians in the Ottoman Empire.

The Turkish government officially turned down the tsar's offer of involvement, which was seen for what it was, a naked act of aggrandisement, in May 1853 and in reprisal, Nicholas ordered his troops into Moldavia and Wallachia – Turkish vassal states – two months later. The porte, unwisely, declared war and the Turkish fleet was seriously battered by the new Russian ironclads at Sinope in November.

A furious round of diplomacy now ensued, de Redcliffe keen to bolster the Turks' position, Aberdeen looking for a compromise. In the meantime, the issue of the protection of the holy places took centre stage, France championing the Catholic Church's claims and Russia that of the Orthodox Church.

Endlessly poring over the maps in Whitehall, the mandarins there, including the Horse Guards (War Office) and the Admiralty, could see at a glance what the problem was. If the Russian bear knocked out 'poor little Turkey', the way was open to the eastern Mediterranean and the British overland route to India. The Russians already had a sizeable naval base at Sebastopol in the Crimea. All they had to do was to cross the Black Sea, seen as a glorified Russian lake, sail through the straits of the Dardanelles and they would be in the Aegean. From there, it was only a few days' voyage to Egypt and the desert crossing to the Red Sea, which led, in turn, to the Indian Ocean. At all costs, this Russian expansion to the south-west must not be allowed to happen.

Accordingly, Britain and France both declared war on Russia on 27 March 1854, making them allies for the first time in nearly a thousand years; that, in itself, was going to cause potential problems in the future.

The satirical magazine *Punch or the London Charivari* made much of this new alliance. 'Our volume,' the editor wrote, 'Mr Punch's Twenty-Seventh … shall be sent, an alliance-offering, to the people of France.' As always, *Punch* was marvellously tongue-in-cheek – 'And thus was England and France bound together, with nothing but good fellowship and give and take jest and good humour … And as it is in 1854, so may it ever be!' Throughout the year, the magazine featured accounts 'from the seat of war', written by 'our very own Bashi-Bozouk', a reference to the roguish (and wholly unreliable) Turkish light cavalry. There was a whole plethora of weak jokes at the expense of 'Old Nick' (the tsar) and the vacillation of Aberdeen, whose heart seemed not to be in a war at all.

J.H. Stocqueler, writing a history of the British army in 1871, saw it, as most Englishmen did, in terms of black and white: 'The Czar … addressed [his people] in the language most calculated to stimulate their zeal – "England and France have taken up the cause of Turkey; [they] have ranged themselves by the side of the enemies of Christianity" – thus turning the whole thing into an old-fashioned crusade.'

But the Turks checked the Russians at Silistria – 'The Turkish soldiers were not deficient in a wild courage strengthened by religious fanaticism.' And they were led by Omar Pasha, 'a German' Stocqueler calls him. In fact, he was a Croatian Moslem convert, whose real name was Mihajlo Latas. Every British soldier who saw or met him was impressed. Captain Nigel Kingscote, ADC (aide-de-camp) to the commander-in-chief, Lord Raglan, wrote, 'He is a capital fellow. Quite different to the Turks in general, hates all display … He is a sporting looking fellow and sits well on his horse in a plain grey frock coat and long jack boots; he is very fond of horses' – which, of course, endeared him to the whole officer class.

Stocqueler is more interested in the advance British contingent, 4,000 strong, which was sent out to stiffen the Turks. No one believed that the Turkish army could hold out by themselves, but gallant officers like Colonel Cannon of the Honourable East India Company and Captains Nasmyth and Butler, made all the difference. The writer had a rather rose-tinted view of the men about to be sent to the East:

> Education and the Reform Bill had wrought an important metamorphosis in the character of the British soldier – he had become a thinking member of society and cared to know 'the reason why' when the Government deemed it necessary that he should take the field against a political enemy.

Apart from jumping the gun a little by referring to Tennyson's 'reason why', the Reform Bill of 1832 had made no difference at all to the average 'Ranker'. It had doubled the electorate, but the voting qualification still depended on the ownership of property and that excluded virtually all of them. Similarly, improvements to education were severely limited to the Sunday and Board schools. There was no Education Act until 1870 and no compulsory attendance until several years after that. According to Helen Rappaport, in *No Place for Ladies: the Untold Story of Women in the Crimean War*, a fifth of the army was illiterate and a higher percentage still could only write their name. For example, Private Joseph Tagg, who rode the charge of the Heavy Brigade with the 5th Dragoon Guards, had five good conduct medals, but he 'signed' his name with an 'X' on his discharge. Understanding complex politics was beyond men like him. And they knew virtually nothing of Russia; ironically, the Russian exhibit bound for the Great Exhibition at Hyde Park's Crystal Palace in 1851, which some of them may have attended, never turned up!

Victoria's government, as well as that of the Austrian emperor, Franz Josef; the king of Prussia, Wilhelm; the French emperor, Napoleon III had all urged the tsar to reconsider his action against the Turks, but he refused. Negotiations dragged on throughout the spring and summer and as Nicholas became ever more entrenched and stubborn, especially as the Turks were more than holding their own, a mood of Russophobia gripped Britain which Aberdeen and the queen could not contain. Because of her parentage and her marriage (her mother and husband were both German) Victoria had an unusually European outlook, which contrasted with that of the majority of her subjects.

By that time, the two armed camps were in place. Each of the five powers – Britain, France, Austria, Prussia and Piedmont – had their own agendas and their own reasons for reining in Russian ambitions. Britain was concerned with the tsar's southern expansion, especially now that British protectorates of Malta, Corfu and the Ionian islands gave her a real toe-hold in the Mediterranean. France had a commercial interest in the Levant and a long history of friendship with the Sultan; in addition, Napoleon III, anxious to emulate his formidable uncle, the first emperor, was looking for a successful war to wage. The little kingdom of Piedmont was in effect Sardinia and it had ambitions above its size by 1854 to spearhead a move towards Italian unification, which would not become a reality for seven years. Two Piedmontese officers were to ride behind Lord Cardigan in the charge of the Light Brigade. Prussia, in effect, took no part in the war. The move towards a united Germany was already underway but Otto von Bismarck was not yet its leading light. Consolidation and reform were the issues in Prussia, but it was still in her interests to curb any possible westward expansion by the tsar. The Austrian empire had been dominated until 1848 by the arch-reactionary cynic Count Metternich, but the 'coachman of Europe' had been overthrown in the Year of Revolutions and the Austrian empire was a hotbed of intrigue and dissent, especially among the Balkan states. The Austrians saw themselves, rather than the Prussians, as the natural leaders of 'Germany'. They were also opposed to the Turks who had been their natural enemies for three centuries. In the event, like Prussia, Austria effectively watched the events of 1854 from the sidelines.

The opening moves of the war, in April and May, were confined to naval manoeuvres. The British navy at the time was second to none.

A squadron had destroyed the Turkish fleet in Navarino Bay in 1827 and when a British subject, Don Pacifico, asked Lord Palmerston to intervene in 1850 in a quarrel he had with the Greek government, Palmerston sent the fleet! Don Pacifico was quickly recompensed without a shot being fired. Engagements such as the bombardment of Svenborg and Kronstadt were ongoing even as the tsar drew his troops out of Wallachia and Moldavia. It was too little, too late, as Britain's declaration of war in March led to a momentum of its own.

Lord Clarendon, Foreign Secretary under Aberdeen, wrote: 'We are not now engaged in the Eastern Question [the term would not go away until at least 1915] but in the battle of civilization against barbarism ...' Henry V's knights at Agincourt and Harold Godwinson's housecarls at Hastings would probably have expressed broadly similar sentiments. Diplomacy had not worked. Neither, for all the reputation of the British navy, had the arrival of armed paddle-steamers as far as the Black Sea. Now, it was time for regiments to 'sharpen', as it was called in the cavalry and, as Lord Raglan, the 70-year-old commander put it, 'the finest army ever to leave the shores of England' was underway.

The problem was that very few of them had any idea why they were going, still less where. The war had been bubbling on the stove now for months, but it resolutely refused to boil. Various individuals responded in different ways, as is always the case with the men actually tasked with fighting a war. Edward Cooper Hodge, commanding officer of the 4th Dragoon Guards, was pessimistic. In his diary for 14 March, he wrote:

> Received the orders. Now begins a life of neither profit nor pleasure. I expect no more peace, comfort or happiness in this world. I will however do my duty to the utmost of my power and I humbly pray to God to give me health and strength to fulfil my calling.

George Maude, a captain with the Royal Horse Artillery, had read the *Gazette* of senior officers who had been given key appointments. 'There is an old commander-in-chief, an old engineer, old brigadiers – in fact everything old at the top. This makes everything sluggish.'

Ten days before, there had been a sumptuous dinner at Boodle's, one of London's snobbiest gentleman's clubs. The *United Services Gazette* recorded that, with military luminaries like the Duke of Cambridge and Lord Cardigan present, 'the subject of the approaching struggle with Russia was of course alluded to, always with cheers and in hopeful and confident terms.' All of it washed down, no doubt, with copious amounts of champagne!

Back in late February, Henry Aldworth Neville, of the Grenadier Guards, whose little brother Grey was with the 5th Dragoon Guards, wrote to his father: 'I am greatly buoyed up by the hope of seeing you all, well and safe, in the course of a year or eighteen months at the most. They talk, indeed, of our being back by the winter.' Like another, later and far bloodier war, it would all be over by Christmas.

Because of the pattern of literacy in the army, virtually all the letters and diaries that have survived from the Crimea were written by officers. Other Ranks' memoirs are usually shorter, devoid of any emotion and tend to stick to the facts. So, as a typical example, Troop Sergeant Major (TSM) Henry Franks of the 5th Dragoon Guards wrote: 'In the beginning of 1854 we were stationed at Ballincolig, and from there we went to Turkey.'

He would have much more to say later.

Chapter 2

'A Bloody War on a Sickly Season'

The British army of 1854 had not fought a European war for nearly forty years. It was composed of the cavalry, the infantry, the artillery and a variety of auxiliary corps. It was about the same size as today's army, but, because of the rapidly growing empire, was spread out literally around the world.

The officer class of the cavalry, the focus of this chapter, were, almost exclusively, gentlemen, following the Duke of Wellington's precept that the safety of Britain lay in the hands of such men as the natural defenders of queen and country. It was taken for granted that such men were natural leaders. Horsemen and riders to hounds, they took five-barred gates in their stride and had been giving orders to underlings since before they could ride.

Most of them were the product of the public schools; a few were taught at home, first by governesses, then by tutors. The majority of the officers of the five regiments of the Heavy Brigade attended Eton, Harrow or Rugby and although it was not the raison d'être of these institutions, the regimes there fitted boys well for a career in the army. As 'fags' in the Lower School, they ran errands for the older pupils. As prefects in the sixth form, they gave orders and doled out punishments, including flogging with a cane. In that sense, army life was less harsh in that officers were not flogged. The institutional bullying in these schools made men of boys, fitting them for command and authority in their chosen paths. Those who could not take it were deemed failures. At Rugby, the reforming headmaster, Thomas Arnold, not only broadened the ludicrously narrow Classical curriculum to include modern history, mathematics and languages but controlled the violence of 'boy government' by making his prefects personally responsible to him, reporting to him every day. Slowly, Arnold's system of creating what he called 'Christian gentlemen' spread to other schools, but it is difficult to gauge how far this had any effect on the officers of the Heavy Brigade. One officer who certainly benefited directly was Captain Samuel Toosey Williams of the Scots Greys. *Our Heroes of the Crimea*, published in 1855 by George Ryan, includes the fact that 'Williams was educated at Rugby under Dr Arnold …'

Colonel Edward Hodge was taught at Dr Pearson's school in East Sheen until he was 12. His father had been killed at Waterloo; his body was never found. Pearson's was a preparatory school, where the basics would have been taught before Hodge went off to Eton in 1822. Here, because of his short stature (even as an adult, he was less than 5ft 2in tall), he was a cox for the rowing team. Another Etonian, several years younger than Hodge, was Richard Temple Godman, adjutant to the 5th Dragoon Guards. He was a gifted artist, like several officers in the Crimea, but it is doubtful that he was encouraged in that skill at school. He does not mention Eton anywhere in his diary or letters home, probably because schooldays must have seemed largely irrelevant and because the public schools were boarding institutions, often miles from the family home and the family experience.

Several of the officers of the Heavy Brigade joined the army directly from school, but a few attended university. Again, Oxford and Cambridge predominated because this was the pattern for gentlemen's sons. Neither university was at its academic best in these years. Most of the courses offered merely continued the Classical education of the schools and if we can believe the words of Cornet Edward Fisher of the 4th Dragoon Guards once they were in the Crimea, 'We are uncommon jolly here. You never saw such good living,' he wrote to his parents. He *may* have been being ironic or else he wanted his parents not to worry about him. Alternatively, his time at Magdalene College, Cambridge, may have been awful!

In these Medieval universities, college servants cooked, cleaned, laundered and directed mail, exactly as the undergraduate's family servants did at home. In the Crimea, every officer had at least one servant, who doubled as groom and batman, doing his best in difficult conditions to keep animals fed and watered and kit serviceable and clean. For example, Cornet the Honourable Grey Neville had Private James Orr as his servant. Temple Godman had Private Joseph Kilbourne. The man was painted by John Fearnley at Newbridge Barracks, Ireland, in 1852, holding the reins of Godman's charger, the Earl. He appeared again, this time with Godman, in April 1855:

> The Photograph man [Roger Fenton] has taken a picture of our camp, the officers and men standing about, but my hut does not come in well. He has also taken me and my horse (in fighting costume) and Kilburn, the latter likeness is excellent, when I can tell you where to go in London for copies, as many as you please at 5s each.

In the Cambridge colleges and probably at Oxford too, daily attendance in chapel was compulsory. The arrival of Prince Albert as vice-chancellor of Cambridge shook the place up. He was a serious academic, but a thoroughly modern reformer and oversaw the extension of the college curriculum to include philosophy, anatomy, law, chemistry, biology and botany. Even so, the social life of rich young gentlemen at both universities continued unimpeded. They played cards and put on lavish parties, both in the colleges and their respective towns. Breakfasts included ham, chops and pigeon pie. For the Cambridge men in particular, regular trips to the Newmarket racecourse were the norm, as was attendance at bare-knuckle fist-fights.

After that, what sort of career beckoned to young men of this social class? There was a general tendency to follow in father's footsteps, be it politics, the armed forces or the church. Business was out of the question because it smacked of 'trade' which was a sordid word to the aristocracy and gentry. Lieutenant Colonel Thomas Le Marchant, commanding the 5th Dragoon Guards, was the son of John Gaspar

Le Marchant, the Channel Islander who had designed the 1796 pattern Light Cavalry sword and had been killed at Salamanca in 1812. Hodge, as we have seen, was the son of a major killed at Waterloo three years later. James Mouat, surgeon to the 6th Inniskilling Dragoons, was the son of a surgeon to no less than five infantry and two cavalry regiments throughout his career.

But whether a university graduate was going to join the army as the next generation of an established family or whether this was an adventure in a totally new direction, there were formal steps that had to be taken to join. What very rarely happened as early as this was enlistment in the junior department of Sandhurst. This had been set up at High Wycombe in Buckinghamshire in 1801, the brainchild of the Le Marchant who fell at Salamanca. The Royal Military College was set up to fill a gaping void. When Arthur Wellesley, the future Duke of Wellington, joined the army, there was no training ground in Britain and he had to go to France to find one. The move to the village of Sandhurst had taken place in 1822 and the idea was that the juniors, having passed a written examination in arcane matters like practical geometry, trigonometry and mensuration, as well as field fortifications, algebra and 'fortresse', would graduate to the senior department and qualify as staff officers. This was undoubtedly a good career move, but the majority of young men wanted action and adventure, not to end up as a glorified secretary to some stuffy old windbag of a general. Accordingly, most young hopefuls ignored Sandhurst altogether and flicked through the pages of the *London Gazette*.

This was the official list of vacancies in the various army regiments and in the cavalry and infantry; the only means of joining was the purchase of a commission. This system had been laid down in the reign of Queen Anne, but the costs were prohibitive. In 1854, a cornetcy in the Heavy Cavalry (Dragoon Guards and Dragoons) cost £840. Cornet was the most junior rank in a cavalry regiment, later second lieutenant, and originally the cornet had carried the regiment's flag into battle. The annual pay was £50. The thinking behind the purchase system was to find the ablest and 'best' men to officer the army and to guard against military insurrection. Wealthy men of the landowning classes who had bought their ranks were less likely to lead a 1789-style revolution than the lower orders who relied on the pittance paid to them by an ungrateful government. There would be no officer-led rising in Britain like that of the Decembrists in Russia. But the British system was also iniquitous and continued the amateur tradition which would dog the army long after purchase was abolished in 1871. Highly competent officers without the necessary funds may have remained cornets all their working careers, while renowned idiots like James Brudenell, the Earl of Cardigan, rocketed to generalships on the strength of their obscene wealth.

From cornet, the next stop was to lieutenant, which in 1854 cost £1,190. If there was no vacancy, a man might 'exchange', rather as professional footballers do today, into another regiment. At this level, the annual pay was not much more than a cornet's. A captaincy, whereby a man commanded a troop, was far more expensive – £3,225 – and it carried an annual salary of £190. As a major, an officer led a squadron (two or more troops combined) which would hit him with a bill of £4,575. His annual income? £270. The highest rank a gentleman could reach by purchase was lieutenant colonel, at which point, like Hodge of the 4th, Le Marchant of the 5th, Henry Darby Griffith of the 1st Dragoons, Clarke of the Scots Greys and Dalrymple White of the Inniskillings, he commanded a regiment. This would cost a staggering £6,175 and the annual rate of pay was £364. Even this was not the end of it. Such was the prestige of some regiments, especially in the Guards regiments and the cavalry generally, that huge over-regulation prices were paid. Lord Cardigan paid a rumoured £35,000 for the command of the 15th Hussars and over £40,000 for the 11th.

Because commissions were the private property of officers, there was a great deal of clogging within regiments. This explains the title of this chapter; it was a common toast in the mess of cavalry regiments, among men who knew that vacancies were only likely to occur because of death in action or by disease.

But the prohibitive expense of being a cavalry officer did not end there. There was the little matter of uniform, horses and mess bills. Early in Victoria's reign, an officer of the 7th Hussars (Light Cavalry) was riding in escort behind the queen's carriage when the heavens opened in a downpour. His uniform was ruined, his plume destroyed, the fur of his busby draped over his shoulders. And, to add insult to injury, his charger caught a cold and died some days later. Compensation from Her Majesty? None.

Just as the business of buying and selling commissions was handled by an agent – Cox and Co were the most popular – so a variety of tailors, in Savile Row and St James's, provided the complex range of uniforms and accoutrements to make the officers of Her Majesty's armed forces look splendid. Officers' uniforms after 1815 had become ludicrously flamboyant with yards of gold lace, tassels and buttons. They were also increasingly tight, making mounting and dismounting difficult, especially in the Light Cavalry.

The most recent description of officers' clothing was printed in 1846 and was still in use eight years later. Commanding officers were allowed some leeway, but there could be no deviation from established norms. The painting by Francis Grant, currently in the museum of the 5th Dragoon Guards, however, shows General Scarlett wearing a non-regulation helmet and no one seems to have complained. There were a number of orders of dress – review, marching, field day, mounted drill, riding school, horse parade, court, full dress, stable dress, dress for town and dress off duty – all requiring various subtleties.

All the Heavy regiments wore gilt helmets (brass for the men) with horsehair plumes. The exception – and the army was full of little historical inconsistencies – was the 2nd Dragoons, the Scots Greys, who wore bearskin caps of grenadier style. Drawings made in the Crimea by the French general, Vanson, show very little difference in the uniform of these regiments because they are not in colour. All regiments of the Heavies wore scarlet jackets (properly called coatees), worn short to the waist, differentiated by their facing colour (collars and cuffs). In full dress, officers wore expensive epaulettes, embroidered with the regimental badge and the jackets themselves had 'swallow tails' at the back, a vestige of the much longer eighteenth-century uniform. A typical depiction of the Heavy uniform for officers is the painting in the National Army Museum of an officer of the 5th Dragoon Guards. He is wearing his pouch belt, decorated with regimental pattern gold lace and the pouch itself – nominally for holding pistol balls – hung in the small of his back. He wears a gold sash at his waist, with dangling tassels and carries an 1834 pattern Heavy Cavalry sword with its distinctive 'honeysuckle' pattern hilt. The blade was slightly curved and was designed essentially as a thrusting weapon. At the Horse Guards in Whitehall where such decisions were made, arguments raged for a hundred years as to whether thrusting or slashing was the best attack for a cavalryman. Under the officer's arm, he carries the 1849 'Albert' pattern helmet. Prince Albert took a keen interest in army matters and several of the changes about to take place in uniform were under his auspices. One of the most pointless – and elaborate – accoutrements carried by an officer was the sabretache (sword pocket) which, decorated with regimental cyphers, hung from three slings from the sword belt. It was used to carry orders.

In the field, of course, much of this finery was left at home, as various photographs in the Crimea make clear. It is unlikely that the Heavies took their plumes with them and officers carried plain black leather sabretaches. Likewise, horse equipment was simplified. The embroidered *shabracques* worn over saddles were left in store too, the ubiquitous black lambskin covering the leather to make riding as comfortable as possible. All Heavy regiments were given 'booted' overalls, leather inserts on the inside of each leg up to the crotch, which again took the discomfort out of frequent mounting and dismounting, especially in wet weather. The 5th Dragoon Guards, according to Assistant-Surgeon William Cattell, left their epaulettes at Hansen's Bank in Constantinople.

Most officers owned at least two horses and took them to the Crimea with them. Captain Louis Nolan of the 15th Hussars, an acknowledged cavalry expert, was given the task of finding suitable horseflesh in Turkey before the campaign began in earnest. He was disappointed by the result, so the army reluctantly made the decision to transport animals from Britain. Officers' horses were invariably called chargers and they were expensive thoroughbreds, the peculiarly English breed descended from native stock and Arab stallions, like the Darley Arabian and the Byerley Turk, imported in the late seventeenth century. Such animals were routinely sixteen hands high, towering over the shaggy ponies of the Russian Cossacks, and had the stamina for long marches in intense heat as well as the ability to leap obstacles such as five-barred gates (in hunting) and cannon (as at Balaclava).

Louis Nolan could train a troop horse in sixty-four days (it routinely took ten months) by banging drums and firing pistols near them. The natural tendency of these animals was to follow the herd instinct and cling closely to the horses on either side of them. This would prove highly dangerous in the Light Brigade's return from the guns at Balaclava. It is difficult to know how far Nolan's 'system' was used in the cavalry. Lord George Paget, commanding the 4th Light Dragoons and himself the son of a famous cavalry commander, the Earl of Uxbridge, wrote that Nolan was 'an officer ... who writes books and was a great man in his own estimation'. Neither is it easy to gauge the preparedness of officers' mounts for active service, especially if a man had not been with his regiment for long.

All officers had to be proficient at the complex drill movements of the parade ground and it was important that they were seen at the head of their individual troops as role models for the men. Actual preparation for war was limited. Only at the Curragh and Phoenix Park in Ireland was there room for several regiments to carry out manoeuvres in brigades. In June 1853, long before the Crimea became the focus of the government, a camp was set up at Chobham Ridges in Surrey, where an estimated 8,000 men could take part in 'war games'. Of the regiments told to 'sharpen' for the Crimea, only the Scots Greys and the Inniskillings had taken part by the time the fleet sailed.

Each regiment was divided into six or eight troops, each commanded by a captain. These were clumped together in battle formation into three or four squadrons, led by a major or sometimes a lieutenant colonel. A depot troop was left behind to train recruits in the event of a regiment being sent overseas. Each regiment had its own paymaster, a quartermaster (responsible for supplies), two surgeons, a schoolmaster and a veterinary officer. The hierarchy of these officers is fascinating. In Hart's Army List, the official documentation of officers of all regiments, the paymaster is listed first, above the surgeons and veterinary officers who were vital for the regiment's existence. The paymaster, by comparison, was someone who could add up! There is no official mention of the schoolmaster at all.

All these men, even the doctors, were expected to master the round of drills and would probably be called upon to fight. There was the column, the direct echelon, oblique echelon, pivot, attack and charge, all of them directed by bugle calls. The pace of movement was walk, march, trot and gallop, from under four miles an hour to eleven. Such formations were complex enough for the infantry but having to factor in horses made life much more difficult.

There is no doubt that officers' messes in the cavalry were appallingly snobbish places. An officer had to behave like a gentleman, wearing the correct items of uniform, drinking the right sort of wine and holding cutlery in a certain way. The infamous 'black bottle' incident when Lord Cardigan accused one of his officers, John Reynolds, of drinking porter ale at a regimental dinner, reached the national press, making a laughing stock of both Cardigan and his regiment, the 11th Hussars.

But Le Marchant was nearly as bad. TSM Henry Franks recorded, on the 5th's march to Devna:

> [Le Marchant] seemed quite unable to control himself and he upbraided the officers … in language so very unusual on a military parade, that it certainly astonished every one who heard it and he finished his address by … saying 'I am so disgusted with the paltry sentence of twenty-five lashes [given to a private] that I won't go to the trouble of having you tied up; many a schoolboy has got more than that.'

Le Marchant was so furious with his regiment that he threatened first to report them to Sir George Brown, who commanded an infantry division and had nothing to do with the cavalry at all, and then to have the 5th sent home! The extent to which vicious mess politics was not only ugly but routine was borne out by two incidents after the war. In 1862, Captain Arthur Robertson of the 4th Dragoon Guards was court-martialled for 'conduct unbecoming an officer and a gentleman'. This was army-speak for an unpopular officer being 'got at' by his brother officers. Robertson had insulted Colonel Dickson and when the latter offered to fight a duel with him, Robertson refused. Despite the fact that duelling had been illegal in Britain for over 200 years, it was Robertson who was deemed to be the transgressor. He was, according to The Times of 27 March, 'teased, bullied and persecuted until he can hold out no longer'. Since the original insult had been given two years earlier at the Army and Navy Club in London and since Robertson had not gone through proper channels to report the incident, he was found guilty and cashiered. The queen, however, on the advice of the judge advocate general, effectively overturned the verdict.

In the same year, all hell was let loose in the scandal at Mhow, an army barracks in India. A junior officer of the Inniskillings, Richard Renshaw, had brought his wife out with him, as would become more common after the creation of the Raj, but Mrs Renshaw had recently been Mrs Tourle, in the centre of a very messy and public divorce that filled the London papers. Such everyday events today were anathema to the uptight officers of a cavalry regiment and two armed camps formed in the mess – pro- and anti-Renshaw. The kindly old colonel who had ridden the charge with the regiment, Charles Shute, had recently moved on, to be replaced by T.R. Crawley of the 15th Hussars. He blundered into this hotbed of intrigue knowing nothing about it, and the bickering that resulted led to open warfare in the mess and court martials for Crawley and other officers involved. The whole sorry affair cost the country £18,378.

There was one group of officers whose situation was peculiar and that was men elevated without purchase from the ranks and those with specific, generally unmilitary, duties. Colonel Hodge himself had been given a commission in the 13th Light Dragoons free of charge as a 17-year-old because of the loyal career of his father, killed at Waterloo. This was probably unique in the Heavy Brigade, but promotion from the rank of regimental sergeant major was more common. It happened usually for valour in the field, but it created fish out of water. Such appointees were not fully accepted by titled officers because of the gap in social rank. Neither could they still be regarded by their old comrades as equals. And the strain of paying for uniforms and horses, as well as covering mess bills, must have seemed intolerable.

One glaring example was Archibald Weir of the Inniskillings. Involved in the affair at Mhow, a devastating account of him was given by Charles Shute, his former commanding officer:

> Captain Weir has too well succeeded in sowing a vast amount of dissention amongst the staff of the regiment to which he owes everything, and in which, from being an indifferent RSM and a very moderate adjutant, he has risen in the ranks to be, in only six years, a captain without purchase.

Astonishingly, Weir actually commanded the 6th for six weeks before Crawley arrived.

'Paymaster, Duberly, paymaster? That ain't a rank, that's a trade' is the famous line delivered by Trevor Howard's Lord Cardigan in *The Charge of the Light Brigade* and it is fiction. Duberly was not in Cardigan's old regiment and the men must barely have known each other. Even so, the attitude was typical of snobs like Cardigan who had never had to stand in line like the men and 'uncover' to receive a week's pay in his life. The paymaster had at least one orderly to help hand out the cash.

Regimental surgeons and veterinary officers probably had a higher status in their fellow officers' lives, especially when, as in the Crimea, they were called upon to save lives. The extraordinary thing is the number of them who actually rode the charge of the Heavy Brigade, exposing themselves to injury or death and for whom there was no replacement. James Mouat was a case in point. Of an army medical family, he was educated at University College, London and became a member of the College of Surgeons in 1837. He had served with the 44th Foot before transferring to the Inniskillings and won the newly instituted Victoria Cross because of his gallantry on 25 October. Following up the charge of the Light Brigade as the Heavies were, he came across a badly wounded staff officer, his head pouring with blood. This was Captain William Morris who led the 17th Lancers that day and a Russian lance had fractured his skull. Coolly, under fire the whole time, Mouat, watched over by Sergeant Charles Wooden of the 17th, patched Morris's head, stopping a haemorrhage and saving the man's life. In the process, to defend himself, Mouat had to draw his sword, which he found 'a novel experience'.

Mouat was clearly a character. Someone who worked under him referred to his faultless dress, 'whether in uniform or in mufti'. He had 'a very sharp tongue' and was 'formidable in dispute'. He was 'the only … medical officer [I] can recall who made his camp inspections in a well-appointed carriage and pair'.

Assistant-Surgeon William Cattell was another example of a man who took his job seriously. A keen botanist, he collected plants from the Crimean plains when he had time, of which he probably had little. He almost certainly rode the charge, and that was after weeks of work trying to cope with cholera. As TSM Franks wrote: 'Dr Cattell ... was for three successive nights in the hospital tents and it was a miracle how he kept on his feet as during all that time he scarcely got any sleep. He was the kindest of men ...'

'When the Earl of Cardigan,' wrote George Ryan in *Our Heroes of the Crimea* in 1855, 'was ordered to the East in command of our light cavalry, from club to pothouse marvelled how he would behave. Their remembrance of him satisfied all that he had a taste for gunpowder, but they had no experience of how he could wield a sword.'

And that applied to all the officers of the cavalry. Most of them had never seen action before, from General Scarlett to the newest cornet who would ride behind him across the 'valley of Death' at Balaclava. And what even the contemporary George Ryan did not realise, was that the Crimea was a new kind of war, different from any that had gone before.

The mere wielding of a sword would not be enough.

Chapter 3

'Going for a Soldier'

William Robertson holds a unique place in British history. He was the only man before the Second World War to rise through the ranks of the army from the very bottom to the very top. He enlisted in the 16th Lancers in 1877 and became a field marshal by 1920. I hope his mother lived to be proud of him, because she certainly was not when he enlisted. Despite the defeat of Napoleon and the valour displayed in the Crimea and the Indian Mutiny, 'going for a soldier' was a shameful thing for mothers like Mrs Robertson and she was distraught.

Whereas officers bought their commissions because it was seen as an honourable thing to do for queen and country, Other Ranks joined because army life seemed marginally the best of any other option. Most of the rank and file of Scarlett's Heavy Brigade in the Crimea enlisted in the 1840s, a decade known as 'the hungry forties' to social historians today. The free trade policies of Prime Minister Robert Peel and the rapid growth of railway mania were about to pull Britain out of a grim recession, but that took time; and men facing the workhouse saw the army as a means of escape.

Most of the Heavy Brigade gave their occupation in their enlistment papers as 'labourer', but there were other examples. James Brodie of the Scots Greys was a ploughman; John Benison of the 4th Dragoon Guards was a tile-cutter; John Crofts of the 5th was a gardener; William Blackwell of the Inniskillings was a grocer. Most of them were tied to the land, working often on a squire's estates from dawn till sunset at various times of the year, especially harvest. William Hancox of the 4th Dragoon Guards was a case in point. A farm labourer from the village of Bubbenhall in Warwickshire, he would have lived with his parents and siblings in one of the tiny, grim cottages there and perhaps worked on the estates of the Murcott or Grimes families who were the major landowners in the area. Perhaps seeking adventure – or perhaps lured by the flash of the queen's shilling – he enlisted at Coventry on 10 April 1851. He was 19 years and 6 months old, about average for recruits. He was six feet tall, with a fresh complexion, grey eyes and brown hair, with no marks or scars on his body. He had no educational attainments (there was no school in the village until 1864) but could probably write, at least his own name. As Joseph Pardoe, who became a troop sergeant major by the time of the Heavy Brigade's charge wrote: 'I had little schooling, but did learn to read and write and this stood me in good stead, for when I was 23 years old, I fancied a soldier's life ...'

Hancox's recruitment would have gone something like this. In Coventry, where he may have been selling food or livestock at the town's market, he would have been intrigued by the recruiting party, especially the 'bringer', usually a sergeant, no doubt a tall man in scarlet with gold stripes on his sleeve. It was drinks all round for likely lads while the bringer told tall tales of the regiment's glory. The Royal Irish, as they were known at the time, were raised as the Earl of Arran's Regiment of Horse in 1685, to put down the rebellion of the pretender, the Duke of Monmouth. This was not a history lesson, but a list of the dash and fire of a regiment looking for fresh blood. Steenkirk and Landen, neither of which William Hancox would have heard of, became the regiment's first battle honours, in wars against Louis XIV's France. By the middle of the eighteenth century, the regiment was known as the Blue Horse because of the colour of its facings and shortly afterwards, recruiting took place in Ireland. They were now the Dragoon Guards, a matter of pride in their superiority over mere Dragoons and they fought under the future Duke of Wellington in the Peninsula. The regiment's motto was *Quis Separabit*, which the bringer explained meant 'who shall separate us?' and the harp, the crown and the star of St Patrick were embroidered on their battle honours. The stories flowed along with the beer and when Hancox took the queen's shilling, he had automatically signed his life away for twenty years. If he survived, he would be in his forties by the time the army let him go, with dubious skills under his belt and no guarantee of a pension.

The general tendency among commanding officers of regiments was to prefer rural recruits over 'townies'. Robert Peel's early police force had followed the same policy; there was something unsoldierly about urban artisans – they were unhealthy and more politically aware, perhaps, than their country cousins, more likely to be trouble. When the 4th Dragoon Guards sailed for the Crimea three years after Hancox joined, the average height of the men was 5ft 8¼in – so they would have all towered over Colonel Hodge. Their average weight was 11 stone 4lb and their average age 25 years and 7 months. There were 210 Englishmen, 213 Irishmen and 30 Scotsmen. Welshmen would have been lumped in with the English, in that Wales had officially been part of England since 1536. Two hundred and seventy-nine of them were Anglican, 140 were Catholic (exclusively the Irish contingent) and 34 were Presbyterians.

From the Coventry pothouse where Hancox took his shilling, he was marched, still in his labourer's smock with its unique Warwickshire stitching, across to Liverpool, where a steamer would have taken the new men to Kingston in Ireland where the regiment was based. This was almost certainly the first time that William Hancox would have seen the sea or travelled by ship or set foot on Irish soil. The only Irishmen he may have seen were the navvies, employed on the canals – and, increasingly, the railways – of Warwickshire.

Henry Franks had enlisted in the 5th Princess of Wales's Dragoon Guards at Nottingham twelve years before Hancox joined the 4th. His regiment took no one under 5ft 10in tall, adding to the legend of 'big men on big horses' which stayed with the Heavies throughout the century. Franks enlisted on a Saturday and the next day was given a bed in the barracks and was sworn in on the Monday. 'I had been led to believe by the Corporal who had given me the Queen's shilling, that a soldier's life was all "beer and skittles".' He quickly found out that it was not. The bounty, the sum of money promised to augment the shilling, the traditional daily pay of a soldier (in the cavalry, it was slightly more) was a straightforward bribe. In 1831, Alexander Somerville, joining the Scots Greys, was given £2 12s 6d as bounty. He only actually got 10 shillings and with that he had to buy no less than thirty-eight items which were deemed essential for a cavalry soldier. These included uniform items such as a forage cap, a leather stock (to be worn at all times around the neck), shirts, socks, gloves and 'necessaries' (underpants). Then there were the essentials for the horse – brushes and combs, a nosebag, saddle cloth, saddle bags and sponges (for the animal's nostrils). A recruit also had to buy an account book of printed army regulations, whether he could read it or not. In the 1840s, the average bounty was £6 17s 6d; his costs added up to £8 3s 7½d. The shortfall was borrowed, probably from a man's troop commander, and repaid in instalments from his pay. Looking at this financial situation and the gap between officers' pay and the purchase price of their promotions, it can be seen that the government was ripping off its soldiers at every level. Yet they still expected men to die for them.

The makeup of recruits in cavalry regiments, allowing for the 'Celtic fringe' of Irishmen and Scots, was standard. They were over 16 and under 30 – apprentices, colliers, 'stragglers' and vagrants were not allowed.

The first experience of many recruits was an army haircut, a close cropping which appears nowhere in films like *The Charge of the Light Brigade*, so that an army man could be recognised easily should he try to desert. There were 'incorrigible rogues' who deserted as soon as they got the bounty, to enlist in another regiment and start all over again. Deserters (for whatever reason or for however long) had the letter 'D' branded on their foreheads until the 1830s. One man tried the trick eighteen times before he was caught and hanged. William Lucas, who joined the 7th Dragoon Guards in 1845 described what followed the haircut – 'I was sent to Riding School to learn the Art of Equitation and many were the falls I received before I could manage it … We got very bad rations …' Part of the bounty went as pay for the regiment's riding master, usually a junior officer or senior NCO who ran a small, elite group of 'rough-riders', men who broke and trained horses.

On the parade ground, men like Hancox, Somerville and Lucas had to master the manoeuvres that the officers did, at the same time remembering to keep their backs straight (the stock helped) and to wear their stirrups long in the cavalry tradition. Even men who could ride already were re-trained in the army style, virtually standing in the stirrups with legs straight. Manuals of the time compared the 'seat', bizarrely, as 'like sugar tongs astride a wall'.

Concern for a man's horse was far more important than the man himself and various individuals in a troop were also made grooms to officers, so they had at least two horses to look after, probably more. In the Heavies, we have already come across Private Kilbourne who worked for Temple Godman. Irascible masters, like Colonel Hodge, got through a whole succession of servants in a matter of weeks.

There were no dress regulations for Other Ranks, but uniforms were decided upon and rigidly laid down by the Consolidated Board of General Officers, meeting regularly at the Horse Guards in Whitehall. By a government warrant of July 1848, clothing, necessaries and accoutrements were listed, including cost and regularity of replacement. The Albert pattern helmet, a simpler brass version of the officers' pattern, was replaced every four years. The full dress jacket, an undress uniform and a pair of overalls (trousers) were to be worn for two years. Twenty-nine items had to be neatly stored under or around the bed of each man in barracks or in the stables nearby. In many such barracks, the sleeping quarters were built above the stables, to save space, so the ammonia smell of horse urine constantly seeped up through the floorboards. The heavier gear known as accoutrements, which included all belts, hooks and carbine ammunition, was to last anything from ten to eighteen years. In the field, haversacks, water canteens and cooking pots were added to the list.

As with the officers, the soldiers of the Heavy Brigade looked very similar to each other, the exception, as always, being the bearskins of the Scots Greys. The brass shoulder scales, stitched to the jacket, gave some protection from sword cuts, but oddly, they were not worn in the Crimea. Trumpeters, farriers (in charge of horses under the veterinary officer) and all ranks from corporal to regimental sergeant major wore embroidered badges on their sleeves. The undress version consisted of a circular forage cap and stable jacket, the overalls, like those of the officers, fitted with buckled straps to be fastened under the boot.

Because there are no Dress Regulations for this period, information has to be gleaned from photographs and drawings, as well as the rare survival of the accoutrements themselves. A pouch with twenty rounds of ammunition for the carbine was suspended from a white buff leather belt worn over the left shoulder. All leather equipment had to be kept supple and 'blancoed' to keep it white, which was a full-time job in itself. The waist-belt, complete with regimentally cyphered brass buckle, was two inches wide, but the sabretache was not carried by the Heavies. The belt had a cap-pouch for extra ammunition; in some regiments, this was stitched to the jacket.

In marching order, whenever the regiment was on the move, be it at home or overseas, all Other Ranks carried a semi-circular mess-tin in a haversack, as well as a circular wooden water canteen holding half a gallon. These were painted blue for all regiments, with a broad arrow and B.O. (Board of Ordnance) on the front. They were appallingly unhygienic and the water in them quickly became undrinkable.

Horse equipment was standard, the saddle a modification of the traditional hunting variety with fans and bars to keep it steady on the horse's back and to hang equipment from. This gear was not regularly replaced. A saddle was expected to last for fourteen years, girth, surcingle and crupper for nine. Stirrup irons had a life expectancy of twenty years; stirrup leathers, nine. Bridles were to last as long as saddles. Valentine Baker, who reached the Crimea as a captain in the 10th Hussars towards the end of the war was the acknowledged expert who replaced Nolan: 'Ordinary saddles never get out of order and are easily cleaned, and why a dragoon's should be such a complication of moveable straps and buckles, pilches, etc. all made … like a Chinese puzzle, has ever been beyond my comprehension.'

A new cavalry recruit, sometimes referred to as 'Johnny Raw', was taught sword exercise on foot at first. Draw, carry, slope and defence were based on the 1796 regulations drawn up by John Le Marchant. There were seven attack thrusts and seven for defence, one involving swinging the weapon *behind* a soldier, which was extraordinarily difficult. Several survivors of both cavalry charges at Balaclava complained that the Russians were not using the same cuts as they were! When a regimental surgeon was tending one of the Heavy Brigade and asked him how he got his wound, he said, 'I had just cut five at the Russian and the damned fool never guarded at all, but hit me over the head.' At Balaclava, some of the Heavies' swords could not pierce the Russian greatcoats, whereas the Brigade was badly cut up. One private of the 4th Dragoon Guards had fifteen head wounds, but they were all only skin deep. The Other Ranks' sword came into service in 1830, with a hatchet point, a slight curve to the blade and a solid steel bowl to protect the hand.

Sergeants and above were issued with pistols. While officers bought their own, usually expensive new revolvers like the .36 calibre Navy Colt or Deane Adams, the NCOs were issued with musket-bore barrelled versions, nine inches long; they were exceptionally difficult to cock, fire and reload, to the extent that they were rarely used. The carbine was the Victoria pattern, clipped to the pouch belt with a swivel hook. This was twenty-six inches long and was the product of ten years' deliberations as to efficiency by George Lovell, Inspector of Small Arms.

The daily rations for the men of the Heavy Brigade left a lot to be desired. Fixed in 1813, they consisted of three-quarters of a pound of beef and a pound of bread. This was called 'Tommy' and was black or brown, often badly baked and sticky. Sixpence a day was stopped from the men's wages for the two meals a day provided. There were rarely cooks in peace time. The famous cook-house of the 8th Hussars photographed by Fenton in the Crimea, was run, as we shall see, by women. Accordingly, most troops rotated the cooking, producing beef stew called 'skilly'. This was little better than prisoners received at the time and nowhere near the relative haute cuisine enjoyed by railway navvies, who earned nearly three times a soldier's wages. Coppers were provided for cooking and after 1840 a third meal was made obligatory and the men were allowed to choose their own local butchers and bakers. 'Buck' Adams, who enlisted in the 7th Dragoon Guards in 1843, remembered his first meal in the Other Ranks mess. It consisted of boiled meat, soup and a hunk of bread. As was the regimental custom, everybody at his table gave him a potato, until he had forty of them on his plate! In return, Adams was obliged to treat the others at the regiment's canteen, buying beer and tobacco. In less than ten minutes, they had cleaned him out to the tune of half a crown, the equivalent of two days' wages.

One of the first experiences that Henry Franks had when he joined the 5th was a flogging. It was his first morning and he had not yet even been given his uniform. He followed everybody else to form hollow square. 'In their midst stood as fine a specimen of manhood as ever wore Her Majesty's uniform – a young fellow of about twenty-three years of age.' The man had hit a sergeant and the court martial he faced, presided over by the colonel, decided on a punishment of 100 lashes. This was given with a leather-thonged whip with nine 'tails', known as the 'cat' and it was delivered in this case by two trumpeters and two farriers with twenty-five lashes each. The victim was tied by his wrists to the triangle, a portable frame shaped like a capital letter A and a leather pad was rammed into his mouth so that he did not chew his tongue in his agony. 'He took the punishment,' wrote Franks, 'without moving a muscle of his face.'

One man who felt every touch of those nine 'tails' was Alexander Somerville. It has to be said that Somerville was a most unusual soldier – literate, articulate and political. In that sense, he was every officer's worst nightmare, particularly as he joined the Greys at the height of civil disturbance over the forthcoming Reform Bill. Agitators had let ordinary working men believe that they would get the vote – this would not happen finally until 1918. When the Scots Greys were ordered to 'aid the civil power' by controlling crowds, Somerville wrote to the local newspaper, saying that the regiment would not draw its swords against the people. A private soldier had no right to make this statement – in fact, it was unprecedented. Somerville was set up – he was given a fractious horse to ride and when he could not, he was court-martialled and sentenced to 200 lashes.

> I felt an astonishing sensation between the shoulders, under my neck, which went to my toe nails in one direction, my finger nails in another and stung me to the heart, as if a knife had gone through my body ... He [the farrier carrying out the punishment] came on a second time a few inches lower and then I thought the former stroke was sweet and agreeable compared with that one ... and he came on somewhere about the right shoulder blade.

At each stroke, a sergeant major called out the number. 'I felt my flesh quiver in every nerve, from the scalp of my head to my toe nails.' When Somerville heard 'five' he knew he had only reached 'the fortieth part of what I would get'. At twenty-five, the farrier stood back and a young trumpeter took over. 'He then gave me them [the blows] upon the blistered and swollen places where [the farrier] had been practising. The pain in my lungs was now severe' but Somerville resolved that 'I would die before I utter a complaint or a groan ... I almost choked and became black in the face'. The farrier took over again and seemed to be slowing down, until an officer barked, 'Farrier Simpson, do your duty.'

At a hundred lashes, half the sentence, the colonel ordered a halt. 'Stop, take him down, he is a young soldier.' Wet towels were draped over his back and his jacket laid on them. In the barracks hospital, his torn flesh was covered with a lotion of some kind and after six days he was back on duty. Using simple mental arithmetic, Somerville worked out that the individual tails had hit him with 5,400 separate wounds. His skin erupted in boils later, which Somerville took to be a good sign. A beating like this could cause internal complications, as in the case of Frederick White, a 7th Hussar, who had been flogged at Hounslow in 1846. He died as a result of his beating and the case hit the national press. What upset middle England, however, was not White's death, but the fact that Lord Cardigan, who had given out the punishment, had done it on Palm Sunday!

The crimes of which soldiers could be found guilty were many and varied. Mutiny and desertion could carry the death penalty, as did striking superior officers, plundering, burglary with violence, sodomy, child abuse, rape and, bizarrely, 'riotously *beginning* to demolish a house'. Many of these were regarded as serious crimes in the civilian community too, and in the army they probably stemmed from Wellington's attempt to keep his men in check during the Peninsular War. For centuries, it was tradition for commanders to let their troops loose on a town once it had been taken. Wellington hanged men for such misbehaviour. The ease with which various officers resigned their commissions in the Crimea, however, and simply went home, shone a spotlight on the precise definition of desertion. In the case of Lieutenant Colonel Le Marchant, as we shall see, he was *very* lucky to escape censure.

'Being touched over' (army slang for flogging) was merely an extension of the beatings that officers had undergone at their public schools and was not far removed from the belts applied at home by the fathers of the Other Ranks. More than a thousand lashes could not be given by law after 1807, but twenty-five to one hundred remained the norm until corporal punishment was abolished in 1868. Intriguingly, it continued at various public schools until well into the twentieth century.

Minor infringements, such as a dirty carbine barrel, unpolished spurs or a badly made bed, led to 'taps' (an offender's name being called out from dawn to dusk on the parade ground). Then there was 'gagging' (drinking salt water), trotting round the parade ground on foot with full marching pack and carbine, being placed in the stocks or a dark confined space called 'the black hole'.

For drunkenness, which was easily the most common infringement in the barracks, the result was usually demotion to the ranks for an NCO, which would mean loss of immediate status and pension. Ironically, spirits and beer (called 'pongolo' by the men) were available at all hours in the regimental canteen, whereas tea and coffee were in short supply. Pay days were usually staggered to prevent too many men having too much small change at the same time, with the inevitable result. Libraries were becoming common by the time of the Great Exhibition (1851) but with a relatively high rate of illiteracy, they were not all that popular.

With poor food and hygiene in unsanitary living quarters, the health standards of the men of the Heavy Brigade were equally poor. In civilian life in the middle of the century, the average mortality rate was 7½-9/1,000; in the cavalry, it was 11. Tuberculosis was the most common disease – ignoring the 1850s arrival of cholera – and suicides in the army were unusually high. Statistically, in the Heavies as a whole, the figures work out as 1 in 20 of all deaths, compared to 1 in 340 in the civilian population.

The reputation of the cavalry fluctuated. In the army itself, horsed regiments followed their officers' leads and saw themselves as a cut above the 'poor bloody infantry', simply because they rode horses. They were physically higher in the literal sense. Their role was different too. Light cavalry in particular, but often the Heavies too, were the 'feelers and feeders' of the army, in Nolan's phrase, carrying out reconnaissance on campaign for water-supplies, food and enemy troop movements. On the battlefield, their role, particularly the Heavies, was to charge a wavering, rattled infantry unit, driving them from the field in a rout. It did not always work out that way. In the Peninsula, Wellington famously complained that his cavalry 'got him into scrapes', implying that they were more trouble than they were worth.

Among the civilian population, communities *away* from barracks probably thought highly of them, believing the recruiting posters that had begun appearing in the 1790s for the war against Revolutionary France. In army towns, however, or where the cavalry had been sent in by the lord lieutenant to keep order in a potentially tricky situation, they were feared and disliked. In Manchester in 1819, the 15th Hussars had had to rescue the Manchester and Salford Yeomanry when the local troops attacked a large, but unarmed and peaceful, mob. In Bristol in 1832, the 3rd Dragoon Guards were unleashed against the reformers, led, apparently, by the fictional 'Captain Swing'.

Nowhere was the love-hate relationship between civilian and army more apparent than in Ireland. Two of the five Heavy Brigade regiments – the 4th Dragoon Guards and the Inniskillings – were Irish and the Crimean War broke out not long after Ireland had undergone the economic disaster of the potato famine. Between 1843 and 1846, no less than five harvests had failed in a desperately poor country which had gone over to potato production as a cheaper option than corn. The result of the Irish blight was that the 'praties' turned black in the ground and could not be dug. A horrified Robert Peel, now prime minister, sent commissioners who reported on whole villages being deserted, the dead lying in their homes and ditches with no one to bury them. Thousands left Ireland for good, drifting to England via Liverpool in search of work on the canals or railways, or to the brave new world of the United States where they colonised the growing towns like New York and Chicago. Gold struck in Australia in 1851 lured many of them in that direction too, penned like cattle in ships' holds, hoping for a miracle that would never happen. Much more practically, many young men enlisted in the army.

The ranks of the Heavy Brigade are littered with Irishmen. John Donovan and no less than three Dooleys enlisted with the 4th 'Royal Irish'. So did Patrick Byrne who also deserted from the regiment – twice! Edward Finucane was there; so were Michael Fitzgerald and John Fitzpatrick. Two men named Flynn rode with the 4th, as did two Gallaghers, both, confusingly, called Michael; and two Gannons, Martin and Patrick. There were two Gilligans, Mark and John. Connor

Hogan rode the charge of the Heavy Brigade and Patrick Hogan was born in Darley, Kildare. John Keegan and William Kelly enlisted; so did John Leary. Charles Mason hailed from Cork, John McGuire and Garrett McKenna joined up. James Maloney, Francis Moran, the O'Briens (Edward and James) from County Clare; John O'Connor; O'Donnell, O'Hara, O'Keefe, O'Leary – the list goes on. Private Thomas Ryan, who was killed in the charge, came from Cloanch in Tipperary. Lieutenant Fox Strangways of the Royal Artillery reported on the man's head injuries – Ryan had 'red or fair hair, which was cut as close as possible and therefore well suited to show any wounds. His helmet had come off in the fight and he had about fifteen cuts on his head … His death wound was a thrust below the armpit, which had bled profusely.' A similar list of Irishmen can be found in the Inniskillings.

Officers too had Irish links. If not actually Irish themselves, they or their families owned estates there. Most notorious was Lord Lucan, with lands in County Mayo. He was a typical absentee landlord of the kind his tenants hated, ignoring the problems of the famine and doing nothing to help. Assistant-Surgeon Robert Chapple of the Scots Greys was born in Limerick in 1832. Andrew Nugent, of the Greys, born two years later, hailed from Portaferry, County Down. Cornet William Bruce Armstrong of the 4th Dragoon Guards was born in Dublin, as was Lieutenant Christopher McDonnel. McDonnel's father was a paper manufacturer and chairman of the Great Southern and Western Railway in Ireland. Colonel Hodge's diary entry, for 29 May 1854, reads, 'Sir Edward McDonnell, the Lord Mayor of Dublin, has kindly taken charge of all my baggage. He will put it into an empty room and will have fires in it in winter.' Lieutenant John Ferguson of the 5th Dragoon Guards was born in Belfast, County Antrim and baptised in the church of St Anne's there. Captain Richard Thompson came from Wicklow and by all accounts was not very impressive. Temple Godman, serving under him in the 5th, wrote: '… he is as great an ass as ever … as to consulting him on matters connected with the regiment, I might as well talk to a post'. Assistant-Surgeon Henry Boate joined the Inniskillings from Dungavon, County Waterford.

In 1815, the year of Waterloo in which the army triumphed over Napoleon and the Scots Greys rode into history charging the French army with shouts of 'Scotland forever!', notices were pinned to the gates of London parks – 'No soldiers, servants in livery or dogs permitted.'

And, despite the war fever gripping the nation early in 1854, not much had changed since then. People only remembered the first part of Wellington's famous dictum and ignored the last – the British soldier is 'the scum of the earth and the sweepings of the gaols, enlisted for drink; but we have made men of them'.

In the summer of 1854, it remained to be seen what kind of men.

Chapter 4

Heavy Baggage

'The Colonel's lady and Judy O'Grady,' wrote Rudyard Kipling in *The Ladies* (1922), 'are sisters under the skin.' It is only very recently that women have been added to front-line troops. Before that, the traditional picture was of womenfolk waving handkerchiefs and bidding their menfolk a tearful farewell. Even as late as 1914, government propaganda posters appeared in which beautiful wives urged their men to enlist, to do their bit. The music hall song of that year, before the reality of trench warfare became known, ran:

'We don't want to lose you,
But we think you ought to go.
For your king and your country
Both need you so.'

The situation in 1854 was different. One in six of the cavalry Other Ranks' wives were allowed to travel with their husbands – a ballot, usually of coloured stones, was held – and none of them was ready for the hardship of a winter campaign in the Crimea. But for the five left behind, the army provided no support. They had to leave the barracks and find work where they could. For many, that meant the sweated trades involving hours at a treadle, or prostitution or the workhouse.

As always, there was a great social divide. The official terminology read 'Colonels and their ladies, officers and their wives, Other Ranks and their women'. Actual marriage for soldiers was frowned upon by most commanding officers, so most of the women were common-law wives only. Even officers had to ask permission from their colonels to marry. Ladies, themselves often the daughters of army men, lived as close to their officer husbands as possible, coming to London, to their town houses, in the 'season' from May to September. They attended regimental balls and the occasional dinner and even wore 'gala' belts of gold lace with the regimental badge on the twin buckles. Among women of this class, war was a remote and romantic concept, linked with the chivalric Medieval novels of Walter Scott that were hugely popular from the 1820s onwards. For them, the nonsensical advice given by Lord Raglan to Fanny Duberly (through the pen of screenplay writer Charles Wood in *The Charge of the Light Brigade*) made perfect sense: 'Young ladies [Fanny was 25] should concern themselves with things that are pretty. England is pretty. Babies are pretty. Some table linen can be very pretty ... Find a pretty flower and press it in your housebook and watch the pretty valley.'

The 'pretty valley' of course, was the 'valley of Death' where the Light Brigade was about to face destruction. This view of womanhood as frail and otherworldly, inclined to reach for the smelling salts, found its apogee in Dickens' Dora Copperfield. It is appallingly patronising by today's standards and not true for most ladies, who were tougher than most men gave them credit for.

Sightseers of this class were commonplace in many theatres of war in the middle of the century. Titled ladies travelled from Moscow and St Petersburg, as well as Sebastopol itself, taking lavish picnics into the hills to watch the Allied invasion of the Crimea and the creation of camps around Balaclava harbour. Not until the bloodbath of the Alma on 20 September did they pack their bags and go home. By the spring of 1855, however, once the hardships of winter were over, ladies came out in greater numbers from Britain, to be with their officer husbands or merely to 'watch the pretty valley'. The enterprising travel agents Inman & Co ran special cut-price trips. For £5, a civilian of either sex could buy a fourteen-day excursion, including visits to battlefields and to Constantinople. Most soldiers of all ranks were appalled by these people, regarding them as little more than ghouls. The Germans called them *Schlachtenbummler* (battle walkers) and they appeared in droves at the major battles of the American Civil War, like Shiloh, Gettysburg and Antietam.

Few commanding officers approved of ladies' presence in a war zone. Lucan did his level best to keep out Fanny Duberly, but he was outmanoeuvred by Raglan and Cardigan, both of whom had a soft spot for a pretty face. Although she was married to an officer in the Light Brigade (Henry Duberly, Paymaster of the 8th Hussars) she knew several officers in the Heavies and witnessed both cavalry charges on 25 October, which gives her work relevance.

Fanny left the New London Inn, Exeter, at ten o'clock at night on Monday, 25 April, 'with sad heart and eyes full of tears'. She had no idea where the army was going and relied, as they all did, on the constantly shifting swirls of rumour. From the Royal Hotel, Plymouth, having bought a few extras for the sea journey, she went on board the *Shooting Star* in the harbour and the ship travelled downriver until the wind and tide could take them out to sea. We shall look at the perils of the voyage to the Crimea in the next chapter, but whenever possible, Fanny was up on deck, scribbling in her notebook all that was going on around her. On Sunday 30th, the Duberlys attended a church service on board and sadly remembered such days at home, walking through lanes and fields to church. The sea was calm and Fanny saw whales and porpoises, with phosphorescent lights gleaming like stars at night. They sailed past Gibraltar under a 'brilliant moon' and the next day saw 'the mountains of Africa [the Atlas] capped with snow'.

By Monday, 8 May, they were off Malta, listening to the ringing of a matins bell. Fanny could not concentrate, however, because her favourite horse, a grey, had died in the night. They buried the animal at sunset, 'my good horse was lowered to his rest among the nautili and wondrous sea-flowers which floated around the ship'. Reality was beginning to kick in. Several crewmen, drunk with the rum they had bought in Malta, 'became mutinous and several passed the night in irons'. Bad weather threatened to put Fanny off sailing for life. 'Give me the smallest house in England, with a greenhouse and stable and I will sigh no more for the violet waves of a Mediterranean sea ...'

Fanny was having trouble with her servant – clearly, even in 1854, one could not get the staff! 'Today, for the first time since I left England, I induced Mrs Williams, the sergeant-major's wife ... to wash a few of the clothes which had accumulated during our voyage. I mention this, as being the first assistance she has ever thought fit to render me ...'

Having soaked up nearly as much Classical literature as any man of her class, Fanny was fascinated by her first sight of the Greek coast. 'I watched for an hour, my mind dreaming poetic fancies – "I too have been in Arcadia".' She was quoting Virgil. At the mercy of the wind, one day they reached 11 knots, the next they were immobile, becalmed at the entrance to the Dardanelles. She saw cattle, mules and camels grazing on the hills of Gallipoli while the local Turks stood staring at the foreign ships off their shores. At Scutari, with its massive barracks which could hold 6,000 men, she heard the 'Imaum' calling the faithful to prayer from his minaret.

Henry went ashore, to find that Constantinople, the legendary heart of the old Byzantine empire, was just a scruffy Turkish town – 'the filth, stenches and dogs on shore are *indescribable*.' When she herself was taken to the Turkish cavalry barracks at Kulali (which would become a hospital in 1855) Fanny was disgusted anew – 'the dilapidation! the dirt! the rats! the fleas!!' The stables upset the fanatical horsewoman more than the human quarters – 'no straw and no mangers!'

The harbour at Kulali horrified Fanny – it was 'filled with cabbages and refuse of every description – a dead dog floating out and a dead horse drifting close to the shore, on whose swollen and corrupted flanks three dogs were alternately fighting and tearing off the horrible flesh.'

It was now that Lucan put his foot down. He gave orders that Fanny was not to re-embark on the *Shooting Star.* In other words, her journey 'to the East' was over. Henry fretted about this. 'He looks upon the order as a soldier; I look upon it as a woman and laugh at it.' She pointed out that she was there with the authorisation of both the Horse Guards, who managed the army, and the Admiralty, responsible for getting the troops to the Crimea. Undeterred by Lucan's bullying, she did what any woman would do – she went shopping in the bazaar and bought herself a pair of crimson, gold-embroidered slippers.

Fanny mentions the Hotel D'Angleterre 'the resort of English naval and military officers who have "accompanied their husbands to the sear of war".' Marianne Young, the wife of an infantry officer, described it as 'a charming little auberge … a boarding house without its monotony'. And by 1 June, they were disembarking at Varna.

One who did not reach Varna was Miss Bird (forename unknown) who left a written account of her voyage east. She was one of a party of 'cockney excursionists' who left London with picnic hampers, parasols, wide-brimmed hats and plenty of porter! Whoever these ladies were, they do not appear to have been army wives, but if not, their travelling without male chaperones was at once a dangerous and shocking thing to do.

The government's idea, for women travelling to the seat of war, would be for them to be left at a depot somewhere en route – Malta, Varna or, at a pinch, Scutari. No female was supposed to get to the Crimea itself, although an unknown number did. Fanny Duberly, of course, was foremost among them, as was Lady Erroll, the wife of an officer in the 60th Rifles. Outwardly, she and Fanny were courteous to each other, but it probably rankled with the paymaster's wife that both Lady Erroll and her husband far outranked her and Henry. Another 'stowaway' who got to the Crimea was Adelaide Cresswell, the wife of a captain in the 11th Hussars. Bolder even than Fanny, Adelaide told people she intended to ride through the campaign in a leather suit, armed with a brace of pistols (she was a crack shot). Fanny was bitchy about her in the extreme in a letter home (in May 1854):

We expected something rather fashionable and brilliant – but, after waiting some time a woman came from among the troop horses – so dirty – with such uncombed, scurfy hair, such black nails, such a dirty cotton gown open at the neck … Oh, you never had a kitchen maid so dreadful … Mrs Cresswell allows no woman near her tent – so who empties her slops – or how she manages – I can't divine.

Captain Cresswell was still at sea, however, the day before the battle of the Alma, when he died of cholera.

There was only one lady with the Heavy Brigade and that was 'that horrid Mrs Forrest' of the 4th Dragoon Guards. Perhaps it was her bad luck that her husband's commanding officer was little Hodge, who does not seem to have liked anybody, especially women. The only one he respected, apart, arguably, from his wife Ethel, was the head nurse at Scutari, Florence Nightingale.

Major William Forrest was, in effect, Hodge's second-in-command in the 4th and he had a colourful history. He had joined the 11th Light Dragoons as a cornet in 1836 and stayed when the regiment was made hussars four years later. His misfortune was that his colonel was James Brudenell, the Earl of Cardigan. Not content with hounding John Reynolds over the 'black bottle' incident and fighting a duel with Harvey Tuckett, Cardigan also accused Forrest of a whole host of minor infringements and put him under house arrest. Lord 'Daddy' Hill, the octogenarian commander-in-chief, effectively closed ranks with Cardigan and Forrest was censured. The national press had a field day with Cardigan but for the Horse Guards to tolerate him as they did was outrageous. He should have lost command of his regiment and never been given another post. When Forrest's wife was in difficulty, giving birth to their first child, Cardigan refused him compassionate leave until the Duke of Wellington himself upbraided the colonel for his 'foolish quarrels' with his officers. Forrest wisely exchanged into the 4th Dragoon Guards in 1844.

Annie Forrest did not come out to the Crimea until May 1855, but her husband's boss was already dreading it. 'It is quite true,' Hodge wrote to his wife, 'that that foolish woman, Mrs Forrest, has left

England and I dare say is now at a filthy hotel at Pera.' He was furious that Annie had not told Hodge's wife of her plans, 'but perhaps she did not wish me to know it, being well aware how strongly I disapprove of anything of the kind.'

Annie was unhappy at home, so Forrest did everything he could to accommodate her. Hodge, of course, had another take on things. 'I trust that Mrs Forrest will not come up here. He is not a very active officer at any time, and should she come here, the regiment may go to the dogs, for all that he will do for it.'

His worst fears were realised when he agreed to share a hut with Forrest. In his diary, he wrote grumpily, 'Mrs F. here again.' And a week later, she had become 'that woman'. By the end of June, she was 'screaming in her vulgar way for our cook to bring things for her. I was quite driven out of my hut by her. I can hear the two washing and dressing and talking to each other – disgusting!' On the day before Lord Raglan's funeral (he died of cholera in late June) Annie was sponging off Hodge for food, but at least the colonel could gloat that the heavy rain must have made the Forrest's newly erected marquee very uncomfortable. By 6 July, the couple had moved out of Hodge's hut, 'but still she has no female attendant about her. The dragoon still "empties the leather bucket".'

To add insult to injury, the smell of the Forrest's cooking also annoyed Hodge. 'He is a selfish, vulgar man, and I have ever thought so since we were in Glasgow, where he brought his kept woman to reside in the same passage as myself, much to my disgust.' One wonders whether Annie Forrest knew about her husband's extra-curricular activities! Continuing the theme of Mrs Forrest not having a female attendant, on 5 December 1855, Hodge wrote: 'Mrs Forrest and her lady's maid, Private Denis Shine, are storing the goods away in various boxes.' The next day, Forrest did nothing regimentally, but looked after Annie who sat on top of an overloaded cart drawn by two mules bound for Balaclava harbour. The Forrests had three wagons of baggage, two goats and a lot of chickens.

From the time of her arrival in the Crimea, Annie's husband's commanding officer had it in for her. Judging by Hodge's remarks about others, like *his* boss, General Scarlett and a junior officer, Captain Brigstocke, he was a petulant, narrow-minded man of the Cardigan variety and a good example of how *not* to run a regiment. He refused to invite Annie to eat breakfast in the makeshift officers' mess and was appalled that she was partaking of the rum ration designated to Forrest himself. He, on the other hand, worried about her, writing home that she had lost weight – 'she never was so hungry as she is here'. But Hodge never had any sympathy: 'The batman was seen yesterday picking the fleas out of Mrs F's drawers, after which he hung them out to air ... Her infernal cackle nearly drove me out of my hut today. Her laugh is quite that of an idiot.'

While Fanny Duberly quite gave the impression in her journal that she was the only woman with the army in the Crimea, a brighter light arrived – Agnes Paget, the new wife of the commander of the 4th Light Dragoons. She brought so much baggage that they had to hire a brewer's dray to carry it all. George Paget was the son of 'One-Leg', the Earl of Uxbridge, who had famously lost his leg in the closing phase of the battle of Waterloo. Agnes was his cousin and the couple had married in February 1854, only a few months before the cavalry embarked for the Crimea. Although he led the 4th down the 'valley of Death' in the charge of the Light Brigade with a cool nerve, smoking a cigar the whole time, he behaved like a lovesick puppy off the field and went home as soon as he could to join his wife. Public opinion in Britain varied enormously. Cardigan left the Crimea early and was feted and mobbed as a hero; Paget was 'cut' in his Club (White's) as being not much better than a deserter. Accordingly, he went back to the Crimea as soon as possible and Agnes joined him later. The photographer Roger Fenton called Mrs Paget the 'belle of the Crimea' but there appears to be no photograph of her – unlike Fanny Duberly, snapped on her horse with the ubiquitous Henry holding the bridle. Agnes arrived on the *Leander* at the end of April 1855 and, rather like Forrest, Lord George abandoned his regimental duties to spend time with her. They took picnics, watched parades and listened to the various bands. Mrs Paget regularly dined with Raglan, travelling here and there in his carriage and pair. Hodge must have been incandescent, but he was not alone. Captain Henry Percy wrote:

> Lady George Paget is here with a great proportion of the Paget beauty, and, from what I hear, the *whole* of the Paget presumption and insolence ... she is in full plenitude of power and rides out with a cortege ... of officers from every regiment (though principally the Dragoons).

Fanny Duberly criticised Agnes' riding and did not believe she was in love with her boring husband!

On 8 June, Agnes, Fanny and a bevy of touring ladies took up position on a hill to watch a renewed infantry attack on the Malakoff and the Redan, the fortresses that guarded Sebastopol's dockyards and the city itself. Major Roger Barnston was horrified: 'It's bad enough for ladies to be in camp at all, but when they come to see a couple of thousand men put an end to all at once, one might find a better title than "ladies" for them.'

The 'belle of the Crimea' died in childbirth at her London home three years later.

So much for the 'colonel's lady'; what of Judy O'Grady? The one in six who drew the coloured stone at cavalry barracks dotted around Britain had no children. Mothers were exempt from selection, although, in an era of non-existent birth control, it was always possible that childless women could conceive on the journey to the front or in the Crimea itself. While Fanny Duberly was worrying about her horses, the wife of a sergeant in the Coldstream Guards (in another ship) gave birth to a healthy baby; both survived. The government and the army made no provision for any of that.

The numbers are infuriatingly inaccurate. Because we do not know how many of the Heavy Brigade women had children, we cannot even use basic mental arithmetic to add up the numbers who went. We know the 4th had four wives with them; Private Edward O'Brien's son, a soldier himself, wrote to Colonel Hodge on behalf of his father, who was in dire straits by the 1870s: 'I am not unknown to you, having served in the 4th D.G. while under your command, as did my father for 25 years, including the whole of the Crimean campaign, as did my mother who accompanied the regiment there.' We shall meet Mrs Rogers later.

There were wide discrepancies in the army as a whole, with some commanding officers being more generous and understanding than others. *Household Words*, a must-have weekly magazine for which Charles Dickens wrote, summed up the classlessness of the women who were left behind – 'from the rocky fastnesses of the Scottish highlands … to the Cornish headlands …' from 'the Queen's palace and the Grenadiers' barrack-room, the labourer's cottage and the ghillie's sheeling and the bogtrotter's shebeen.'

The women who had married soldiers had a grim existence even at home. They lived with the other men of their husband's troop, on straw mattresses that were changed once a quarter. Privacy was maintained only by a blanket strung across a rope. Rooms were damp and cold, lit after dark by candles and penny dips. Army women were regarded as the lowest of the low; camp followers had always had an appalling reputation. When, by the 1870s, serious studies of prostitution were being carried out, such women were at the bottom of the social heap. And it was no consolation to realise, as many women did, that if army life at Aldershot or Kingston or Canterbury was bad, Varna and Balaclava were so much worse. Food in barracks was one pound of bread a day, along with potatoes and hard tack biscuit that cracked the teeth. Because army wives were not paid, even though they usually slaved at washing, cleaning and cooking, they were effectively living on their husband's wages of less than ten shillings a week. In some regiments, laundry earned the women a pathetic halfpenny a day.

Of the minimum of 750 army wives who accompanied their men to the east, three-quarters of them never came back. In that sense, the female death toll was far higher than that of the men and they were rarely exposed directly to enemy fire. When the officers told them they could go no further than Constantinople or Varna, some of them haggled with locals to get *any* form of transport to take them on to the Crimea; others tried to find some kind of living in towns full of aliens, whose language and religion they did not understand.

When they got to Gallipoli, there were no tents for the women and they had to sleep outside on the ground. It was here that the British contingent met their French allies for the first time and were astonished, not to say furious, that the French had grabbed the best billets in the town and had everything fully organised. Their commissariat (responsible for lodgings and provisions) was particularly impressive, whereas the British equivalent was little more than a joke. What staggered the ragged, suffering British women most were the French *cantinières* who rode with the French army and provided wine and food. Roger Fenton's famous photograph of one such woman says it all. The girl is attractive and vivacious, wearing a pseudo-military jacket and simple cap to hold her hair in place. She carries a riding crop and wears pantaloons under her short dress, enabling her (unlike, for example, Fanny Duberly, Agnes Paget and Mrs Cresswell) to ride astride, like the men. Around Fenton's girl's waist is a ration bag from which she sold tots of brandy to the troops. Britain had *nothing* like this. Most of the *cantinières* were the wives of NCOs, so they knew their regiments and carried a status wholly lacking in the British army.

In Scutari, the heat became obvious for the first time as the army neared the seat of war. 'Turkish cannibals' as they called mosquitoes, buzzed around the stagnant pools near the hospital. Some women turned to drink, especially the local rot-gut raki, which was cheap. Their skin burned in the sun as hats got lost or were ruined by rain. Only ladies carried parasols. They haggled in bazaars and did whatever they could to survive.

Eventually, financial help would arrive for the women from a variety of charitable institutions from home, but in the winter of 1854–5, it was very much a matter of living from hand to mouth and coping with the extremes of weather, from scorching heat to freezing conditions and camp walkways that resembled sheets of glass. One woman of whom even Colonel Hodge approved was Mrs Rogers, the wife of Private John Rogers in his regiment. In Fenton's photograph of the camp of the 4th Dragoon Guards, she is serving tea from a tin can to a group of officers including French Zouaves, lounging about and smoking pipes outside a makeshift hut. She appears again in another photograph taken outside Captain John Webb's hut, where, unsurprisingly, she is wearing the same dress. Her hair is tied back and she has on an astonishingly clean apron (keeping it so was one of her many tasks). Hodge had learned, in early June 1855, that Fanny Duberly had had the gall to ask for a Crimea medal with clasps for Balaclava and Inkerman – 'I will apply for one,' he wrote, 'for Mrs Rogers, who deserves it ten times more than half the men who will get it.'

Think of the Crimea and women and two names occur immediately. We shall look at their exploits later, but we need to establish them in the front ranks of the women who went. The first is Florence Nightingale, an extraordinary, single-minded woman who flouted the convention of her middle-class origins to become a nurse. Before the 1850s, nursing had a very poor reputation. At best, pre-Crimea nurses were cooks and cleaners; the nearest they came to any medical interaction with patients was changing beds. At worst, they were prostitutes, like the Turkish women who were hanging around the hospital at Scutari when Florence arrived.

Because training for nurses in Britain barely existed, Florence went to Kaiserwurth in Germany in 1851 and then to Paris. Two years later, she was superintendent of a hospital for invalid women in London. Florence's grandfather had been an abolitionist at the time when Britain still had a slave trade. She herself had pseudo-religious leanings, intending to set up a 'Protestant sisterhood, without vows, for women of educated feelings'. In 1852, she wrote *Suggestions for Thought to Searchers after Religious Truth* which was published seven years later when she had become famous.

On 14 October 1854, alarmed as most newspaper readers were by the reports from the Crimea, she wrote to Sidney Herbert, a family friend who was also Secretary for War, offering her services as a qualified nurse. Four days before Balaclava, she sailed for Constantinople at the head of thirty-eight nurses, not all of them particularly qualified and none of them prepared for the horrors they found at Scutari, the nearest base hospital to the Crimea, seven days' sailing time away.

It would be fascinating to know what the doctors of the various Heavy Brigade regiments thought of her, men like Chilley Pine, surgeon to the 4th Dragoon Guards; William Cattell of the 5th; Alexander Forteath of the 1st; John Brush of the Scots Greys; and James Mouat of the Inniskillings. They probably agreed with the army's medical department that a woman had no place treating the weak and wounded in a war zone. Florence herself had a great deal of opposition from army doctors and sensibly stood back until they had no choice but to ask for her help. Her arrival at Scutari coincided with a huge influx of wounded from Inkerman early in November.

One of the volunteer nurses whom Florence turned down was Mary Seacole, the Creole woman whose astonishing life captivated her contemporaries as it still does today. Her book *The Wonderful Adventures of Mrs Seacole in Many Lands*, published in 1857, was a runaway best seller and in the foreword written by the Crimean war correspondent William Russell, he explains Mary's importance:

> She is the first who has redeemed the name of 'sutler' from the suspicion of worthlessness, mercenary business and plunder; and I trust that England will not forget one who nursed her sick, who sought out her wounded to aid and succour them and who performed the last offices for some of her illustrious dead.

Unforgivably, Mary is not listed in the *New Universal Encyclopaedia* published in 1955. Neither is she recorded in *Chambers Biographical Dictionary*, 1992. This last volume is a reprint of an 1897 original, by which time, Mrs Seacole seems to have vanished. The reason is, sadly, obvious – Mary Seacole was a Creole, whose father was a Scottish army officer but whose mother was a free-born black Jamaican. This was undoubtedly why Florence Nightingale turned down her offer to join her nurses, even though Mary actually knew personally several of the officers camped outside Sebastopol by November 1854. Florence wrote: 'Anyone who employs Mrs Seacole will introduce much kindness – also much drunkenness and improper conduct.' Traipsing around London that autumn, Mary got the same cold shoulder from everyone in officialdom that she met. Luckily, she had enough funds – and tenacity – to get to the Crimea herself and off she went on board the screw-steamer *Hollander*. Enterprisingly, she sent business cards on ahead:

> Mrs Mary Seacole, late of Kingston, Jamaica, respectfully announces to her former kind friends, and to the officers of the army and navy generally, that she has taken her passage in the screw-steamer 'Hollander' … intending on her arrival at Balaclava to establish a mess table and comfortable quarters for sick and convalescent officers.

The artist William Simpson sketched her in the Crimea and, in the weeks and months that followed, and in their different ways, Mary and Florence would take the 'seat of war' by storm.

Chapter 5

The Troopers

The logistical problems in getting the army out to 'the east' (the generic term constantly used well into August 1854) were huge, especially in the cavalry. Louis Nolan had failed to find suitable cavalry horses in Turkey, so the five regiments of the Heavy Brigade had to take their animals with them, which was never easy. In his book *Cavalry: Its History and Tactics* (1853), Nolan ignores the problem of transporting horses, even though the work is crammed full of useful, common-sense advice on virtually every other matter. Although the term 'trooper' became synonymous with the cavalry soldier in both the British and American armies, in the 1850s, it either meant a troop horse or a troopship, depending on the context.

The 4th Dragoon Guards had been on home service since their return from the Peninsula in 1813. Twenty officers and 297 Other Ranks left Kingston (now Dunlaoghaire) Ireland on 2 June. Commanding them on board the 1,033 ton *Deva* was Colonel Hodge and his staff. He was pleased with the condition of the men's swords, but horrified that many of his officers had no idea how to pack their horses for campaign. After all, as they would probably have argued, as officers with grooms and servants, they had people for that! In particular, he was unimpressed with Cornet John Webb, his new adjutant, 'who is quite ignorant, but has not, I fear, much wish to learn'. Hodge worried, too, that too many of his horses – fifty-three, in fact – were too old for efficient active service at four years; and many of his men were too heavy, at 13 or 14 stone. 'I see,' he grumbled, 'an infinity of bother before me.' He had bought another horse for £80 and various bits and pieces for life in the field, including a little cooking stove. Intriguingly, Hodge was short of cash and had to write to his uncle, who was a baronet, to lend him £100. His field allowance, as lieutenant colonel, was 4s 6d a day and horse rations were free. He had just got hold of Colonel Arthur Shirley's new book on the treatment of horses at sea and intended that all his officers should buy one.

Hodge's servant was a private in his regiment who 'understands washing linen, cooking, can repair my saddlery ...'

The *Deva* carried 58 soldiers and 60 horses with four spare stalls, each animal, as in all the ships, slung by canvas harnesses so that, when the sea became rough, they were not knocked against the stall partitions. The *Maori*, which had already left on the 25th under Captain Francis Forster, had 3 officers, 48 men and 50 horses. The *Burmah* left two days later. It weighed 718 tons and carried 47 men and 45 horses as well as the usual complement of officers. The *Sir Robert Sale*, 721 tons, left three days after that. The *William Jackson*, the *Palmyra* and the *Libertas* made up the regiment's complement.

The Scots Greys set sail on the *Himalaya*, the newest transport in the fleet and at that time the largest passenger-carrying ship afloat. She belonged to the P&O line but had never made money for the company and there was relief all round when the government bought her as a troopship. The regiment left Nottingham with 14 officers, 299 Other Ranks and 294 horses, sailing from Liverpool on 25 July. The speed of this vessel, as opposed, for example, to Hodge's *Deva*, meant that the Greys were shipped direct from Constantinople to the Crimea, avoiding the camp at Varna which turned into a disease-ridden hell hole.

The Royals, on board their troopers the *Gertrude*, the *Pedestrian*, the *Arabia*, *Rip Van Winkle*, *Coronetta* and *Command* sailed from Liverpool. *The Times* reported on 12 May that the *Gertrude* and the *Pedestrian* were in the Mersey, waiting for the tide. Major Robert Wardlaw commanded the troops on board the *Rip Van Winkle*. The *Command*, the property of Edward Oliver, a local shipping magnate, left Liverpool on 1 June, with 50 tons of hay on board. The total numbers for the 1st Dragoons were 14 officers, 294 men and 296 horses.

The 5th Dragoon Guards were at Ballincolig, west of Cork. Four of six troops were ordered to embark, the remaining two staying behind as a depot troop. Since one of the majors had to stay behind with this unit and since James Scarlett had recently been given the command of the Heavy Cavalry, a replacement lieutenant colonel, Thomas Le Marchant of the 7th Dragoon Guards, was drafted in at the last moment. We already know from Sergeant Major Franks how unpopular this man was and nobody felt very hopeful for the opening of the campaign. The regiment's strength was 19 officers and 295 men. A unit of the Royal Artillery and a company of the 68th Foot were also on board.

The 6th Inniskilling Dragoons sailed from Plymouth at the end of May in five ships – the *Europa*, the *Escort*, the *Sutlej*, *Lord Raglan* and *Talavera*. All but the *Europa* carried a single troop.

The problem with troopships bound ultimately for the Crimea was that some were steam-driven, others powered by sail. In the rapidly evolving technology of the mid-century, this was inevitable. Ships were expensive to build, which is why the navy, for example, kept them in service for so long. One of the troopers used in the Crimea was blown up during the Second World War. The *Himalaya*, probably the most impressive of them all, reached Constantinople in eleven days, nineteen hours. She was spacious and comfortable, known to the men of the 5th as 'Her Majesty's Floating Mess'. The 13th Light Dragoons by contrast took eight weeks to accomplish the same journey and they and their horses were wrecks when they arrived. The other problem was that several of the troopships were far past their best, worn out by the long voyage to India over the past twenty years. They were cold, damp and infested with rats.

At first, as with Fanny Duberly on the *Shooting Star*, all went well. 'I like my ship,' wrote Hodge. The captain was a 'funny old brandy-faced cove' who kindly gave the colonel his cabin. The officers ate four meals a day including a pint of wine. Lieutenant Robert Hunter of the

Scots Greys was enjoying life too. On board the *Himalaya* on 27 July, he wrote to his sister Molly:

> This is a most splendid ship and the best idea I can give of her size is that she is 80 feet longer than the *Duke of Wellington* [a Royal Navy warship]. We are now getting near the Bay of Biscay and the ship, as you may see by my writing, is rolling a few. Besides our screw makes such a thumping that it really is not easy to get the letters straight.

Only Lieutenant William Miller, the adjutant, had been seasick and the horses were well. Breakfast was at nine, lunch at twelve, tea at (blank) and grog at nine. 'We have been allowed to take off uniform and go about the queerest figures imaginable, with all sorts of hats, wide-awakes, caps, boots etc. ... We all expect to be at Malta this day week – July 31st.'

For the historian, the most important source travelling with the army was William Russell of *The Times*. This was the first British war covered by a newspaper correspondent and Russell was very conscious of that. Photographs of him in the Crimea show him trying to blend in with a peaked forage cap (he spent most of his time camped with the Light Infantry Division) and knee-high boots. Most officers resented his presence and some, like Raglan, ignored him entirely. Russell was 33 and had a wide journalistic experience, having covered parliamentary debates, Irish political trials and even a brief war between Prussia and Denmark in 1850, in which he had been slightly wounded. Four days before he embarked, he was the guest of honour at a drunken party hosted by literary luminaries Charles Dickens and William Thackeray.

'Soon after daylight anchors were tripped,' he wrote in the first of his reports for *The Times*, 'and with full steam off dashed our little fleet ... They ran past the Needles [Isle of Wight] at 8.15 and were soon bowling along with a fresh breeze on the bow' called by the sailors (inexplicably to Russell), 'moderate to fine'. Russell's hammock (he was travelling with the Guards) was eighteen inches wide (for the naval crew it was only fourteen) and he had one blanket, using his greatcoat as an extra cover to keep warm.

Three days out and the rough seas began to take their toll. 'The figureheads plunged into the waters and the heads of the poor soldiers hung despondently over gunwale, portsill, stay and mess-tin, as their bodies bobbed to and fro with the swaying, creaking, trembling tabernacle in which they were encamped.' They all felt better the next day when the seas calmed and they sighted their first whale!

In the cavalry ships, the situation below decks contrasted sharply with the holiday atmosphere 'up top'. The ammonia from the horse urine and the vinegar used to soothe their nostrils stank to high heaven and this worsened as the temperature rose in the Mediterranean. Rough seas, and especially storms, saw the animals panicking, thrashing and kicking in their stalls, the slings that held them scraping their flanks and drawing blood. Even on Russell's infantry ship, five officers' horses died. In an ominous sign of the more that was to come, Russell wrote: 'The commissariat are blamed for these deficiencies [specifically a lack of candles and blankets] ... the despatch of these troops was determined several months ago.'

By 6 June, Hodge's *Deva* was nearing Cape Finisterre and one horse had to be put down – 'The men worked well at it but the animal was so injured that we could not get it up. We therefore threw him overboard after knocking him on the head. It was a fine and good horse.' What concerned the ever-petulant Hodge was the table manners of Lieutenant Robert Gunter – 'He is dreadful ... eats with his elbows on the table ...' Gunter was the son of a chocolatier, so what could anyone expect? In Hodge's words 'the old story of silk purse and sow's ear'. In a later letter to his mother, the colonel called him 'the nobby pieman', but was put out that, having returned to the Crimea after a leave of absence at home, Gunter had not brought his colonel a box of chocolates! On the *Deva*, the officers continued to eat well, but the men were on 'salt provisions' and the notorious hardtack that had been the fodder of the navy since long before Nelson's day. The colonel spent his days reading until they reached Malta when he went ashore to reunite briefly with his mother and sisters. His mother had apparently moved to the island on the advice of her doctor.

Fanny Duberly, who had left England long before the 4th Dragoon Guards, was already beside herself over her horses, on the *Shooting Star*:

> A fourth horse died last night. They tell me he went absolutely mad and raved himself to death. The hold where our horses are stored … appears to me horrible beyond words. The slings begin to gall the horses under the shoulder and breastbone; and the heat and bad atmosphere must be felt to be understood.

The day after this, Fanny's grey – 'Missus's Horse' – was ill. The animal was, of course, in a nation renowned as animal lovers, perfect – 'with faultless action, faultless mouth and faultless temper'. The horse died two days later, off Malta; and Fanny could not bear to talk of it again.

Lieutenant Hunter was still drooling over the size and majesty of the ship as they rounded the straits of Gibraltar and with almost childlike glee, he once again babbled to his sister, 'This screw propellor [*sic*] goes thump, thump so that it is next to impossible to write.'

But however much Hodge grumbled about Gunter and Fanny Duberly fretted over her horses, all that was put into perspective by the fate of the *Europa*, carrying the colonel and staff of the Inniskillings. The troopship left Plymouth with the regiment's other four transports on Tuesday morning, 30 May. The *Europa* belonged to Somers and Wheaton, a London shipping company and weighed 841 tons.

On board were five sergeants and fifty-four Other Ranks, as well as an unspecified number of women. This was the staff ship carrying: Lieutenant Colonel Willoughby Moore; the adjutant, Lieutenant Archibald Weir (who later failed to impress Colonel Shute); Cornet Henry Timson; Surgeon Alexander MacGregor and probationary veterinary surgeon Kelly. There were thirteen officers' chargers in the hold, along with forty-four troop horses. It may have been the extra hay that was being carried that began the fire that would sink the ship.

From the depositions given at Gibraltar by the survivors, we can piece together the events of 31 May when disaster struck the *Europa* 200 miles out from Plymouth. About ten o'clock that night, Captain Gardner's steward reported to Weir, as adjutant, that the ship was on fire. Weir went at once to Colonel Moore's cabin on the quarter deck and asked what his orders were. According to Weir, the colonel had no orders, which seems unlikely, except to 'keep the men quiet and prevent them from getting into the boats'. It is not known how many lifeboats the *Europa* had, but in all probability, not enough for every life on board. There was suspicion at the time that some of the crew grabbed those boats and left the *Europa* and the cavalry to fend for themselves. Weir and MacGregor did their best to maintain some semblance of order, but when they saw some of the lifeboats pulling away, the men in effect mutinied and grabbed what boats they could. Weir along with MacGregor, Lieutenant Black and Cornet Henry Timson, were herded into the boats with the others.

Whether Colonel Moore was unlucky or whether he chose to go down with the ship is not clear, but he and veterinary surgeon Kelly were the officers who did not survive. Charles Mountray, the quartermaster sergeant, two hospital sergeants, William Johnson and Thomas Gore, made up the dead NCOs and there were twelve Other Ranks. Perhaps most shocking of all was the death of Mrs Parsons, the wife of Private William Parsons who also went down with the ship. She became the first female casualty of the war. Memorials to the dead were erected by a shocked nation in the Royal Hospital, Chelsea and at York Minster.

On 23 June, the RSM of the Inniskillings, John Mountain, and eleven men from the *Europa* were put onto Hodge's *Deva* at Malta. Hodge questioned them and concluded: 'Had the sailors behaved properly every man would have been saved. There was nothing saved at all … The two mates and three able seamen at once deserted the ship in a boat. The rest of the crew took to their boats. The soldiers behaved well.'

Beyond Malta, the classically educated cavalry officers were in their element. On board the *Himalaya*, Temple Godman with the 5th wrote to his mother, 'We saw the tombs of Ajax, Achilles and Hector on the shore.' Considering that those ancient warriors were fictional characters from Homer's *Iliad*, Godman must have been a tour operator's dream! The horses on board were coping, he says, because they are French and show no feisty spirit at all. The *Himalaya*, of course, being a sleek steamship, easily passed the older, slower vessels. 'We overtook today [9 June] several large cavalry transports, which sailed long before us, but which are not likely to be in till long after us, as the wind is dead against them.' Despite attempts by these troopships – by using flag signals – to persuade the *Himalaya* to tow them, the steamship would have none of it and ploughed on regardless.

Temple Godman was reminded of the Sussex downs by the scenery he saw (apart, presumably, from the myrtles and olives) but Hodge found something to moan about. 'I have no baggage horses, no native servant and I do not like the things I have brought to carry my luggage in.' Even he, however, was impressed with the boats, lights and painted houses of the Bosphorus.

While William Russell lost many of his belongings to an unscrupulous 'servant' hiring himself out in Valetta, Malta, as the correspondent changed ship there, Fanny Duberly marvelled at the current at the entrance to the Dardanelles and Hodge complained about the soaring temperatures. 'Very hot last night,' he wrote in his diary on 27 June, 'No air. The horse hold and the men's decks like ovens. 82 [degrees Fahrenheit] in my cabin.' Fanny noted the Turkish women staring transfixed at the huge ships passing them and while she was entranced again listening to the 'Imaum' summoning the faithful to prayer at sunset; soldiers following in the troopships behind were less enchanted, mimicking the strange cry and shouting 'What's up, mate?'

And it was not only Mrs Duberly, the paymaster's wife, who had brought all kinds of baggage, real and metaphorical, with her. The whole army, rutted in the false reality of forty years of peace, was about to have a severe shake-up.

Chapter 6

Cholera

'The cholera is come amongst us!' Fanny Duberly wrote in her journal on Sunday, 23 July. 'Sixteen men have died of it this day in the Rifles.'

Weeks before the terrifying disease appeared, first in the French lines, then in the English, William Russell was pointing out in a furious flurry of despatches to John Delane, his editor at *The Times*, the extraordinary shortcomings of the 'finest army ever to have left the shores of England'. He watched as officers, completely unprepared for a campaign in the east, tried to haggle with 'apathetic Turks' and 'stupid arabi drivers'. They used sign language or attempted to work with interpreters who spoke neither English nor Turkish! And it did not help that the French, from Gallipoli onwards, seemed to accomplish everything with effortless ease.

'Let us have plenty of doctors,' Russell wrote from Malta. 'Let us have an overwhelming army of medical men to combat disease. Let us have a staff, full and strong, of young and active and experienced men. Do not suffer our soldiers to be killed by antiquated imbecility ... give the sick every chance ...'

Beyond the scope of the strictly medical, the Heavy Cavalry was as lacking as every other unit in such young expertise. The brigadier, James Scarlett, had been about to retire when war was declared. He had never seen a shot fired in anger in his life. Under him, on the brigade staff, Major General William Beatson was an experienced veteran of numerous Indian campaigns. The Crimea was a brief sideshow for him as his real interest was in commanding irregular Indian cavalry for the Nizam of Hyderabad. He was effectively a volunteer in the Crimea and Scarlett needed him desperately. Even so, Beatson was 50 in 1854 – too old, by Russell's yardstick, for a field command.

Scarlett's brigade major was James Conolly of the 5th Dragoon Guards. A competent and loyal officer, he, like Scarlett, had never seen action. Captain Alexander Elliot was different. Originally with the 9th Lancers, he had transferred to the 5th Dragoon Guards in 1850 and had served for five years before that in India. He had fought at Punniar and Ferozeshah and was wounded at Sobraon, earning him the Gwalior Star medal. He and Beatson were the only officers with the Heavy Brigade to have seen Indian service. Lord Cardigan's well-known contempt for 'Indian officers' precluded him from using the experience of men like these. In his own Light Brigade, the staff officer William Morris, who led the 17th Lancers at Balaclava, was another 'Indian', a personal friend of Elliot who had seen similar service in Gwalior.

Above Scarlett, on Lucan's staff at Headquarters, the lack of experience and the age problem was very acute. Lucan, as we have seen, had fought briefly against the Turks in 1829, but he was 54 at the time of Balaclava and had spent most of his army career berating and belittling everybody in sight. His son, Captain Charles Bingham, was the exact opposite of his father, a sensible cavalry officer and a good landlord in the years ahead. He was only 24 at Balaclava, with no military experience at all and held his post because of Lucan's nepotism. Captain the Honourable Walter Charteris had no experience either. He suffered badly from seasickness on the journey east and was Lucan's nephew.

A better bet was Captain Arthur Hardinge. Son of the joint commander-in-chief with Raglan, he had also fought in India on the Sutlej 1845–6 and had been a company commander with the Coldstream Guards. So too was AQMG (Assistant Quartermaster General) Thomas Westropp who also wore the Sutlej medal. He had experience in three cavalry regiments, but at the time of the Crimea he was 74, making him arguably the oldest serving officer in the entire army. William Paulet, Assistant Adjutant General (AAG), was a child by comparison, at 54. Most of his army career had been spent sharpening up a particularly sloppy regiment, the 68th Light Infantry. Lieutenant Colonel Charles

Walker had served around the world with the 33rd Foot, in Gibraltar, the West Indies and even America, but none of it involved any action.

These were the men, among others, about whom Russell of *The Times* was complaining, but even the few experienced among them had no idea what to do about cholera.

From Gallipoli, a dirty town near the Sea of Marmara that was crammed with British, French and Turkish troops, as well as the camp followers who were drawn to such army towns, the Heavy Brigade was posted to Varna, on the Bulgarian coast of the Black Sea. Junior officers and even more so the men, had no idea what was going on. Diplomacy to avert a war was still happening behind the scenes, even as late as mid-June. Temple Godman, noting that the Bulgarian coast reminded him of Greenwich, quickly became disillusioned with Gallipoli. General Scarlett and Alexander Elliot were living in a half-flooded storeroom full of rubbish. 'Our Brigadier's rooms … swarm with all manner of creeping things, so much so that one would be covered by sitting there only a few minutes.'

Varna was not much better. Officers of the 17th Lancers, already there, told Temple Godman on his arrival that the place was crawling with snakes and centipedes. Wild dogs howled at night and there were rumours of Cossack patrols to the north. By 12 July, the temperatures were reaching 115 Fahrenheit (46 Celsius) at midday. Unlike some infantry units, the cavalry had no lightweight canvas trousers, but had to make do with their hot, leather-gussetted overalls. 'Fever is becoming more prevalent,' Temple Godman wrote, 'a sort of low fever and many men with cholera, diarrhoea etc.' He resorted to wine, which made him ill, then beer, which did the same 'and to take very weak brandy and water, and water when I can't get brandy.' And it was the water that carried cholera. It was the water that killed.

The official history of the war, written in nine volumes by the 'travelling gentleman' Alexander Kinglake, writes sombrely in Volume 2: 'But another and more dreadful enemy had now entered the camp of the Allies.' Cholera first appeared in the French army shortly after their leaving Marseilles. It broke out in the French lines at Gallipoli and 'followed their battalions into Bulgaria'. It hit the British army in the last week of July. There was something deeply ironic about this: the efficient, organised and suave French bringing death and destruction, not only to themselves but to their allies too. 'The disease that walketh by noonday was among us,' wrote Marianne Young, the infantry officer's wife, and it was a painful reminder that in the Crimea, as in every other theatre of war in history, it was disease, not the battlefield, that killed the greatest number.

Cholera morbus had first hit London in 1831, probably originating in India. Whether troops returning from active duty there or trading ships which brought it west is unclear. From October of that year, there were over 6,000 deaths in the capital. A particularly virulent outbreak occurred in 1848–9 when there were 30,000 recorded cases leading to 14,000 deaths. In the year that the Crimean War broke out, there were 10,675 fatalities, although there is no suggestion that the troops sent to the east took it with them.

The first symptoms were diarrhoea, followed by vomiting and severe dehydration. Overall, the mortality rate was about 50 per cent; the cause was unknown and there was no cure. Not until the third epidemic outbreak in 1866 did Dr John Snow, vice-president of the Westminster Medical Society, identify the disease as water-borne. He was even able to pinpoint the pump that lay at the epicentre of the outbreak in Broad Street. The worst-hit areas then were Vauxhall and Southwark, both districts using water from the Thames containing effluent from Baltic ships moored along the river.

What alarmed everybody connected with the disease, either in London or Bulgaria, was the speed with which it claimed lives. Two days was the most some people had, but often it was only a few hours. The navy was hit as badly as the army. On the *Britannia* in the Black Sea on 14 August, fifty men died in twenty hours.

The only solution that the army doctors had was to move camp constantly, believing that 'miasmic' odours from pools and marshes were responsible. Such places were the haunts of mosquitoes and carried the risk of malaria, but the water itself was poured unthinkingly into cavalry soldiers' canteens and taken to the next campsite. Hodge was ill at the end of September and whatever he had merely confused the bewildered medics who were trying to cope with it all. 'Felt very unwell,' he wrote on the 23rd, 'with pain in my stomach and dysentery.' Two days later, 'Fomented my stomack several times, which seems to do me good.' And the next day, 'In my bed all day. Much purged and very ill.' Two days after that, he could not get up. As a Christian gentleman he was stoical about it. 'God's will be done. He does everything for the best.'

Kinglake wrote at greater length after the war was over. By 19 August, the army had lost 532 men. On the march from one camp to another, soldiers doubled up with stomach cramps, falling by the wayside and desperately thirsty. In the French divisions, an estimated 10,000 were ill or dead. Kinglake knew Dr Rees of the *Britannia* personally, citing fifty-five deaths on board out of sixty infections. Bizarrely, the ship's officers were not affected (perhaps because they drank champagne and wine rather than water) and they went among the sick, soothing them and talking to them as mothers did to their frightened children.

In the army, those who survived cholera were weak for weeks, barely able to pitch and dismantle tents, saddle their horses or march with rifle and pack. The invasion of the Crimea went ahead in the hopes that the climate there would be better than the swamp-infested Bulgarian coast of the Black Sea.

Temple Godman remained positive – at least in his letters home. From Devna in the middle of July, he wrote:

> We have changed our ground a quarter of a mile, which is necessary in this climate now and then … Some fever and dysentery had laid up many of our men, but they got over it in a day or two … Nearly all our officers have been laid up from some cause; [Lieutenant Charles] Halford has been very ill.

At least, in the Bulgarian heat, the cavalry were told they need not wear their leather stocks. When he wrote to his brother Joseph at the end of the month, Temple Godman admitted that he had not mentioned cholera to their parents. Sixteen men of the Light Division died in half a day. And the lieutenant was nearer the truth than he knew when he wrote, 'I expect this valley is unhealthy and the men *would* drink the river water, which is very bad, and also the country wine; all warning is useless.' The Light Division had lost thirty-five men and two women; the 5th had lost three soldiers, although the cause, according to the regiment's doctor, George McCullogh, was a heart condition and typhus. The third death was indeed cholera and because of the paucity of officers, Temple Godman expected to have to perform the funeral ceremony himself:

> I can tell you, this work is anything but lively, when you see a man go to hospital [actually a field tent] and die in a few hours, then put in his grave with nothing but his blanket rolled around him and not knowing who may be next.

Temple Godman's concern was that his parents would worry about cholera because of Russell's presence with the Light Division and the fact that everybody was reading *The Times*. All the medical orderlies could do was to keep victims' extremities warm with hot compresses and rubbing.

TSM Franks remembered in his memoirs that the regiment was mercifully free from disease until several men reported sick simultaneously to the hospital tent. The surgeon with the 5th, although he seems not to have gone to the Crimea, was Dr Trousdale and under him, William Cattell. The patients' symptoms were all the same – vomiting and purging with pain in the bowels. Neither doctor had seen this before and ordered that the first to die be buried in his clothes so that everything connected with him was destroyed, to prevent the spread of infection.

Trousdale, Cattell and Colonel Le Marchant held an urgent council of war and, using interpreters, asked the locals what they knew of the disease. The whole area, they were told, was unhealthy and that resulted in a move to Kotlubie, 8 miles away. For a few days, all was well and the cholera seemed to have been left behind. Then, of course, it came back. There was no hospital corps in the army at that time, so a number of volunteers from the 5th offered to help the doctors and orderlies. The number of sick quickly spiralled, filling a marquee and several bell tents. There were usually about seventy patients at any one time. Fifteen died in twelve hours on one day and the regiment was digging mass grave pits three times a day to accommodate the corpses. 'It is occasions like these,' wrote Franks, 'that try a man's nerves and show what sort of metal he is made of.' A lump still rose in Franks' throat years later when he remembered the words of Brigade Major John Conolly, an ex-5th officer himself. 'Men, I hope you will not think me in any way "womanish" but … what would they think in England if they could see that?' He was pointing at a grave of seven men who, at reveille that morning, had been, in Franks' words, 'as fine soldiers as ever the sun shone on … in the bloom of health and manhood.'

To make matters worse, there were rumours in the 5th that two medicine chests, containing drugs that could cure cholera, had been left behind in Varna, and that, somehow, this was the fault of the colonel. It was this that led to the extraordinary 'disappearance' of Thomas Le Marchant from the scene and it explains why he never reached the Crimea at all. Today's vague and generic accounts of the 5th Dragoon Guards, particularly on websites, make no mention of Le Marchant; his impressive father dominates the news. Some versions have the colonel falling ill and going home, as several other officers did, but this clearly glosses over a scandal. We have seen already that Le Marchant was given command of the 5th when James Scarlett was promoted and his arrogant behaviour to his officers contrasted unfavourably with Scarlett's popularity.

On 28 August, Temple Godman, who could be expected, as adjutant, to be loyal to Le Marchant, wrote:

> I don't expect ever to see Le Marchant again, nor do I wish it, he is not at all liked, and no one would have much confidence in a man who left us as he did, just when the cholera was raging (being ill himself) when everyone was required to be present. I think at such a moment it was every man's duty to remain, however ill, unless his doctors insisted on his going.

There is no suggestion that either McCullogh or Cattell gave Le Marchant any such advice. Just a week later, Temple Godman wrote:

> I hope [Le Marchant] will never rejoin, for I think that no one will speak to him after what he has done. Finding himself quite incapable of commanding a regiment, he went to Lord Raglan and reported the regiment to him as unfit for service, thereby trying to escape himself at our expense, but everyone has found him out.

TSM Franks provides the details. Having found fault with his officers several times already, berating them in front of the men and claiming that the punishment they recommended for the men was too lenient, Le Marchant threatened them with reporting the entire regiment first to Sir George Brown of the infantry, then to Raglan himself. Even if accusations of inefficiency by the regiment were true (and there is nothing to substantiate them), the commander-in-chief could hardly accede to Le Marchant's request to send them home, as that would reduce the cavalry's strength by 10 per cent. What with the loss of men owing to cholera, such a notion was nonsensical. Clearly, Raglan agreed.

But what *really* happened in the 5th Dragoon Guards? When the rumours spread about the medicine chests, the men decided to form a deputation to ask the colonel outright whether the rumours were true and whose fault it was. One of the men involved was Surgeon McCullogh's servant and he reported all this to the doctor who duly passed it on to Le Marchant. Three men went to the colonel's hut to have it out with him, only to find that he had gone, hidden under horse-forage hay in an arabi driven by his servant, Private James Gamble, so that he could smuggle him away on board a ship at Varna.

Franks wrote:

> He had deserted his regiment in a mean and cowardly manner ... This was the last time we ever saw Colonel Le Marchant, nor did we hear anything more of him. It is not often that we hear of a Colonel of a Regiment deserting and of course, it was a surprise to many people who had no knowledge of the man; but he was an exception to all the Colonels I ever saw – he never seemed to take the slightest interest in the Corps from the day he joined us at Ballincollig. I don't think he ever once visited the Hospital tents, which were crowded with sick men, and they got it into their heads that he did not care whether they lived or died.

The following day, Captain Duckworth, 'one of the best officers in the service' according to Franks, died of cholera; so did the veterinary officer Fisher, who was dead within the hour after exhibiting symptoms. Franks himself fell ill, but pulled through. Command of his regiment devolved on the senior captain, Adolphus Burton 'who was', Franks wrote with some trepidation, 'a very young man'.

What of Le Marchant? At the end of November, Temple Godman heard a rumour that he was going to return to the Crimea. However, the men of the 5th were saying that Le Marchant's return was unlikely: 'He would not come here, because he would not like the noise of the cannon.' Godman was saying the same thing to his father in December – 'as for that greatest of all humbugs Le Marchant, it is very easy to get your doctor to tell you that the Crimea climate will kill you, when one doesn't want to come back.'

There had been reports at the end of September that Le Marchant had died, which Temple Godman repudiated. What he clearly did was to lie low while the war rumbled on. With the actions of the Alma, Balaclava and Inkerman following in quick succession in the autumn and the shambles of organisation that followed in the winter, Le Marchant may have been forgotten very quickly. In fact, he should have been court-martialled for desertion.

The hospital at Varna, rat-infested as all such communal buildings were, could not remotely cope with the number of sick. Hospitals at home were generally regarded with dread, increasing the risk of infection rather than curing disease. The French set up a hospital at Galeta near Constantinople, run by the advanced and highly effective Sisters of Charity of St Vincent de Paul.

As the army moved on from one camp to another, what appalled those who saw it was the robbing of newly dug graves by the local Turks. The men whom Temple Godman buried very probably had their blankets taken out of the ground as the cavalry moved on. Two thousand British soldiers were transported to Scutari, on the Bosphorus shore opposite Constantinople, but there was no Florence Nightingale there then and even when she arrived, she was powerless against a disease that no one understood. Lady Errol attended to the needs of the women of her husband's regiment, the 60th Rifles, but Fanny Duberly offered no such comforts. The women in general were badly hit by cholera and William Russell commented on it. Before the disease struck, he wrote that they 'seemed the happiest and most contented beings in the camp, where their services as excellent foragers and washerwomen were fully appreciated'.

Russell had been critical of the army's commissariat since day one and he was also acutely aware of the dirty conditions in every place where the army camped. Stagnant water, dead animals and general filth pervaded everything and *The Times'* man was not slow to include it all in his despatches. He pointed out that the locals in Varna were as badly hit as the army by cholera and painted a grim picture of the French camp, where General François Canrobert came back from a reconnaissance sortie to find his camp at Constanta looking like a hospital. There were not enough standing men to bury the dead. 'Fear,' wrote Russell, 'almost as demoralising as the disease itself, swept through the camps.' When he visited Varna hospital, largely occupied by the French who were waiting, shivering and retching on carts outside, he asked a *sous-officier* what the empty carts were for. The man looked at him and told him, in English, 'For the dead, Monsieur.' Russell talked to orderlies who had not seen their own beds for fifty-six hours. Even the doctors were crammed into tiny rooms, plagued by a howling wind from the sea. One of them slept in a passageway.

The fire that broke out in Varna on the night of 10 August caused panic – and a great deal of drunkenness among the rank and file of all three armies camped there. When a Greek civilian was seen deliberately setting fire to the alcohol running down the gutters, a French officer split the man's skull with his sword and left him to burn. Although it had no actual bearing, cholera seemed to recede after this, rather as it was generally imagined that the great fire of London in 1666 destroyed the plague. What was particularly galling to Russell was the natural beauty of Bulgaria compared with its dangers: 'the lake and the stream exhaled death and at night, fat unctuous vapours rose fold after fold from the valleys and crept up in the dark and stole into the tent of the sleeper and wrapped him in their deadly embrace.' There is little doubt that Russell believed this; so did his readers.

So weak was the Brigade of Guards that even the short march from Aladyn to Varna (less than 10 miles) wore them out and their rifles and packs had to be carried by civilians on arabis. Russell urged a Crimean invasion because 'the sound of the cannon and the sight of the Russians would do more to rouse [the men] from this gloomy mood than all the "doctor's stuff" as the men term medicine, or change of air in the world.'

Fanny Duberly recorded that the 5th Dragoon Guards 'are suffering terribly from cholera. Two days ago (9 August) eleven men died.' She and Henry took long rides, trying to escape the 'nervous apprehension' which cholera brought. By Friday, 18 August, Mrs Blades was ill. The wife of Private John Blades of the 8th Hussars, she had replaced the ineffectual Mrs Williams and had perhaps done her job as Fanny's maid rather too well. She was recovering from a fever but relapsed 'from over-anxiety to attend to my comforts'. She was unconscious for a day and died on the morning of the 20th. 'Truly we are in God's hands,' Fanny wrote, 'and far enough from the help of man.' She sounded like Russell, bemoaning the lack of medical supplies, good food and doctors. The next day, however, she cheered herself up by shooting quail with Henry and Captain George Chetwode of the 8th.

What they all needed, the officers believed, was a jolly good invasion!

Chapter 7

'A Name That Will Ever be Memorable'

'**B**efore we left Varna,' Temple Godman wrote to his father, 'we heard of an engagement … I don't think from what I heard, the cavalry were in for much.'

The aim of British and French strategy was to land somewhere to the north of Sebastopol, the naval base, march south and lay siege to the city, with a harbour nearby for seaborne supplies and, if necessary, reinforcements. It was considered too dangerous to sail into Sebastopol harbour itself, even with a fleet as superior as the British. The best place for a defender to stop an invasion is at the coast, as the Cantii and Regni tribes of southern Britain had stopped Caesar's exploratory raid in 55BC. Had the Russians attacked the chaotic landings at Kalamita Bay on 14 September 1854, there would probably have been no siege of Sebastopol at all. As it was, the constant harassment of coastal defences by the British and French navies made the Russians wary and they could not be sure, until it happened, exactly where the landing would take place.

Despite the outbreak of cholera, the loss of the *Europa* and growing concern among the more discerning officers in all arms of the service, both the British and French armies had an unassailable sense of their own invincibility which bordered on complacency. Raglan's army was, after all, the one that had defeated Napoleon. He himself had had his arm shattered at Waterloo, riding as a staff officer behind Wellington and everybody knew the story of his asking for the arm, amputated on the field without anaesthetic, so that he could reclaim the ring his wife had given him. The fact that virtually no one serving under him had been involved in a European war (Lucan, arguably, the exception) for forty years seems to have passed everybody by. The French, for their part, glossed over Waterloo. Even Wellington had called it 'a near-run thing' and the inimitable emperor had, the French believed, only been defeated by a Europe-wide coalition against him and plain, old-fashioned bad luck.

Nobody knew what the attitude of the Turks was, except that they were fighting a war of self-preservation against an overweening bully, Tsar Nicholas and his grey-coated Russians. Throughout the war, British and French troops consistently berated the Turks, especially after Balaclava when their abandonment of forts on the Causeway Heights led directly to the loss of the Light Brigade. As for the 15,000 strong Piedmontese and Sardinian army, nobody had much of a clue why they were there at all.

One witness who watched the landing at Kalamita Bay was William Russell: 'The vast armada which had moved on during the night in perfect order, studding the horizon with a second heaven of stars and covering the face of the sea with innumerable lights, advanced parallel with the coast till it gradually closed in to the shore.'

The French landed first, each infantry company sent forward in light marching order to check the dunes above the beach. In two hours, 6,000 men were on the sand, the officers in full dress, being watched by tiny knots of Cossack horsemen with telescopes, ready to report back to Sebastopol what they had seen. No shots were fired and Russell found the whole spectacle, of senior officers carried ashore by sailors, quite amusing. Each man had three days' rations, a spare pair of boots in his knapsack, a shirt, greatcoat, forage cap and water canteen. The infantry carried their rifles or smooth-bored muskets, together with shot and ball-cartridge.

Some of the British infantry had been at sea for seventeen days and their legs were, at first, unsteady on firm ground. Many of them had been eating nothing but salt pork and hardtack for the last five days. There were no ambulances for the sick and wounded – and some of the soldiers stumbling inland were still shaking and vomiting with cholera. Junior officers marched with their men, as their horses had not landed.

Senior officers sat on upturned barrels or in the sand, waiting for their animals to arrive. Doctors from the rudimentary hospital corps and the regimental surgeons did what they could as the numbers on the beach grew; 150 men had been buried at sea on the week's voyage from Varna and it was clear that the healthier air of the Crimea was not going to help an army barely fit for active service.

'Seldom or never,' wrote Russell, 'were 27,000 Englishmen more miserable.' There were no tents and little food; and to cap it all, the rain came down in torrents as night fell. There was no grog, no fires, no prospect of breakfast. Russell found some shelter under a cart, but the incessant rain and the roar of the surf kept him awake. Recently, a school of younger historians have played situations like this down. The Crimea, they argue, seemed worse than it was because Russell reported it. Mistakes and disasters happened in the Peninsula too, as they did and do in all wars; it was merely that Wellington did not have an annoying newspaperman to pass comment. Some of this is true, but an efficient army, well organised and ably led, would not have spent its first night on enemy soil, exposed in the open, with inadequate provisions, unaware of where the enemy was, what numbers he had or where the next food supply, after the three-day rations ran out, was coming from. When he landed in the Crimea, one of the first things Temple Godman asked his mother to send was a map because the 5th Dragoon Guards, at least, did not possess one!

The Light Cavalry and the artillery landed the next day, but the surf was up and a number of horses were lost, including one of Raglan's chargers. There was confusion over the landing of tents; first they were ordered off the ships, then returned to the holds. The French, of course, already had their tents with them, as did the Turks.

Still on board ship off Bulgaria, Temple Godman was lashed by the same rain that hit the beaches and he realised grimly that his winter gear was in storage in Constantinople. He had got hold of some brandy, but it was not very good and Lieutenant Halford had sent for more from Fortnum and Mason's in Piccadilly. Hodge, too, had no warm clothing or thick socks – 'I much fear I shall never be able to stand the cold.' He only heard about the Kalamita Bay landing on the 17th and, since he had received no orders, had to conclude that the Heavy Brigade would be the last to leave Varna.

Fanny Duberly watched events from the deck of the *Shooting Star.* She reported that Lord Cardigan was itching to get ashore and to 'get at' the Russians. He had already made a fool of himself back in July when he had taken the 8th Hussars and the 13th Light Dragoons on the 'soreback reconnaissance', chasing reports of Russian cavalry north of Varna. The two regiments were gone for seventeen days, covering, according to Hodge, 60 miles one day and saw no Russians at all. In the process, Cardigan lost five horses and another seventy-five were unrideable for weeks.

On Monday 18th, Fanny wrote: 'Today I set my foot in the Crimea.' Her husband's 8th Hussars were already 7 miles inland. This discrepancy infuriated Temple Godman who wished, in a letter home, that he had joined the Light Cavalry instead of the Heavies. He reports that Marshal St Arnaud, the aged French commander-in-chief, who was far from well, had prophesied that the French eagles (he did not mention the Union Jack!) would be flying over Sebastopol in less than three weeks. Because the 5th had been so decimated with cholera, it had been decided to amalgamate them with Hodge's 4th. Some wag commented that the new unit should be called the 9th.

Godman would have been even more annoyed had he known at the time what happened on 19 September. A thirsty and exhausted advance guard of the army with a screen of Light Cavalry at its head reached the Bulganek river. Colin Campbell, with his terrifying voice, kept his Highlanders in check but the others ran headlong to the water to gulp it down. They were still drinking when Russian cavalry were spotted approaching over the brow of a hill. Cardigan at last had the fight he was longing for and he threw out a skirmish line of his crimson-overalled 'cherrybums', the 11th Hussars. They fired their carbines at the Russians who fired back. William Russell was there, as were Raglan, Richard Airey and Louis Nolan, who remarked what bad shots the Russians were. Colonel John Douglas, commanding the 11th, ordered them to fall back to the river; there was no telling the size of the Russian contingent facing them. The enemy artillery opened up with round shot, balls of iron that could be seen bouncing over the ground as they reached the end of their trajectory. The impact of those balls was terrifying and could snap a man's leg like a twig. One soldier of the 11th, with his leg dangling by the skin, the bone shattered, wheeled his horse out of line and told the regimental surgeon he was reporting to have his leg dressed. In all, four men were wounded and six horses killed. Rations of meat and grog were served out as the Russians pulled back, but their camp fires – and the blaze of villages put to the torch in the kind of scorched-earth policy they had used against Napoleon in 1812 – reddened the night sky.

It is difficult to know why Raglan left the Heavy Brigade behind at Varna. Not only was it unhealthy ground, it was seven days' sailing time away from the Crimea. In effect, half the British cavalry were not available at the front for two weeks. It was perhaps just as well that the first major clash of the war was a hard infantry slog, in which neither side used its cavalry. Raglan is notorious today for his phrase 'We really should keep our cavalry in a bandbox'. It is true that his numbers were small, less than 2,000 sabres, but keeping them out of harm's way across a sea seems to be taking care a little too far.

At first sight, the battle of the Alma, fought overlooking that river on Wednesday, 20 September, was an impossible undertaking for the Allies. The Russians, under the command of Alexander Menshikov, had taken up position on steep hilltops above the Alma's banks. Menshikov, an arrogant aristocrat of the old school, was Cardigan's age (56) and had fought the Turks in 1828 before taking over command of the navy. As Russian ambassador at Constantinople, he had played his part in the breakdown of diplomacy that had led directly to the Crimea. Like Raglan, he had faced Napoleon, in the emperor's disastrous Moscow campaign of 1812. But even a man of Menshikov's experience could not forge an efficient fighting army out of the Russian peasantry. He subscribed to the ridiculous maxim of an older general, Suvorov, who believed 'the bullet is a fool, but the bayonet is a fine fellow'. This notion, ignoring the technical improvement of firearms while sending thousands of men, badly equipped, to their deaths, was still being carried out by Josef Stalin and his generals in the Second World War.

The Allied army at the Alma perhaps numbered 60,000 – twice the number that Wellington had at Waterloo. Because of Raglan's rabid mistrust of spies, no one in the Allied camp had any clear idea of the number of Menshikov's troops. He may have had 39,000 infantry and 3,600 cavalry. The British cavalry, by contrast, was made up of the five regiments of the Light Brigade and a unit of the Royal Horse Artillery. Both sides had about 130 field guns, firing various sizes of shot, from 9 to 32lb in weight.

At first sight, from the Alma plain where the Allies were drawn up, the height looked almost impregnable. No one there had any idea of the fighting abilities of the men who faced them. One of two men who had even seen a Russian soldier in action before that day was Lord Lucan, sitting his horse with his detested brother-in-law, Cardigan, on the British left flank, beyond a burned out village caked Tarkhanler. Next to him were the scarlet-coated infantry divisions of Sir George Cathcart (4th), the Duke of Cambridge (1st) and Sir George Brown (Light Division). Cathcart was the other man who knew the Russians. Now in his sixties, he had served with them against Napoleon and had relatively wide experience in Canada and Africa. The Duke of Cambridge was by far the youngest of the British generals and was really only there because he was the queen's cousin. Rather as Florence Nightingale lived on for years, stultifying the progress of nursing in the process, so Cambridge lived on as commander-in-chief until 1904, opposing new ideas in the army for as long as he could. George Brown was something of an enigma. He was one of the oldest generals in the army, at 72, but he had fought under Wellington in the Peninsula and was always impeccably turned out – 'like a piece of well-washed china', somebody said. Even so, he was notoriously churlish and generally unpopular with anyone who knew him.

Beyond the narrow trunk road were the Second and Third Divisions of George de Lacy Evans and Richard England. De Lacy Evans was another old man with a distinguished record. The Peninsula, Waterloo, even the American War of 1812, could be added to his battle honours. He was an author and a radical MP when not serving with the army and his lean, scruffy features in the Roger Fenton photograph taken of him back in London after the war shows a man of determination. England, by comparison, although nine years younger, was 'of no particular career'. All that Fenton could think to say about him was 'he's not a bad rider'.

The other units north of the Alma were the Turks, 9,000 strong, nearest the sea, and the French. The divisional commanders here were a mixed bunch. In the centre, the ground was held by Prince Napoleon, the nephew of the former emperor. Like all the Bonapartes, this Napoleon did his best to *look* like the scourge of Europe and, according to Kinglake, who devotes nearly an entire volume to this one battle, he had at least *some* of the emperor's legendary ability to multi-task. General Forey's division stood between Richard England and the Turks, and the Allies' right wing was commanded by the most competent and dazzling general of the war, François Canrobert, a product of the academy at St Cyr with years of active service in Algeria.

Facing them, the Russian army was an unknown. With hindsight, Tsar Nicholas's autocracy meant that in the army, like every other element of Russian society, there was no modern thinking and no willingness to change. Menshikov, whom Kinglake describes as a 'wayward, presumptuous man' had taken no precautions in the positions that he had chosen, believing that the heights on which his troops were drawn up were virtually impregnable. In fact, there was a wooden bridge, still intact, over the river which was, anyway, after a dry summer, perfectly fordable by men on foot. Even though the Allied artillery would have problems, and this was no country for cavalry (which of course worked against the Russians too), a determined infantry assault was likely to succeed.

Kinglake estimates that the French numbers at the Alma were 30,000, but he concedes that cholera had seriously reduced that. St Arnaud, the commander-in-chief, personally commanded the Turkish contingent. Raglan had 25,000 infantrymen and 1,000 cavalry, together with 65 guns. Off the coast lay nine battleships, their guns trained on Menshikov's positions. Because of the layout of the Russian divisions, the British found themselves facing the toughest opposition across the river, where the enemy had thrown up two earthworks called the Greater and Lesser Redoubts.

On the morning of the 20th, without drums and trumpets or even reveille, the Allied army moved forward. General Pierre Bosquet led the French advance guard and the British lines had to manoeuvre to face front. There was a delay while the British baggage train was secured, bullock carts lumbering across the field that would become a killing ground later. Accordingly, Bosquet halted his advance and let his men brew coffee. In all the battles of the Crimean War, orders were sent by 'gallopers', staff officers carrying the written word of generals from one part of the field to another. At twenty past ten the warships opened fire. The timings of this day's events were recorded by the judge advocate, William Romaine, the most senior civilian on Raglan's staff, who had incredibly long sight and was called by Raglan 'the eye of the army'. Romaine stayed in the saddle all day, using his pocket watch and making notes. By half past eleven, British and French lines were advancing together.

The weather was good, like England in June as some men remembered it. There was a sudden silence, of which Kinglake poetically wrote 'it was now, after near forty years of peace, the great nations of Europe were once more meeting for battle'. Colin Campbell's Highlanders were ordered to 'shake loose' their cartridges ready for the attack. His men responded 'with beaming joy', Kinglake wrote, 'for they came of a warlike race; yet not without emotion of a graver kind – they were young soldiers, new to battle'. St Arnaud and Raglan met in the middle of the front line, two old men, one dying, but full of confidence in their troops. 'Hurrah for Old England!' St Arnaud shouted, in English with virtually no French accent, and everybody cheered him.

The general assault began at shortly after one o'clock, Russian artillery testing its range from the heights and skirmishers taking pot-shots at the advancing line. Despite the improvement in the range and accuracy of rifles, as opposed to muskets (which not all the infantry had in 1854), the tactics were still essentially those of Waterloo. With flags flying, trumpets blaring and drums beating to keep the pace, men marched forward in line, shoulder to shoulder. As they went down to rifle- or cannon-fire, the ranks closed in, orchestrated by the officers marching ahead and the NCOs on the wings. As in any battle, survival was a lottery based on the physics of random flying lead.

The Russians were amazed to see the British coming towards them in line formation. In the years of Napoleon, every other European army, including the Russians, fought in close column, only extending to line when within musket range of the enemy. Although a column could crash through a formation if delivered with enough guts, it considerably cut down the fire power of the ranks at the rear, for fear of hitting their own men.

At half past one, cannons opened up on Raglan's front, the balls bouncing around the commander-in-chief. The front ranks were ordered to lie down to minimise casualties, while Raglan gave orders that his 'gallopers' should go about their business quietly. They were within telescope range of the Russians now who could see everything they did; it was important to be seen to be behaving well. Kinglake praised the attitude of the men, a few of whom were being picked off by now – 'a game where death is the forfeit has a strange, gloomy charm for them'. They made up girls' names for the artillery pieces facing them – Mary and Elizabeth were the favourites.

In the centre, near the bridge, the abandoned village of Burlyuk suddenly burst into flames, clearly having been fitted with Russian incendiary devices. It was mistimed, however, going up too soon for the British lines and even providing a black smoke cover for their approach. At ten past two, Bosquet, ahead of Canrobert's division, crossed the Alma and trudged on up the slopes. His Zouaves, the colourful North African troops who fascinated everybody who had never seen them before, were particularly adept at scrambling through the vineyards and the watching sailors in the ships cheered them on. There were no Russians ahead of Bosquet because the Minsk battalion had not come across quickly enough and the scattered *sotnyas* (regiments) of Cossacks were not able to charge down the steep ravines. Bosquet took the Heights and hammered away at the Russian centre with his artillery.

'With men like you,' St Arnaud yelled at Canrobert and Prince Napoleon, 'I have no orders to give. I have but to point to the enemy!' While this was buttering Napoleon up above his reputation level, it was true of Canrobert and the 1st and 3rd divisions splashed their way across the river. French skirmishers hid in the vineyards and picked off their targets on the Heights, nibbling from their rations and swigging from their canteens until they had clear shots.

To the left of the British line, which was still lying down and still under fire, the Light Brigade, headed by Lucan and Cardigan, fumed. Other than the pointless 'soreback reconnaissance' and the skirmish at the Bulganek, the cavalry had done nothing yet and the events of this day were to win Lucan the sneering nickname 'Lord Look-On' because of his inactivity. They had two troops of horse artillery with them under the command of Captains George Maude and John Brandling and the shot was now reaching them. An artilleryman had his head blown off and George Paget's 4th Light Dragoons, who had been dozing in a melon field, now mounted and drew their swords for action. None was forthcoming. Lucan was nearly hit and Cardigan moved his front line back to keep out of range. Louis Nolan, on Airey's staff, spoke fluent French and he galloped between Raglan and St Arnaud with messages, the leopard-skin saddle flounces of the 15th Hussars very obvious to the Russian telescopes.

It was a French galloper who got the British line moving, however. Bosquet could be cut off and Canrobert's and Prince Napoleon's divisions were now under galling fire. 'The infantry will advance,' Raglan said. It may have been the only order he gave throughout the entire battle. Nolan took the news to the divisional commanders, but his horse was killed under him as he reached George Brown's Light Division and another staff officer took it up.

As they crossed the river (the bridge was too narrow and too tempting a target for the Russians), it was obvious that the Alma had little tricks of its own. In places, men were only in water up to their ankles; in others, the current swirled around their chests and some men lost their footing with the weight of their equipment and were drowned. Musket balls ripped through the ranks, bouncing on the water and thudding into mud. Above it all, the thud of drums and the skirl of the Highlanders' pipes.

Some men had grabbed bunches of grapes as they reached the vineyards. General William Codrington ordered 'Fix bayonets' (which would, presumably, have delighted Menshikov) and Colonel Yeo, rather destroying 200 years of training and drill in the process, yelled to his men, 'Never mind forming! Come on anyhow!'

The Alma was William Russell's first major battle, as it was for nearly everybody who crossed the river that day. George Brown rode past him, calling 'in a very jaunty, Hyde Park manner, "It's a very fine day, Mr Russell".' He was blown out of the saddle moments later, yelling to his men, 'I'm all right, Twenty Third. Be sure to remember this day.' A bandsman near the reporter had his face ripped off by a shell 'and he fell dead – a horrible sight'. Russell watched the Light Division, 'scrambling, rushing, foaming like a bloody surge up the ascent and in a storm of fire, bright steel and whirling smoke, charge …'

Contrary to what future generations of soldiers observed, the birds did not stop singing, but flitted about in the smoke, terrified by the noise and screaming at each other. Russell gave his brandy flask to a soldier who hobbled by him, his foot blown away – 'Thank you kindly, sir'. He could not see the Highlanders in the smoke, but he heard their battle cries and saw the Light Division and the Guards hurl themselves on the dense mass of Russians, bayonetting them and blasting their guns at close range. The volleys of the Guards, in particular, were so devastating that the ridge was suddenly covered in dead and wounded and the Russians were falling back.

'It was near five o'clock,' Russell wrote, unaware that Romaine was somewhere noting the time exactly. 'The Battle of the Alma was won. The men halted … and as the Commander-in-Chief, the duke of Cambridge, Sir de Lacy Evans and other popular generals rode in front of the line, the soldiers shouted and … the whole army burst into a tremendous cheer which made one's heart leap. The effect of that cheer can never be forgotten by those who heard it.'

Now, every horseman in the field knew, by training or instinct, was the time for a cavalry charge. Rattled artillerymen, busy carting away their guns to the south; shattered infantry, their ranks decimated by shot and bayonet – these were the natural targets in a battlefield situation for a cavalry attack. But there was no bugle call, no order to Lucan for the cavalry to advance. All day, the Light Brigade had sat and watched. And now, General James Estcourt rode up with explicit orders to the contrary – 'Mind, now, the cavalry are *not* to attack.'

Instead, the Light Brigade rounded up Russian prisoners, dazed and shell-shocked. An officer fired his pistol at Private James Whiteman of the 17th Lancers, but the shot missed and Wightman felled the man with his lance butt. Colonel Lawrenson, commanding the regiment, upbraided the soldier for cowardice and even allowing for the fact that he was suffering from cholera, Lawrenson seems to have missed the point spectacularly; the Russians were, after all, the enemy. Another order from Raglan even called a halt to the collection of prisoners, and Lucan, in disgust, led his cavalry from the field.

Because of his caution, his age, the lack of instinct that a great commander should possess, Raglan missed a chance. He had no way of knowing how many Russians were on their way to support Menshikov or where they were. In fact, the only reserve that the Russian commander had was positioned so close to his rear divisions that they were soon absorbed in the fighting and ceased to be a reserve at all. It was also true that the British cavalry (there was no mention of the French in any of this) were less than 1,000 strong and riddled with cholera. Even so, a *show* of strength would have worked wonders on the Allied side and underlined the size and importance of their victory.

As Kinglake pointed out, battles like the Alma ended usually before nightfall, with marauding scavengers from the countryside. First, victorious soldiers helped themselves to dead men's belongings, weapons, trinkets, food. There was still, in Britain, a brisk trade in 'Waterloo teeth', most of which had been nowhere near the Belgian battlefield. But the Alma was too cut off from the riff-raff of Sebastopol and the local villages had largely been destroyed, so men lay where they had fallen. Bodies lay on their backs, carried backwards by the weight of their packs. Some had their arms held high, reaching for the sky when their rifles had dropped from their grip. The groaning wounded stirred slightly, asking for water and 'for dignity and composure they were almost the equals of the dead'.

William Sankey and William Romaine, with the quartermaster general's (QMG) staff, set about providing food and bandages for the wounded. Those who could not walk were carried to the coast to be put on board ship; the Russians had to wait a while longer, before being shipped to Odessa under a flag of truce. Russell of *The Times* watched the burial parties going about their grim business and could not believe the piles of greatcoats, bearskins, helmets, slings, belts, swords, muskets and bayonets strewn all over the Heights. No Russian standards were taken.

But on the following night, it was business as usual. 'Many men died of cholera,' Russell wrote. 'My sleep was disturbed by the groans of the dying …'

And, as usual, rumours flew thick and fast. Fanny Duberly was on board ship off Eupatoria on the 22nd when news came in via Mrs Blades that 'there has been a dreadful battle – 500 English killed and 5,000 Russians; and all our poor cavalry fellows are all killed; and, the

Lord be good to us, we're all widows.' The next day, more information reached Fanny. '2,090 English killed and wounded; the 7th and 23rd Fusiliers almost destroyed and, thank God! the Cavalry were not engaged.'

Their time would come.

Chapter 8

'This is the Way to Make War'

The casualties from the Alma were horrendous, but they were not as bad as expected and the Russian losses were so much worse. The Allied army, patched up as well as it could be (the most senior officer badly injured was de Lacy Evans) marched south for Sebastopol, with Cardigan's Light Brigade a foraging screen to the front.

Although the information from Sebastopol was thin, Raglan and St Arnaud considered an attack from the north on the city to be too dangerous, so they swung east to perform the 'flank march', as it came to be known, passing the area called Mackenzie's Farm after a Scotsman who had settled there years before and linking up with the road across the Tchernaya river that led directly to Sebastopol. The fleet, in the meantime, had secured a port to the south which would do for another landing and the provision of supplies.

'We land in a bay,' Temple Godman wrote to his father, 'I believe called Balaklava.'

The 5th were suffering badly from what Godman calls 'remittent fever' but he did not think it was actually cholera. Only three subalterns (junior officers) were left at Varna. McNeile was in a bad way and should never have come out; his family wanted him to leave the army, as he was clearly not cut out for it. As for Godman himself, he was feeling much better, taking a bath every day. He was not happy with the new arrivals among the officers – 'our second captain … knows about as much as you do of his profession'. The Scots Greys were due to come up from Scutari and Godman was looking forward to the *Himalaya* again, with good dinners and comfortable beds. Lieutenant German Wheatcroft of the Inniskillings had been out shooting boar and was due to get his own troop.

Godman was appalled by the behaviour of the Bashi-bazouks, the Turkish irregular cavalry. These lawless brigands had been disbanded as a fighting force because they lacked much discipline, but they continued to rob and cut the throats of civilians in the area around Varna. He was also outraged that he was liable for income tax – 'it takes £1 off my monthly pay'. The guilty party here was Robert Peel, who had been dead for four years; as prime minister, he had instituted the routine peacetime payment of income tax as opposed to the emergency measures advocated originally by William Pitt and abandoned in 1816. Godman's horses were doing well, especially the cob that was outside his tent as he wrote, rolling in the sand.

Ten days after the Alma, the 5th were on board the *Jason*, by no means as impressive as the *Himalaya* and other regiments were on the *Simla*. Godman seems to have drawn the short straw and was left behind for a night with no tent. At least his fifty men got hold of some meat and biscuits and they were able to cook over open fires. The *Jason* towed a ship of the Royals, but a severe storm hit them, snapping the two cables like string. The next day, the convoy had broken up completely, with most of the ships out of sight. The *Jason* lost eight horses.

It was now that Godman had his first glimpse of the enemy. While a solitary duel was going on between HMS *Retribution* and the shore battalions, he saw cavalry on the ramparts and assumed they were Cossacks. Having heard the news with letters that arrived on 30 September, Godman was full of praise for the infantry at the Alma. 'The French were quite astonished, as were the Russians too, I expect'; they believed they could hold the heights for six weeks against 80,000 men. Brigade Major John Conolly had lost his brother with the decimated 23rd Foot.

Cholera still lingered, but it hit newly arrived regiments harder than the old sweats, which Godman no doubt believed he was by this time. The Scots Greys had lost an officer, but the 21st Foot, which had not been engaged at the Alma, had already buried 200 men. As for that battle, the adjutant voiced the opinion of virtually everyone except Raglan – 'They certainly should have waited for the cavalry …'

Once on shore in the Crimea, Godman could feel that, at last, the war had started. He slept under a cart the first night because the tents had not unloaded and the cavalry were harassed during the hours of darkness by Russian cavalry patrols probing their defences. Balaclava harbour, which, it would soon be apparent, was far too small for the requisite number of ships, was 7 miles from Sebastopol, the first cavalry camps 3 or 4 miles nearer. The Cossacks were not impressive, largely because Godman misunderstood their tactics. They were light horsemen, used for foraging and lightning raids. They 'know better than to stand a charge of even a dozen of our men. They come near and shoot at us.' There was nothing like the Cossacks in the British army. They were a race apart, originally independent tribesmen from the Steppes, linked by history and sometimes genealogy to the hard-riding Mongols of Genghis Khan, the Medieval warlord. They had to provide their own horses (little more than ponies alongside the English thoroughbreds), uniforms and swords. Only their firearms were provided by the tsar's government and these were not very good. As far as the bulk of the Russian army was concerned, especially the officers of the elite regiments, the Cossacks were regarded in much the same way as the British looked upon the Bashi-bazouks.

At the end of August, Hodge had been told that he was now in command of Temple Godman's regiment as well as his own. The 5th's surgeon, Pitcairn, had died, as had Captain George Duckworth, 'one of the best officers in the service', according to TSM Franks. The veterinary officer, Lieutenant Fisher, followed him and Temple Godman attended his funeral. As Hodge wrote on 28 August, the temperature in his tent at Varna was 95 Fahrenheit (35 Celsius). There was a great deal of grumbling in the Heavy Brigade, what with sickness and a lack of activity. TSM George Cruse would become Riding Master of the 1st Royals in March 1855, but before he became, effectively, one of the 'establishment', he was a professional moaner. He wrote to his wife Eliza that the men's boots were disgusting and there was no coal to light fires hot enough to re-shoe the horses. Hodge was aware of this problem and offered to buy the coal himself, but permission was refused as it was not 'the system'.

What *really* annoyed Hodge, however, was that news that ought to have been top secret was banner headlines in the British press. '*The Times* newspaper [Hodge must have been aware of Russell's presence with the army] ... has informed the Russians long ago of all we *did*, or rather *did not* ... Believe nothing,' he urged his father, 'you read in the 'Morning Lie' or the 'Daily Liar' or any other papers.'

There was a sale of horses and belongings of the dead of the 5th Dragoon Guards. The horses went for very little in the auction, but shirts did well. Hodge was furious that he could only take two horses to the Crimea, but by 2 September, he was ill. His adjutant, the unimpressive Lieutenant Webb, had gone down too, but was making himself worse by drinking champagne – 'poisonous kind of liquid at best. It will not do to play these tricks out here.'

'Hurrah for the Crimea!' Cornet Fisher of the 4th wrote home. 'Take Sebastopol in a week or two and then into winter quarters.' Hodge knew better, but this was the attitude of most young men at the beginning of a campaign; the 'lost generation' of 1914 felt the same. The Heavy Brigade, kicking its heels at Varna, was too well fed, according to Hodge. Each man had 1½lb of beef a day and the same of biscuit, as well as rice, sugar, coffee and rum. The wooden water canteens, by comparison, were falling apart. Contemplating the Crimean landing, Hodge wrote: 'I hope this may not prove a second Walcheren affair.' He was referring to a disastrous attack by Britain on the French-held island at the mouth of the river Scheldt in 1809, which achieved nothing and racked up huge casualties. It did not happen at Kalamita Bay because the Russians missed the chance to oppose the landing in force. It *was* to happen again, equally disastrously, in 1915 when the British landed in open rowing boats at Gallipoli under heavy Turkish heavy gun- and machine-gun fire. History *does* repeat itself and we do not learn from our mistakes.

The rain in mid-September took its toll on horses and saddlery. 'The poor brutes had scraped away all the sand and were all standing in canals of muddy water, their coats staring, themselves shivering and looking only fit for dogs.'

Two days after the Alma, Hodge was on board the *Simla*. He had 230 troop horses, 47 officers' chargers and 17 baggage animals. Somehow, he had managed to wangle five horses for himself, one of many examples of how the organisation of the war was being mishandled. The men's quarters were in total darkness below decks and the noise of the horses' stamping hoofs was deafening.

Storms continued to batter the Heavy Brigade ships. The Royals were down to a single squadron in terms of horses. On 26 September, they lost more than the regiment had lost at Waterloo. Their commanding officer, Lieutenant Colonel John Yorke, noted that the total loss was 150 animals. Altogether, the Heavy Brigade had lost 226 horses and the rest horrified Lucan when he saw them. Hodge, ill and even more inclined to grumble than usual, was appalled by the laxity of his officers of the 4th, especially Forrest. The man was supposedly Hodge's 'number two', but 'he seems to think he is to do nothing'. The men landed in the Crimea in their full dress uniforms, as well as a shirt, a pair of drawers, a vest and a pair of socks. The valises in which these things should have been stored behind their saddles were still on board ship and stayed there throughout the winter.

It would have been possible to launch an assault on Sebastopol once the Heavy Cavalry had arrived. Despite the build-up to this war, the Russians had not defended the town adequately other than sinking ships in Sebastopol harbour to deny the Allies access to it. The French, despite their heroism under Canrobert, were wary of an attack on the town and set up their camps at Kamiesch. Hodge whinged about the lack of private servants, which had been disallowed. Such men, he knew, turned to drink anyway. The colonel felt a little better when he went on board the

Sans Pareil, a 70-gun ship of the line commanded by a relative, Captain Sidney Dacres. He felt better still when he steamed out of Balaclava along the coast to Yalta, passing the summer palaces of the Russian aristocracy, 'all in white marble'. They landed to find some bad flour, a little wine and no cattle. The sailors got drunk and Dacres was furious.

On 7 October, Hodge heard that St Arnaud, the French commander, had died of cholera a week earlier and that Canrobert now ran the show. St Arnaud was an experienced soldier and, like most senior French officers, a political one, having supported the emperor in his *coup d'état* in Paris three years earlier. He was not at his best in the Crimea, however, and Canrobert was widely seen as a better option.

TSM Franks described the camp around Kadikoi. There were vineyards everywhere and empty houses where the inhabitants had got out fast, even leaving prepared meals on their tables. Medical officers who believed that grapes caused cholera issued stern warnings to the men.

Temple Godman was explaining to his father on 6 October the difference between outlying piquets, inlying piquets and videttes. All the cavalry, not just the Light Brigade, were involved in this, scouting up to 5 miles ahead of the camps to keep watch on enemy troop movements. Because so many officers were ill, Godman was on duty every day. He had clear views of Sebastopol, the warships in the harbour and an army of people, soldiers and civilians, scurrying like ants to build earthworks, ramparts and ditches to keep the Allies out. Unbeknown to Godman, the man in charge of all this was a German engineer officer, Colonel Franz Todleben, a 'natural' who was the best thing that Menshikov had under his command. In true Russian fashion, the commander-in-chief disliked Todleben and almost sacked him before the fortification work began.

Captain Adolphus Burton, not much older than Godman and now in command of the 5th, was nearly killed when a shell from the town burst on the hillside, killing a sergeant and two soldiers of the 63rd Foot. Godman described the monotony of the salt pork and biscuit.

They got 'some very skinny mutton' and it was boiled up in a pot into a mess resembling what the Godmans' groundskeeper fed to his dogs. He was annoyed that the Scots Greys, having bypassed Varna entirely, were far better off than any other unit. They 'look first rate, but then they have lost no men ... have done no work and had the best of forage'.

Godman was very impressed with the local civilians. They were Crim Tartars, not Russians at all and most of them were Muslims rather than Russian Orthodox. They were polite and doffed their caps, which was probably a sensible move in the presence of *any* army of occupation. Local houses were stripped of their timber to make fires, but the French were particularly vandalistic, burning beds and wardrobes. A winery near Kadikoi furnished huge barrels that served the 5th as makeshift beds.

The British lines were within 1,400 yards of Sebastopol by 12 October and lines of trenches had been dug by the infantry, which were guarded all night as the temperatures plummeted. The flashes of gunfire and the hiss of shells was particularly obvious after dark. Without enough tents, the cavalry still slept largely in the open, their clothes wet through with dew by the morning. Godman's servant, Private Kilbourne, had got himself a large cupboard into which he climbed each night to keep dry. Only three officers, including Godman, remained fit enough for duty throughout this period.

Constant rumours filled the camps that a massive army of reinforcements was on the way to Sebastopol from Perekop. In theory, the Russians had the entire resources of their vast country to draw on, but this does not take into account the unbelievable sluggishness of Russian organisation. Somewhere behind Sebastopol's earthworks, Leo Tolstoy was a junior officer serving with the artillery. Later in the war, he spoke to British and French prisoners and was able to contrast their sangfroid with the cloying pessimism of his own people:

> Every soldier [among the Allies] is proud of his position and has a sense of his value, he feels he is a positive asset to his army. He

has good weapons and he knows how to use them, he is young, he has ideas about politics and art and this gives him a feeling of dignity. On our side; senseless training, useless weapons, ill treatment, delay everywhere, ignorance and shocking hygiene and food stifle the last spark of pride in a man …

This was precisely why, in 1917, the Russians were so susceptible to the propaganda and lies of the Bolsheviks; it is also why the tsar's army fell apart in the First World War.

Godman rallied at the arrival of food from home – ham, cheese and chocolate – and was very prescient when he wrote to his mother, 'I am sure if we get [the Russians] in the open they will remember it.'

Ridiculous rumours were circulating even in the ships off Balaclava. Fanny Duberly, first on the *Simoom*, then the *Danube*, saw the bloody and battered trophies of the Alma and heard that 'our army have taken Balaklava, after a slight resistance'. All this, of course, had happened days before and there was no resistance at all. In a rare glimpse of Fanny's empathy for her sex, she noted '… Lord Erroll is wounded; and poor Mrs Cresswell is a widow. God help and support her under a blow that would crush me to my grave!'

It was Fanny's birthday – 'I saw my first battlefield. How many more shall I see ere I am a year older? Shall I ever live to see another year? Look on into the winter, with its foreboding of suffering, cold, privation and gloom.'

She missed Henry and a death's head moth given to her by Captain Fraser of the *Simoom* filled her with dread. On Wednesday, 4 October, she visited the Light Brigade camp and realised that she could not possibly share a tent with Henry, who was already under canvas with three other men. She rode back through the French lines, who were astonished to see an English lady, even though they had plenty of *cantinières* of their own. She got her own saddle (side-saddle) the next day, finding Henry's regulation version very tiring.

Fanny Duberly's diary entries for these October days sound like some long holiday. Because, as a lady, she was a rarity in the Crimea, she was constantly being asked to dine, mostly on board various ships in Balaclava harbour. On the 10th, she ate with Captain (soon to be Major) Alexander Low who would often feature in Roger Fenton's photographs the following spring. With them was Captain Robert Portal, of Eton and Trinity College, Oxford, whose wedding Lord Cardigan would boorishly gatecrash at home shortly after the war. The three of them rode out to watch the random exchange of shots with the Sebastopol defences after dark. And still the 'fake news' kept coming. Captain George Lockwood of the 8th Hussars, whose body would not be found after Balaclava, told Fanny 'with a melancholy face' that Eupatoria had fallen to the Russians. In fact, the assault had been driven back.

Cardigan's yacht, the *Dryad*, appeared in the harbour on the 19th, along with Walter Carew's *Maraquita*. 'What a satire is the appearance of these fairy ships amidst all the rough work of war! They seem as out of place as a London belle would be.' I saw a similar incongruity in 2008, when Balaclava harbour was crowded with the 'superyachts' of Russian millionaires while the locals were trying to get by on their hopelessly inadequate currency. On Sunday the 15th, Fanny had a long chat with Louis Nolan and borrowed his horse with 'a tiger-skin [*sic*] over the holsters' to visit Henry in camp. Nolan, on Airey's staff and therefore 'in the know', told Fanny that the long-awaited bombardment would open up on the Tuesday.

'At half past six o'clock,' she wrote in her diary for that day, 'began that fearful rain of shot and shell, which poured incessantly on the forts and batteries of Sebastopol.'

Temple Godman saw it too. 'We are getting on well,' he wrote to his sister Caroline, 'the round tower was silenced in an hour or so and I believe we have sunk the *Twelve Apostles*, their largest ship.' The Heavy Brigade was in the saddle all day but were forbidden to leave the camp without orders. Clearly, Raglan still wanted them in a bandbox.

TSM Franks was impressed with the work of the navy, the Sailors' Battery, attached to the army, dragging twenty-one heavy ships' guns into position on the hills, hauling them for 6 miles. One of the party, unbeknownst to Franks at the time, was a midshipman, Evelyn Wood, who would later exchange into the 17th Lancers and end up as one of Victoria's most distinguished generals.

A mark of how unpopular Hodge was with his regiment was obvious from his own diary and a letter from Cornet Fisher. 'I have not heard one word of or from the regiment since I left them,' Hodge wrote, and Fisher – 'I have heard nothing of the colonel since we landed, and do not care how long it is before he joins us again.'

By coincidence, Hodge was convalescing aboard the *Sans Pareil*, so he found himself in the thick of naval action on the 17th. For all the positives in Fanny Duberly's breathless narrative, the bombardment did not go to plan. The French, lacking ammunition for their big guns, held off the attack until mid-morning. The British admiral, James Dundas, was far too old and cautious and simply gave in to the French demands. To add insult to injury, the French anchored 1,200 yards from the shore, out of effective range of Sebastopol. Dundas pulled his ships back too. The French land battalions, having been hit by two lucky Russian shots, lost their nerve and stopped firing by mid-morning. So while Fanny was thrilled by the thunder of the guns and the whining of shells, very little damage was actually done. After three hours' firing, six guns in the Russian forts had been silenced. Eleven men had been killed and thirty-nine wounded. As Kinglake said in his official history, 'If this was the heaviest sea cannonade that … had been known, it was also, in proportion to its greatness, the most harmless one ever delivered.'

The *Sans Pareil* was part of the inshore squadron and, as a steamer, was to tow the older sailing ships to within shot of the shore batteries. Hodge was trying to write letters below decks when the shelling started and the ship took a terrific pounding. One midshipman and eleven men were killed. Two lieutenants and fifty-eight men were wounded, including Sidney Dacres, knocked over by round shot. The windows were smashed, the masts shattered and the rigging dragging on the deck. Hodge was furious with Dundas – 'He took care not to expose himself. Oh, that Sir E[dmund] Lyons had commanded the force. Dundas is a disgrace to it.' HMS *Albion* was a write-off and had to be sent to Malta for a refit. The *Arethusa* limped back to Constantinople.

'The English papers,' Hodge wrote, 'are teeming with lies about the capture of Sebastopol. We are, I fear, a long way from it and a bloody business it will be when it, if it ever, does happen.'

And of course, he was blaming everybody in sight – 'The French, they say, went at the Russians a day or so back, but the English did not show. This must be Lord Lucan's fault.'

On the 22nd, the colonel cheered himself up by dining with Lord Cardigan on board the *Dryad*. 'This is the way,' he wrote, 'to make war.'

Chapter 9

The Thin Red Streak

Fanny Duberly was not feeling well on Wednesday, 25 October. She decided to stay on board ship, but, glancing out of the stern cabin windows, saw her horse saddled and waiting on the beach. Within minutes, a note arrived from Henry – 'The battle of Balaclava has begun and promises to be a hot one. I send you the horse. Lose no time, but come up as quickly as you can; do not wait for breakfast.'

Colonel Hodge was back in action by now, checking on the men in hospital, dining with his regimental surgeon, Chilley Pine. The horses of the 5th were all right, although one of Hodge's own animals had worms. What pleased the colonel, however, was that he was now the senior officer in the Heavy Brigade. In fact, only Lord George Paget of the 4th Light Dragoons and Lieutenant Colonel Frederick Shewell (known to the men as 'the old woman') of the 8th Hussars were ahead of him in the cavalry in terms of length of service. The additional burden of commanding the 5th was not much of an imposition and he left the day-to-day running of them to young Burton. On the 23rd, he was under the weather again, but rallied a little when Captain Robertson brought a parcel from home to him that had turned up at Constantinople. On the night before Balaclava, he slept well, despite a gusting wind – 'The troops have passed another quiet day.'

Five days earlier, Temple Godman had been writing to his father, filling him in on the *real* situation, as opposed to yet another announcement of the fall of Sebastopol in *The Times*. Since the failure of the bombardment, the Russians had been probing the Allied lines with more bravado and the cavalry were turned out, saddled, if not actually mounted, every morning early. On the 22nd, they stood to their bridles all night, Godman being only too aware of the havoc wrought by a night attack. Sleeping in the open, as the cavalry were, was taking its toll on the men and Kilbourne, Godman's servant, was ill with 'Crimean fever', whatever that actually was.

The adjutant was particularly annoyed by the false reports of how the sick and wounded were being looked after. Five hundred men were loaded onto a ship after the Alma with two surgeons and five orderlies, one of whom died on the way to Scutari. In the hospital, Godman had heard, there were 4,000 and many deaths in the transports to and from the place. Reading between the lines, it was obvious that the constant strain of waiting was shredding everybody's nerves.

That waiting came to an end on the morning of the 25th. Fanny Duberly spurred her Bob up the winding road that led from Balaclava harbour. A commissariat officer told her that the Turks had abandoned their batteries and were running towards the harbour itself. 'For God's sake,' the officer said, 'ride fast or you may not reach the camp alive.'

The battlefield of Balaclava is a complicated one, made more so today by vineyards, clusters of houses and trees where there were none in 1854. Essentially, Fanny would have ridden up the road past Kadikoi, across the South Valley where the Light Brigade had camped next to the Heavies. Ahead of her was the vineyard, much smaller than today, and a range of hills called the Causeway Heights. To her left, marked with the union flag on the summit, were the Sapouné Heights, Lord Raglan's position. There are at least eight photographs of the cavalry camps, taken from various angles, but these are Roger Fenton's work from the spring and summer of 1855 and nothing exists before that. Battlefield plans are notoriously difficult in terms of accuracy. Even one or two sketches made by men who were there (such as TSM Solomon Williams of the 4th) have to be taken with pinches of salt. From the Light Brigade camp, had she looked ahead at the Causeway Heights, Fanny Duberly would have seen Redoubt Number 6, with the others to her right. At the foot of the Heights waited Captain Maude's battery of the Horse Artillery.

The cavalry had been saddled since an hour before dawn, as was the custom. The colonels checked their regiments, not prepared, even at a moment like this, to let things slip. Two men of the Light Brigade, who would feature heavily in what was about to happen, did not expect any action at all. Welshman Henry Hope, an epileptic, was in the guard tent of the 11th Hussars awaiting court martial. He was always in trouble, largely because the bullying TSM George Loy Smith had it in for him. In the 17th Lancers, John Vahey was the regimental butcher and was in his shirt sleeves up to his elbows in cattle offal when he heard the trumpets. As was also the custom by now, Lord Lucan was riding up to Cathcart's Hill, as it was now called, the closest vantage point overlooking Sebastopol. Those who rode behind him that day probably included: his nephew, Captain Charles Bingham; Captain Walter Charteris (Lucan's ADC); Captain Arthur Hardinge, the son of the former commander-in-chief, India; Assistant Adjutant General Lord William Paulet; Lieutenant Colonel Charles Walker (Lucan's extra ADC) and Henry Joy, Lucan's orderly trumpeter, riding his grey. One of them noticed two flags flying from the top of No 1 redoubt, the signal that the Russians were advancing. The redoubts were a string of six forts, built by the Royal Engineers and manned by the Turks at the highest point of the Causeway Heights along the Woronzoff road.

A spy had come forward to Raglan's headquarters the previous day to warn of the attack. As usual, given his innate mistrust of spies, Raglan had ignored him. At five o'clock, as Lucan was beginning his rounds, 25,000 men and 78 guns moved on the redoubts under the command of General Pavel Liprandi, who had been given orders by Menshikov to drive the Allies back to Balaclava harbour. Despite the Cossack sorties of the past two weeks, there is no doubt that Raglan was caught wrong-footed by this move. His infantry, cold and wet in the trenches, were too far away and his immediate defences, in the path of the Russian advance, were meagre. The two brigades of cavalry were augmented by the Horse Artillery troop, 2,500 Turkish infantry of dubious staying power and perhaps 500 men of the 93rd Foot – the Argyll and Sutherland Highlanders as they would become in the years ahead.

As soon as the two flags waving were seen on the Causeway Heights, Lucan sent Charteris galloping back to Raglan, and Lord George Paget was sent to galvanise the cavalry. It is unclear where Paget was at this point. His own camp was in the South Valley and he must, from there, have had the same view that Fanny Duberly had when she arrived. Today's historians have been kinder than the British at the time. Faced with an overwhelming Russian force, the Turks in No 1 redoubt returned cannon-fire and held on for as long as they could. Inevitably, they broke, however, and panic set in along the Heights. Fanny's road was suddenly blocked with 'flying Turks, some running hard, vociferating "ship Johnny! Ship Johnny!" while others came along laden with pots, kettles, arms and plunder of every description, chiefly old bottles, for which the Turks seem to have a great appreciation.' This is the image carried to the newspaper readers at home and it has never gone away. Given the right conditions, the Turks were perfectly capable of holding their own. They had driven the Russians back in Silistria even before the Allies had set sail and were to prove an effective and stubborn enemy (albeit with a *lot* of German help) at Gallipoli in 1915. However, 25 October was not their day.

Maude's Horse Artillery opened up on the Russians as fort after fort fell. They only had six guns and were soon out of ammunition. A shell hit Maude's horse and exploded, blowing the animal to bits and badly injuring his rider. Lucan ordered the Horse Artillery to withdraw; they were hopelessly outgunned.

The Turks had held on for the best part of an hour, but their casualties had reached over 170 and the Russians were hauling their field guns into position in the now-abandoned forts. Lucan pulled his cavalry back on the written order from Raglan, the first of four that was to be fired off by the commander that day. Timed at half past eight, it read: 'Cavalry to take ground on the left of the second line of redoubts occupied by Turks.' Even allowing for a kind of shorthand which everybody understood at the time, this message, like all the others, was infuriatingly vague. It was carried by a staff officer named Wetherall.

We have no idea whether Lucan queried it with him (which was the usual practice to avoid misunderstandings), but the general did as he was told. In the meantime, of course, vital time was being lost. It was generally agreed that the ride from Raglan, on the Sapouné Heights, to Lucan on the South Valley floor, would take about fifteen minutes. Much was made of this ride when the fourth and final order was carried to the Light Brigade by Louis Nolan, but having stood where Raglan did in October 1854, I am astonished that it took so long. An expert horseman (as Wetherall and Nolan both were) could make the descent in a little over five minutes. The ground is nothing like the steep scarp used in the 1968 film *The Charge of the Light Brigade*.

The cavalry were pulling back as Fanny Duberly reached the Light Brigade camp. She could clearly see, beyond the running Turks, grey-coated Cossacks, swarming over the Causeway Heights, making, it seemed, directly for her. She and Henry were desperately trying to salvage what they could from Henry's tent. Seeing the danger, Henry threw Fanny onto Bob's back and she rode across the ditch-strewn vineyard to be out of harm's way. Henry himself was still loading Whisker, but musket balls were now pinging around him and he got out of there, fast.

'Presently,' wrote Fanny, as though describing a picnic, 'came the Russian Cavalry charging, over the hillside and across the valley, right against the little line of Highlanders.' With the cavalry pulled back and the Horse Artillery out of action, Colin Campbell's 93rd and 42nd were all that lay between Balaclava harbour and the Russian advance. Raglan had, of course, rattled off orders to the infantry too, but their advance was sluggish to say the least, especially the Duke of Cambridge's First Division. In a modern re-enactment carried out on BBC television by a 1970s general, the officer concerned said that had he been Raglan that day, he would have had Cambridge court-martialled for his slowness. Not that there was the remotest chance of that at the time; the man was the queen's cousin.

As the cavalry pulled back, watching with growing disgust as the Turkish refugee trickle became a torrent, shot and shell began to hit the horse lines. An animal of the Scots Greys, its leg blown off, hobbled into the ranks of the 5th Dragoon Guards, as terrified and injured horses tend to, and Temple Godman shot it in the head with his revolver. TSM Franks reminisced in 1904 how kind an act this was – 'the lieutenant Godman of the day is, I think, a General Officer now'. Campbell's Highlanders would have been mortified to read Godman's brief account of what happened next – 'They [the Russian cavalry] never expected to meet *English* there, I am sure.' My italics.

The 93rd, augmented at the last moment by the 42nd and a handful of guardsmen under Ensigns Verschayle and Hamilton, took up position under a hail of gunfire. Campbell, mounted in front of them, ordered them to lie down but there is no record of his dismounting. There were 100 invalids there, under Colonel Daveney, who were waiting to be transported to hospital. Presumably, these men were armed, but the fact that they were walking wounded and perhaps cholera victims, spoke volumes for how useful they were likely to be in the forthcoming clash. Campbell also had a force of some 2,000 Turks formed in two battalions. If he was right, that the Russian cavalry facing him was only a wing, nine sotnyas, perhaps 400 men strong, then the infantry clearly outnumbered the cavalry. But all that was about to change.

TSM Franks was watching. Like everybody else, he was appalled by the cowardice of the Turks. Impressed as everyone was by Omar Pasha riding with his cavalry escort from camp to camp, they believed his assurances about the bravery of the soldiers under his command. 'The cowardly rascals had never made any attempt to defend themselves, but scuttled off like a lot of sheep.' Franks was horrified still further when the Turkish contingent with Campbell broke ranks in the face of the Russian cavalry and bolted, making, like their comrades from the redoubts, for the harbour.

The traditional tactic for infantry facing cavalry was to form square, as Wellington had at Waterloo. What happened in June 1815 was that Marshal Michel Ney, 'the bravest of the brave' misunderstood Wellington's manoeuvre in pulling back out of range and, assuming that he was retreating, ordered the entire French cavalry to charge. The British formed square, every side bristling with Brown Bess muskets and fired salvo after salvo into the French horsemen. Not a single square broke.

'Charging and surging around,' wrote Fanny Duberly, at once thrilled and horrified to be watching, 'what could that little wall of men do against such numbers and such speed? There they stood.' The hyperbole of Fanny's account – and that of William Russell that followed it – carried the day. By his own account, Campbell reckoned that, even with the loss of the Turks, he still, marginally, outnumbered the Russians. The speed that Fanny alludes to is questionable. The cavalry were riding downhill, so momentum was with them, but probably only a third of them were Saxe-Weimar Hussars; the rest were Cossacks, either from the Urals or the Don, not used to charging determined infantry in formation.

Campbell rode along the front of his first line (they were only two lines deep) barking in his gruff voice, 'Remember, there is no retreat from here, men! You must die where you stand!'

'Ay, ay, Sir Colin,' a Highlander called back. 'We'll do that.'

The Cossacks probably checked their speed, imagining that an ambush lay ahead. The lines of Highlanders were edging forward, keen to get at the Russians with their bayonets. 'Ninety Third!' Campbell thundered above the roar of the horses' hoofs and the battle cries of his own men, 'Ninety third! Damn all that eagerness!' and the lines steadied and the first volley crashed out. Horse and rider went down and some squadrons wheeled to the left as though to outflank Campbell's right. 'Shadwell,' Campbell muttered to his ADC, 'that man understands his business,' but so did Captain Ross of the 93rd's grenadier company. They changed front and blasted away again. A further wheel to the left and the cavalry were retreating, not in tight echelon formation as prescribed in the British cavalry drill book but in total chaos and disorder.

William Russell wrote:

> The silence was oppressive, between the cannon bursts [the naval gun battery that was too far away to do any damage] we could hear the champing of the bits and the clink of sabres in the valley below. The Russians on their left drew breath for a moment and then in one good line charged in towards Balaclava. The ground flew beneath their horses' feet; gathering speed at every stride, they dashed on towards that thin red streak tipped with a line of steel … As the Russians came within six hundred yards, down went the line of steel in front and out rang a rolling volley of Minié musketry … With breathless suspense everyone waited the bursting of the wave upon the line of Gaelic rock: but ere they came within two hundred and fifty yards, another deadly volley flashed from the levelled rifles and carried terror among the Russians. They wheeled about, opened files right and left and fled faster than they came.

'No,' Colin Campbell wrote later, 'I did not think it worthwhile to form them even four deep.'

In one of the many ironies of British journalism over the years, it was not the 'line of steel' or the 'Gaelic rock' that caught on, but the 'thin red streak' and that, of course, became, over time, the 'thin red line' used to imply the gallantry and heroism of outnumbered British troops facing impossible odds in various colonial 'small wars' for the rest of the century. Incomprehensibly, it was even the title of a 1964 American film (remade in 1998) about the Second World War, at a time and about an army where scarlet was never worn.

But the Turks who had run were not going to get away with it entirely. Several of the women in the Highlanders' camp assumed that they were intent on looting the abandoned tents and they went for them. 'The fortunes of Islam,' Kinglake wrote, 'waned low beneath the manifest ascendant of the cross,' as Mrs Smith, the wife of Lieutenant Sinclair's soldier-servant and Mrs Ross, a sergeant's wife, both grabbed passing men by the lapels and kicked them. 'Ye cowardly misbelievers, to leave the bravest Christian Highlanders to fecht when ye run awa!' The Highlanders themselves, watching the cavalry turning tail, found this hilarious. Lieutenant Sinclair dashed to Mrs Smith's defence, only to find that she was more than holding her own, with a big stick in her hand. He heard the Turks muttering 'Kokana' (which was a polite form of 'lady') but Mrs Smith did not understand that and took it for an insult – 'Kokana, indeed! I'll kokana ye!'

Years later, Surgeon General Munro of the 93rd remembered Mrs Smith vividly (who would not?) – 'a stalwart wife' with a 'tender, honest heart'. She was 'large and massive, with brawny arms and hands as hard as horn'. Her face, 'though bronzed and weather-beaten and deeply freckled, was comely and lighted up by a pair of kindly hazel eyes'.

'Kokana' Smith survived the war and went home with her husband.

Chapter 10

'A Fight of Heroes'

The bulk of the Russian cavalry, commanded by General Ivan Ryzhov, had not broken off to attack Campbell's 93rd but moved forward, probably at the walk pace, down the North Valley beyond the Causeway Heights. From information obtained after the war, we know that this was the 6th Hussar Brigade, comprising the 11th Kiev Hussars, the 12th Ingermanland Hussars and the First Ural Cossacks. They had with them sixteen field guns of two Horse Batteries. From his position on the Sapouné, Raglan could see them clearly. So could Russell, who noted that, as two shells from the Chersonese battery hit the ground ahead of them, the cavalry swung left, crossing the Woronzoff road and into the South Valley.

It was at this point that Raglan's second order of the day reached Lucan – 'Eight squadrons of Heavy Dragoons to be detached towards Balaclava to support the Turks who are wavering.' This message was carried by Captain Hardinge and again, it was vague. The Turks were not wave*ring*; they had well and truly wavered. And when Hardinge arrived, neither the Heavy Brigade nor Lucan, who was with them, could see any advancing cavalry at all. Raglan's second order had made no mention of them. Lucan probably sent Hardinge to the North Valley (a ride of five minutes or so) to tell Cardigan's Light Brigade to stay put.

Scarlett's Brigade was to ride south-east, in parallel to the Causeway Heights, but to do that they had to manoeuvre around their own tents. This effectively split the Inniskillings; one squadron moved to the left, the other to the right. Behind them, the 5th Dragoon Guards and the Scots Greys followed suit, so that, for several minutes, the Brigade was split into two columns, at least from Kinglake's point of view. The left-hand column was having to pick its way around the guy ropes of the Light Brigade's tents; the camp had not been properly struck.

It was Alexander Elliot, Scarlett's ADC, who saw the danger first. Pennons of Russian lances bobbed over the top of the Causeway Heights and were making for the flank of the Heavy Brigade. These were Colonel Jeropkine's uhlans. Scarlett was notoriously short-sighted and took Elliot's word for what he had seen. He wheeled his horse and shouted, 'Are you right in front?' because half his Brigade was still riding in column of threes *away* from the Russians. 'Left wheel into line.' In the bitter months that followed, Lord Lucan swore that *he* had given orders to Scarlett's Brigade to charge, whereas in fact he was at this stage close to Cardigan's Light Brigade, *yards* from the action. Kinglake, ever the circumspect gentleman, does not take sides in this squabble. The petulant and overbearing Lucan was not a man many people would cross – and that was a shame for the cavalry in the Crimea.

At the head of his Brigade, James Scarlett looked an imposing sight. The famous photograph of him, taken by Fenton the following spring, shows him sitting in the saddle of a grey pony, but this was not the horse he rode at Balaclava. The painting by Francis Grant, currently in the possession of the 5th Royal Inniskilling Dragoon Guards, is probably as accurate as we are likely to get. The charger is a 15- or 16-hand bay with four white 'socks' and Scarlett is wearing the undress frock coat of a general – in all probability the one in the Fenton photograph. He wears the booted overalls common to the cavalry and appears to be carrying a Heavy Cavalry pattern sword. His helmet has attracted much comment over the years because it is not regulation pattern but looks more like a yeomanry helmet (where bizarre alternatives were often selected by commanding officers). There is no doubt, however, that this helmet saved his life in what was to follow.

Behind him rode Alexander Elliot, wearing the plumed cocked hat that almost got him killed. In the melee of the charge, the Russians

Above: 'There is your enemy, there are your guns!' The author on the Sapouné Heights pointing down the Valley of Death. (*Carol Trow*)

Below: Soldier's pipe found in the British Lines near Balaclava. The shamrock design clearly implies an Irish connection which may link it with the 4th Royal Irish Dragoon Guards or the 6th Inniskillings. (*Author's collection*)

1834 pattern British cavalry sword with the distinctive honeysuckle hilt. It was carried by all officers of the Heavy Brigade at Balaclava. (*Author's collection*)

The grave of Captain George Brigstocke, 4th Dragoon Guards, Ryde Cemetery, Isle of Wight. (*Robin Whitehead*)

Above: The uniform trunk of Captain George Brigstocke of the 4th Dragoon Guards. Some officers took four of these to the Crimea. (*Robin Whitehead*)

Right: General James Scarlett, in the uniform he wore at Balaclava, October 1854. Engraving after Sir Francis Grant.

Roughrider Private Michael McNamara, 5th Dragoon Guards on the 2nd class stamp issued to commemorate heroes of the Crimea, 12 October 2004. (*Robin Whitehead*)

Above: The Charge we never saw. This still from Tony Richardson's *The Charge of the Light Brigade* shows the Heavy Brigade engaging the Russian cavalry. The director cut the sequence before the film was released. (*Author's collection*)

Below: *Punch*'s view of the 'whitewashing board' enquiry into the state of the army before Sebastopol, referring in particular to the bad treatment of the cavalry horses. (*Author's collection*)

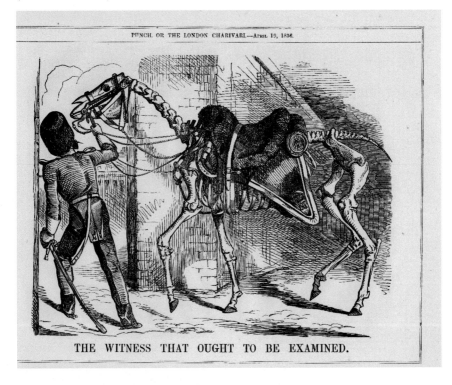

PUNCH, OR THE LONDON CHARIVARI.—April 19, 1856.

THE WITNESS THAT OUGHT TO BE EXAMINED.

Above left: Troop Sergeant Major John Norris, 1st Royal Dragoons. Norris is shown in the full dress uniform for NCOs after the Crimean War, just before the introduction of the tunic. He is wearing the brass shoulder scales which were not worn in the Crimea, but has not refitted the plume to his helmet. He wears his Crimean medals on his left breast, while the chevrons and crown on his right upper arm denote his rank. Regimental sergeant majors wore these on the forearm. (*Author*)

Above right: Private John McCabe, 5th Dragoon Guards. The brass helmet of the Heavies could save lives, but McCabe was badly wounded during the Charge. In the black leather pouch at his back, he carries the bullets for his regulation pattern carbine, slung by a swivel hook from his shoulder belt. In theory, this could be fired with one hand, but loading was more complicated and would rarely be carried out during a cavalry charge. (*Author*)

Lieutenant Colonel John Yorke, 1st Royal Dragoons. It is not certain whether officers took their Mess uniforms to the Crimea with them, but some of them used the jackets as stable dress and even wore them in action. Each regiment, as well as having its own distinctive pattern of lace, had a uniquely designed Mess waistcoat. This portrait is based on a photograph taken after the war, by which time Yorke had an artificial left leg. (*Author*)

Above left: Trumpeter John Nichol, 4th Dragoon Guards. Nichol is dressed in Marching Order, essentially the uniform he wore for the Charge. He carries his bugle (for field calls) in his hand and his trumpet (for camp calls) is slung over his back. He carries the water canteen and food haversack common to all ranks. (*Author*)

Above right: Private John Meikle, 2nd Dragoons, Scots Greys. Uniquely in the Heavy Cavalry, the Greys wore Grenadier style fur caps rather than brass helmets. These probably gave less protection than the 'pots' and they – and the regiment's grey horses – may have made them a target on the battlefield. Meikle would have looked like this on the morning of the Charge. (*Author*)

Captain James Mouat, Surgeon, 6th Inniskilling Dragoons. Astonishingly, regimental surgeons were expected to fight along with their men. We know for certain that Mouat rode down the Valley of Death behind the Light Brigade because he saved the life of Captain Morris of the 17th Lancers. He wears a useless cocked hat as opposed to a helmet and it is likely that his bullet pouch contained laudanum or wound dressings. Note the yellow facings (collar and cuffs) of the Inniskillings. (*Author*)

Lieutenant and Adjutant Richard Temple Godman, 5th Dragoon Guards. Godman is shown in the uniform he wore at Balaclava, with the horse he rode, The Earl. Horse 'furniture' was complicated and under the lambskin flounces over his saddle he carried two pistol holsters. All Heavy Cavalry wore gauntlets that gave some protection to wrists and forearms. His boots are not regulation pattern but privately purchased and sent out to the Crimea by his family. (*Author*)

Lieutenant Andrew Nugent, 2nd Dragoons Scots Greys. Although this portrait is based on a photograph taken after the war, the stable dress shown here has not changed since 1854. Nugent's 'zig-zag' patterned pill box cap was unique to the Greys. (*Author*)

Major William Forrest, 4th Dragoon Guards. Forrest is shown wearing the undress frock coat worn by all cavalry officers in the Crimea. His field cap has a stiffened peak but a peakless variety was also worn. His sword belt is the undress leather pattern, blancoed and he wears booted overalls with leather inserts to protect breeches and legs from constant mounting and dismounting. His sword is the 1834 honeysuckle hilt pattern. (*Author*)

Captain Edward D'Arcy Hunt, 6th Inniskilling Dragoons. No officer in the Crimea looked *quite* as flamboyant as this. Full dress for officers was expensive and reserved for field days and reviews. The tasselled epaulettes and horsehair helmet plumes were left behind and the gold laced belts were replaced in the field by plain white leather. The sabretache dangling from Hunt's left hip, which carried the regiment's battle honours, was plain black leather on campaign. (*Author*)

mistook Elliot for the Brigade's commander because of his cocked hat and he was badly cut as a result. William Morris, a friend of his who was leading the 17th Lancers on that October day, wrote to his wife later that Elliot was 'doing great work ... till his hat was knocked off and he got three cuts – one bad one, right into the bone at the back of the head, one on his forehead and his nose nearly cut off ...'

What Morris did not know is that Elliot had asked Scarlett's permission to wear the staff peaked forage cap, which was more comfortable. Scarlett refused. 'Damn the order!' he grunted. 'My staff shall be properly dressed!' The cocked hat was too big for Elliot and he stuffed a handkerchief inside it to secure it. That too may have saved his life.

Alongside Elliot sat Captain John Conolly, Scarlett's brigade major, in the uniform of the 5th Dragoon Guards. It is impossible, after all this time, to be accurate about the appearance of these men at Balaclava, but the Fenton photograph of Major Adolphus Burton, taken in the spring of 1855, is probably the best likeness. Conolly would have worn his scarlet jacket, without epaulettes, his booted overalls, helmet without plume and would have carried his 'honeysuckle' hilted sword. Under the lambskin flounces over his saddle was a brace of pistols, although only one man in the charge that followed remembers firing one that day, despite Temple Godman's testimony that pistols were going off all over the place. Officers often had privately purchased carbines too, but, again, none seems to have been fired at Balaclava. As I write, the Beckwith-made version belonging to Captain Forster, 4th Dragoon Guards, is on sale for £15,000.

Two Other Ranks rode with the general at the head of the Brigade. One was Sergeant James Shegog, 5th Dragoon Guards, a rough-rider from County Monaghan, who was Scarlett's orderly. The other was the brigadier's trumpeter, Thomas Monks, of the same regiment, whose job it was to blast his bugle on Scarlett's orders to change the pace or direction of the Brigade. It is likely that he carried two instruments – the bugle for 'field calls' and the trumpet for 'camp calls'.

Fanning out to Scarlett's left were the Scots Greys. Artists portraying the charge in the years ahead concentrated on these men because of their distinctive and striking appearance. Interestingly, one of the earliest such artists was Alexander Elliot. Lucan, of course, criticised the man's work for inaccuracy, but then, Lucan did not ride in the charge of the Heavy Brigade; Elliot did. The Greys had achieved a kind of immortality at Waterloo when they captured an eagle standard from a French infantry regiment. Napoleon's famous comment was 'ces terribles chevaux grises' (those terrible grey horses) but, along with other regiments, the Greys exhausted themselves in the charge. At Balaclava, the Scots Greys were the only regiment to have their valises, the blanket rolls worn behind their saddles.

On the march, Other Ranks carried corn sacks and hay nets for the horses, but these would have been left in the tents at Balaclava. Even so, every man would have carried his water canteen and haversack slung over his right shoulder. Carbines were worn suspended from the pouch belt, but it is unlikely they were fired that day. In an action like a charge, the sword was the only weapon routinely used. It is not clear whether the Greys' officers wore their undress leather sabretaches that day. If they did, they were plain black leather with the eagle badge of the regiment in gilt metal. The Greys were led that day by Lieutenant Colonel Henry Darby Griffith.

To Scarlett's right was the second squadron of the Inniskillings, Lieutenant Colonel White at their head. They almost certainly wore their full dress jackets because their stable dress had not yet been shipped from Varna. The Inniskillings were distinguishable from the other units by the yellow facings of their jackets. It is possible that the 6th had discontinued the wearing of gauntlets for some reason; neither Elliot's painting nor sketches of the regiment made at Varna by the French general, Vanson, show them in use.

The 4th Dragoon Guards, Hodge at their head, sat their horses behind the Greys. A number of paintings show officers' chargers complete with black horsehair throat plumes, but, like helmet plumes, these were an additional frippery totally unnecessary on campaign and would probably have been ditched beforehand. Hodge, peculiarly, believed that swords should not be drawn except on the parade ground. Accordingly, while all other units had their sabres 'at the slope', blades resting on their shoulders, the 4th were technically unarmed as they advanced! Alongside the 4th, behind the leading squadron of the Inniskillings, the 5th Dragoon Guards waited. Temple Godman says nothing of this moment in the account of the charge he wrote for his father, but TSM Franks described the Russians moving towards them – '… we saw a mass of Russian cavalry in close columns of squadrons, ten deep – that is, five squadrons in double ranks, advancing to attack us.'

In line with the 5th, the first squadron of the Inniskillings extended to the right. They had been furthest down the South Valley when the Russians were sighted and had to turn tightly to wheel into line. At the rear, behind the 4th on the left, came the Royal Dragoons, Lieutenant Colonel Yorke at their head. Like all units that day, all ranks of the Royals had their stirrup leathers worn at double thickness to prevent cutting by infantry bayonets. A cavalryman without stirrups was very vulnerable, returning to the problems of horsemen in the ancient world, before such things were invented.

It is not possible now to reconstruct exactly where each man of the Heavy Brigade sat. The troop commanders, like Boyd and Buchanan of the Greys or Elmsall and Wardlaw of the Royals, sat in front of their respective troops, men they had known and worked with, in some cases, for years. On the wings of each squadron were the regimental and troop sergeant majors, the tough old veterans who had seen it all and kept their men steady – men like Franks and George Griffiths of the 5th and James Dearden and John Grieve of the Greys; the old sweats who were at once feared and respected by the men of their troops. Behind each squadron rode the serrefiles, the cornets still green and wet behind the ears, the product of the public schools and the universities – like Richard Glyn and William Hartopp of the Royals and the Honourable M. Fitzmaurice Deane and Edward Fisher of the

4th. Their job was to keep the lines steady and, although it was never quite spelt out, to whip stragglers and would-be deserters into line.

There too, somewhere in those lines of scarlet facing a Russian army three or four times their size that day, were the regimental specialists – the rough-riders who trained the horses, the farriers who looked after them, the hospital orderlies who tended the sick, and, most bizarrely of all, the surgeons whose skill after any engagement was vital. It is difficult to know exactly who rode the charge of the Heavy Brigade because no accurate roll call was taken. I estimate that at least three-quarters of the Brigade's doctors actually rode the charge themselves.

Totting up the men listed by Roy Dutton in his *Forgotten Heroes* (see Appendix), we have nearly 1,200 men listed as serving with the Heavies in the Crimea – nearly twice as many as in the Light Brigade. Figures are notoriously inaccurate: for instance, by 25 October, an uncertain number of men had died from cholera and other diseases. A handful had been killed by random shells from Sebastopol. Still more were too sick to ride that day and lay either in camp or at sea or at Scutari. Even so, removing a certain number that way, it is difficult to reduce the Brigade to 'Scarlett's Three Hundred'. Neither was the phrase, like the Six Hundred of the Light Brigade, merely a poetic device by Tennyson; Kinglake uses the phrase in his *The Invasion of the Crimea*. In that, the 'travelling gent' is clearly talking about the leading squadrons – the Inniskillings and the Greys – 'Those three squadrons were the force which constituted "Scarlett's Three Hundred".'

Scarlett may have intended to post the 5th Dragoon Guards to the left of the Greys to form an extended front rank but the vineyard precluded that. Perhaps the arrival of the Allied armies had prevented the grapes being harvested and pruned and trailing vines would seriously impede cavalry who would never be able to gallop, so the 5th were placed in the second line. Elliot gave them this order, which Scarlett did not remember later, but it is unlikely that a mere captain, albeit an experienced one, would take an initiative like this without the nod from his boss.

If Scarlett felt himself facing the dilemma that Kinglake poses – should a cavalry commander lead from the front or direct from the rear? – he barely had time to reflect. He had never seen action before and was just as green as the newest 'Johnny Raw' behind him. In the event, he chose to lead – 'as,' writes Kinglake, 'did Murat himself, for when the great cavalry chief was a king and a commander of mighty numbers, he still used to charge in person … at the head of his squadron.' Joachim Murat was Napoleon's brother-in-law and king of Naples. He was also *the* cavalry commander of the nineteenth century; when driving the Prussians from the field at Jena in 1806, he did not bother to draw his sword but just shook his riding crop at the enemy.

It was now that Lucan turned up. Leaving Cardigan to fume that the Heavies were having all the fun, he rode off after Scarlett's men and gave the same orders that the brigadier had already given! It was this that Lucan referred to later when he tried to steal Scarlett's thunder and at least one survivor of the charge, TSM Franks, fell for it, even though he was *yards* away from Lucan when the order was given. The Greys may have heard Lucan but the Inniskillings certainly did not and neither could Franks.

'General Scarlett, take these four squadrons [there were actually three] and at once attack the column of the enemy.' He might just as well have said, 'Now, then, Scarlett, do as you like' because the Brigade was already poised to charge as Trumpeter Monks' bugle rang out.

Facing the Brigade were 3,500 cavalry, hussars, lancers and Cossacks, including some of the men who had already backed down from Campbell's Highlanders. To make matters worse, they were moving downhill, with momentum behind them and, judging by the way they manoeuvred in front of the redoubts, were efficient and well-led.

Astonishingly, even as this huge force was moving to the sound of their trumpets, the officers of the Greys were still sitting their horses with their backs to them, facing their men. Not until they heard Conolly's barked order 'Eyes right!' did they wheel their horses into position. Even more astonishingly, the Russian bugles sounded again and the charge slowed to a trot and finally a halt. No one, on either side at the time, or since, has explained this manoeuvre. Had the Russian cavalry hit the Brigade at the gallop, sheer weight of numbers would have destroyed them. Perhaps Ryzhov thought the Light Brigade camp, still half standing, was some kind of trap. Perhaps he was unnerved by the parade-ground fiddling about of the Greys. Perhaps he intended to throw out his cavalry into wings to encircle Scarlett's men.

Lucan, positioned somewhere behind the Royals and quite a way back, ordered his own field trumpeter, Henry Joy of the 17th Lancers, to sound the charge. Nobody moved because two of the regiments were still forming up. Scarlett, rookie though he was, knew perfectly well that, from a standing start, riding uphill over broken ground and tent ropes, he could not possibly deliver a crashing charge at the gallop that was designed to panic and destroy an enemy.

By now, the world and his wife had gathered to watch the action. The Light Brigade could see it all because the Heavies were drawn up to their right front. The French and the Turks could see it too, on the Chersonese uplands. So, although they were still marching, could the British infantry. Watchers with spyglasses could make out Elliot in his cocked hat, Scarlett, 'the warm summer hue of his features and a drooping mustache white as snow'.

The Inniskillings at the front were edging forward and Scarlett held them back with a wave of his sword. The Brigade would charge, but it would do it altogether and on his say-so. The Russians were now about 400 yards away, stationary in the extraordinary lull that their halt had caused. The routine commands that *should* have been delivered were 'The line will advance at a walk'. After that, the bugle commands should ring out for increasing the speed – 'Trot. Gallop. Charge.' Scarlett had no time for this. He turned to Monks. 'Sound the charge!'

And the trumpeter did.

Scarlett rammed his spurs home and the bay moved off, rising to a trot and ignoring the tangle of roots under its hoofs. Elliot, Conolly, Shegog and Monks were with him. In parade-ground formation, each trumpeter of the various regiments should have repeated Monks' call, but it is unclear whether this happened at Balaclava. The Greys moved forward, immediately tangling with the edge of the vineyard.

'Come on!' Scarlett yelled at them, turning in his saddle and waving his sword. He was by now at least 50 yards ahead of them. He crashed into the centre of the now advancing Russian cavalry, bowling over an officer who swung his sword at Elliot and riding over him. The brigadier remembered later that the Russians seemed to be throwing themselves out of their saddles, but it is more likely that he hacked them down, just to stay alive. He was so far ahead of his men that the Russian horsemen now crowding around him in effect cushioned him from the impact of the Greys and Inniskillings. Scarlett was the first to admit that he was no swordsman, but he whirled the blade around, striking right and left and the Russians were astounded. This old man was giving them the hiding of their lives.

Elliot skewered a Russian officer and for an instant, panicked as he could not withdraw the blade. Ironically, his friend William Morris would have an identical experience later when the Light Brigade charged. Neither man would 'give point' in such a situation again, they promised each other.

Kinglake waxes lyrical about the long friendship of the Scots Greys and the Inniskillings, the thistle and the shamrock, but never the rose, and here they were again, thudding into the enemy, probably at no more than a canter, side by side. The two ranks of each regiment had melded into one by the pressure of the nearly immobile force facing them and the blades flashed in the morning, the roar of battle cries and the flash of steel obvious to the watchers on the hills.

The Russians were firing their carbines but, in the chaos of the melee, were probably hitting as many of their own men as the enemy. Darby Griffith of the Greys slashed in all directions, Major Clarke and Captain Williams riding knee to knee with him. Handley, Hunter, Buchanan and Sutherland led their troops, perhaps reaching the gallop as they arrived. RSM John Grieve saved an officer's life as the lines clashed. He decapitated a Russian with a single sweep of his sword and drove the others back. For that, he won the Medaille Militaire and even earned praise from Charles Dickens in his journal *All the Year Round*:

> It is not a thing that should be suffered to die away. When he cut off a soldier's head at a blow and disabled and dispersed several others, he had no very exciting motives of self-devotion. Pay, promotion or popularity could not well enter his head, for he knew the rules of the Service about rising from the ranks, and he knew too, that the British public rarely asks the names of the poor privates and non-commissioned officers who fall.

In fact, the officers of the 2nd clubbed together and bought his commission for him.

At some point in the next few minutes, Darby Griffith was hit in the head with a pistol ball. His bearskin cap gave him no protection at all and he was lucky that the bullet ricocheted off. In the years ahead, John Brush, the Greys' surgeon, had to correct Kinglake's version of events. Kinglake believed that the colonel's injury had been bad enough to mean that Major Clarke, his number two, took command in the chaos. In fact, Griffith rode right through the Russians and only then, looking at the profusely bleeding wound, did Brush tell Trumpeter Edward Farrell to find Clarke and tell him the news. Kinglake was happy to print a correction in a later edition of his book.

Clarke himself, riding Sultan, led the right-hand squadron of the Greys. Man and horse were photographed by Roger Fenton the following spring. Sultan was a nervy animal and in trying to control him, Clarke lost his bearskin. The sight of a bare-headed man, especially one bleeding from a head wound, terrified the superstitious Russians, who believed that he had satanic powers, particularly as his sword was doing so much damage.

Samuel Williams had been ill in bed two days before Balaclava. He led the left-hand squadron – 'how they slashed, cut, thrust and pistolled the immense masses of Russian cavalry', as George Ryan put it in his *Our Heroes of the Crimea* (1855). Unlike Scarlett, Williams was an excellent swordsman and beat off four attacks, one of them from six Russians. 'Out of that bloody encounter he came without a scratch.' He saved the lives of two of his men into the bargain. Henry Handley was 19 at Balaclava and carried an Adams and Deane revolver in his saddle holster. This was just as well because, wounded by a Cossack lance, he had probably lost his sword. He shot three of the enemy in rapid succession, which would have been impossible with the older percussion-cap pistol.

We have heard from Robert Hunter before, in the letters he wrote to his sister Molly, complaining about the thump of the ship's engines and excusing his dreadful handwriting. His account of the charge is one of the most detailed on record:

> We came trotting up, wheeled into line and our little regt and one squadron of the Enniskillens charged and broke 4 regiments of regular cavalry and about 100 Cossacks. They were 5 to 1. They were 2 regts. of blue hussars and 2 of Light Dragoons. The latter were fine fellows and my squadron (I commanded the left troop) was opposed to their right regt. And one squadron of the second. The scene was awful, we were so outnumbered and there was nothing but to fight our way through them, cut and slash. I made a hack at one and my sword bounced off his thick coat, so I gave him the point and knocked him off his horse. Another fellow just made a slash at me and just touched my bearskin, so I made a rush at him and took him just on the back of his helmet. I didn't wait to see what became of him, as a lot of fellows were riding at me but I only know that he fell forward on his horse and if his head tingled like my wrist, he must have had it hard and, as I was riding out [through the Russian ranks] another fellow came past me, whom I caught a slap in the face. I'll be bound his own mother wouldn't have known him.

George Buchanan was twenty-four. The citation for his Sardinian war medal, presented after the war, reads, 'This officer's conduct in the heavy cavalry charge at the action of Balaklava was cool and gallant and by his example great execution was done against the enemy …'

Francis Sutherland, from Forse, Caithness, was a lieutenant in the Greys in 1851, having left Eton for the regiment four years earlier. It may have been from him that we have Kinglake's account of the officers of the Greys 'dressing the ranks' with their backs to the enemy. Interestingly, a number of personal items belonging to Sutherland have survived, including watercolours of fellow officers he painted in the Crimea, a passport for the same period, a pair of black gloves he wore to the Duke of Wellington's funeral in November 1852, a cheroot case and penknife and the full dress silver-fronted pouch he wore during the war.

The serrefiles that Kinglake singles out are lieutenants Miller, Boyd, Nugent and Prendergast. He also mentions John Wilson, 'now a cornet' and acting adjutant 'for he took a signal part in the fight'. William Miller had risen, unusually, from the ranks. He had actually been a captain for three weeks by the time of the charge but presumably had no troop to lead. He had a famously loud voice which he had used to thunderous effect as a sergeant major. This could be heard at Balaclava – 'Rally! The Greys!' he bellowed. He was a big man riding a big horse and he loomed over the Russians. Andrew Nugent came from an old Scots family that had changed its name from Savage in 1812. An old uncle did not approve – 'I would rather be an old savage than a new gent' – but the change remained. He was not impressed by the Russians – 'the 93rd fired a volley into [them] … the horse Artillery fired shots into them and both times they ran away in a most dreadful manner. I won't go through another campaign, but if the war continues, they will not catch me out here a third year.'

Lennox Prendergast, the son of an MP and official in the Indian civil service was still a cornet at Balaclava and, like Nugent, rode a huge grey. His left foot was smashed by a pistol ball and Fanny Duberly saw him later in the day, riding down to a hospital ship in the harbour, his booted overalls stiff with blood. She marvelled at the fortitude of mankind – 'the pluck with which an Englishman puts pain out of the question is as wonderful as it is admirable'.

Sergeant Wilson was under arrest on the morning of the 25th for a minor infringement. Whatever it was might have broken him to private, or at best corporal, but the events of the day changed all that. He left the guard tent, which seems not to have been guarded, grabbed his horse and reported to Daniel Moodie, the adjutant. He said, 'I have broken my arrest, sir, as I could not see my regiment going into action and remain quiet in camp. I have come to report myself and wish to join and do my duty.' Moodie gave him the nod and Wilson, with something to prove, laid about him 'using his sword with great exertion'.

In the Inniskillings, Kinglake singles out Manley, Rawlinson and Weir for special mention. Harry Dalrymple White had taken over command of the regiment on the death of Willoughby Moore. He had only been in the Crimea for three weeks by the time of the charge, disembarking from the steamer *Trent*. He led the Inniskillings, who crashed into the Russians with their wild Irish battle-cry and took a vicious cut to his helmet. Earlier in the day, as the Brigade was drawn up, a stray shell had burst near his horse, but he was unhurt. As for the helmet, it – and its owner – survived the day; it is on display in the 5th Royal Inniskilling Guards Museum. Robert Manley, who led his troop at Balaclava, had lost two horses at sea crossing to the Crimea on the *Tyrone*. Archibald Weir was the 'indifferent RSM and very moderate adjutant' who survived the sinking of the *Europa*. All reports on him suggest an unpopular and bumptious man. Arguably one of the shortest men in the battle (apart from Hodge) was Private William Patterson. His father had fought under Wellington in the Peninsula and William was born in the Ringmer barracks, Sussex. When his father died, he was 8 and was taught at the Royal Hibernian school in Dublin. He had enlisted in the Inniskillings at 14, when he was 4ft 6in, one of two boys in the regiment. For a while, he was a bandsman.

Such was the force of the Three Hundred's impact that it would have shattered any formation facing them, but the Russian cavalry, largely the Ingermanland Hussars, were wedged tightly in formation and had nowhere to go. To the watchers on the hills, like Raglan, it looked as though Scarlett and his leading squadrons had been swallowed up by the mass of the enemy. In the thick of it, the heavier men and horses of the Brigade were cutting up the Russians and punching holes in the lines, even if the thick Russian overcoats actually bent some cavalry blades; they were made in Birmingham. Because of the press, most of the Brigade used the 'moulinet', a circular sweep of the blade virtually unknown at Maidstone, which snapped off the probing lance-heads and sliced through the tough leather shakos of the Russians.

Kinglake reaches poetic heights in his description of the Scots Greys being descended from the tough Covenanter clansmen of the seventeenth century, full of fire and pent-up rage, cracking the heads of 'docile', obedient Russians. As an attempt to describe the psychology of battle, it falls a little short. Raglan would say later that the outcome 'was never for a moment doubtful' but he cannot have believed it at the time.

What struck Kinglake was the noise. Above the clash of steel and squeals of injured horses, the yelling of the Greys and Inniskillings was clearly audible, much of it unprintable in a Victorian book! The Russians on the other hand gave out a 'sustained and continuous "zizz" of the kind that is made with clenched teeth'. It reminded Kinglake of an English factory, with the hum of machines.

Scarlett barely noticed the hacking around him. One blow hit his helmet but missed his head; the rest were scratches. It was now that Elliot was hit. His horse lashed out with its hind legs, clearing any attack from behind, but one Russian, blue-nosed and savage-eyed, according to Kinglake, drove the point of his sabre into the ADC's head. Two more cuts hit him simultaneously, but Kinglake was happy to report that 'the wound which divided his face was so well sewn up that it has not much marred his good looks'. It says something about the quality of Crimean medical care that Elliot's fourteen cuts constituted 'slightly wounded' in the official records.

Dalrymple White, unaware of the dent in his helmet and presumably hearing ringing in his ears, came face to face with a Russian who could not have been more than 17. 'He looked like an Eton boy,' he recalled later, but as the Inniskillings swept through the ranks, the lad was felled, his skull split in half. White himself had another narrow escape when a shell burst near his horse, peppering his saddle flap with lead but somehow missing his leg.

It was the Greys who cut their way out first. A line of Cossacks in open formation probably had no idea the British would ever reach them and they dithered. It was now that Darby Griffith got his head wound.

But Scarlett's Three Hundred were only the tip of the cavalry iceberg. Lucan, sitting his horse at the edge of the vineyard from which the Greys had launched their attack, gave orders to Hodge and the 4th Dragoon Guards to attack in flank. Many historians have assumed that the Heavy Brigade charged together, all nine squadrons, but there was clearly a gap, in time and space, between the charge of the Three Hundred and the rest of the Brigade. Hodge did not move and later, when under a great deal of pressure to explain umpteen failures on his part, Lucan claimed that he gave the order to the Royals, not the 4th. Kinglake tries to mollify the situation by saying that one Heavy Dragoon regiment looks very like another, but Lucan was *there and* he was commander of the cavalry. He gave no orders for the other regiments to advance.

Hodge had already drawn up the 4th in open column and ordered 'Left in front'. With him were Major Forrest, Captains Forster, McCreagh, Webb, Robertson and five cornets – Brigstocke, the acting adjutant, McDonnel, Fisher, Muttlebury and Deane. We have heard of most of these men already, but their actions in the charge itself are less well recorded. William Forrest wrote two days after the battle:

> Another body of cavalry came down towards us … and was charged by the Greys and, I think, the Inniskillings were in

the first line. The Russians met them well and outflanking them, wrapped around both flanks and took them in front, flank and rear ... Our first line [the 4th] upon this retreated ... upon which [we] charged the Russians in flank ... For my part I think the Heavies might have done much better. The Greys charged at a trot and our pace was but very little better, but we had very bad ground to advance over, first this vineyard and over two fences, brush and ditch, then through the camp of the 17th and we were scarcely formed when we attacked ... Once in we did better but the confusion was worse than I had expected, the men of all regiments were mixed and we were a long time reforming. If we do it again, I hope we shall do it better ...

No wonder Cardigan hated him!

Ten years after Balaclava, Francis Forster wrote to Hodge:

When we moved down the side of the vineyard to attack the Russians, we were in column of troops or squadrons left in front. At the bottom of the vineyard where we wheeled to the left, we were certainly in column of troops as I remember perfectly your ordering me ... to front-form my squadron and charge immediately on the flank of the Russians and that you would being up the second squadron after me.

Hodge put Michael McCreagh forward for the French Legion d'Honneur as particularly outstanding at Balaclava, commanding, as he did, the second squadron (although, as we have just heard, Forster thought that Hodge did that!)

Hodge did not like John Webb, his adjutant, criticising him for drinking champagne to try to cure cholera. There is no record of Webb's behaviour in the battle, but he was in serious trouble with Hodge – and Lord Lucan – some days later, as we shall see. Other than recording that Arthur Robertson was 'mounted, present in the field' at Balaclava, Hodge makes no mention of the man at all. He had, however, been absent with leave for the whole month until the 23rd; exactly where he was and why he had gone, is not recorded.

Hodge did not like Brigstocke either. He does not list him as being present at Balaclava, though as adjutant, it is unlikely he was not there. Christopher McDonnel, whose father, the Irish paper manufacturer, was looking after Hodge's things in Dublin, receives only the 'present' mention. Edward Fisher wrote to his father the day after the battle:

> A second force of cavalry about the same size [as the unit that had attacked the Highlanders, clearly Fisher was wrong about this] made for our camp and baggage, which were in great danger. The Heavy Brigade, however, were loosed at them and rolled them over and cleared the plain.

George Muttlebury merits no special mention from Hodge, and neither does M. Fitzmaurice Deane.

The 4th instinctively drew their swords without orders from the colonel and prepared to advance, whether or not Lucan had told them to. 'Forster,' Hodge yelled to the captain, 'I am going on with the left squadron. As soon as your squadron gets clear of the vineyard, front, form and charge.'

Too late, the Russian right wing tried to extricate itself from the melee, but the 4th gave them no time to do this. 'Hard all across!' Hodge yelled, although nobody who heard this understood him. It was an Eton boating command, not one used by the cavalry; and, even for Hodge, Eton was a long time ago!

The Royals, behind Hodge, had received no orders at all, despite Lucan's later contention. Instinctively, they formed front and trotted forward in support of the 4th. They could see the Russian flank threatening to cut off Scarlett's Three Hundred. 'By God, the Greys are cut off!' somebody shouted, 'Gallop! Gallop!' and the bugle took up the challenge. As the Royals crashed into the Russian line, Sergeant George Pattenden was hit with a sabre cut. October was not his month. Four days later, he was court-martialled for a third offence and was busted to corporal, losing his one penny a day good conduct pay.

Colonel John Yorke was not happy with the regiment's line – one squadron had far outpaced the other and he ordered a halt to reform. The officers singled out by Kinglake are Major Wardlaw, captains Elmsall, Campbell and Stocks; and cornets Pepys, Charlton, Basset, Glyn, Coney, Robertson, Hartopp and Sandeman.

Robert Wardlaw was ill on 25 October, probably with cholera. He had withdrawn from the regiment at some point during the morning but seeing the enemy cavalry forming up from his tent, he remounted the charger he had kept saddled nearby and galloped to take up his post. William Elmsall would be badly wounded in the next few minutes, as would George Campbell. Despite this, both men stayed in the saddle until the Russians fell back. Michael Stocks left no account of the charge, but he was generally gung-ho about the Russians. 'They remind you of rabbits,' he wrote home, 'only not quite so harmless.' No special mention is made of St John Charlton but Richard Glyn was shot through the leg during the charge. He lived to tell the tale. Walter Coney was 'mounted in the field' and Gilbert Robertson had his horse shot from under him. William Hartopp was wounded in the leg in the battle and was still in hospital at Scutari two weeks later. John Sandeman, of the 'port beverage' family, went down when his horse Toby was shot through the neck. He had the animal preserved and shipped back to Hayling Island where it was buried near the sea. Of Cornet Pepys, there is no mention at all.

At some point during the Royals' charge, TSM John Norris found himself cut off by four Russian hussars. He hacked one down with his sword and drove the others off, capturing the dead man's horse in the process. For that he was awarded the French Medaille Militaire.

One of the most detailed accounts of the charge comes from TSM Joseph Pardoe, who had 'fancied a soldier's life' and had enlisted in London in 1844. He concentrates on the second phase of the cavalry encounter (see next chapter) but has a few words on the cowardice of the Turks:

> The runaway Turks taking refuge behind [Campbell's Highlanders] and, when the danger was past, clapped them on the back and shouted 'Bono, Johnny, Bono, Johnny!' Then came the Heavy Brigade charge … It was a short and decisive struggle, there were some of their saddles emptied, but only one of the Heavies killed [*sic*].

Alongside the 4th, the 5th Princess Charlotte's Dragoon Guards were waiting under the command of Captain Adolphus Burton, whom TSM Franks (and several others) felt was far too young for a field command like this.

With him, at the head of their respective troops, were captains Campbell, Inglis and Halford. The lieutenants were Swinfen and Godman and the cornets Montgomery, Neville, Ferguson and Hampton. Hodge had nominally been in command of the regiment along with his own and Scarlett, feeling for Burton's youth – he was actually 27, eleven years older than Edward, the Black Prince, who commanded an entire wing at Crecy in 1346 – had moved his headquarters closer to those of the 5th. Today, however, Burton was on his own. William Campbell was not well during this period. An old injury to his leg gave him gyp and although he had quite wide experience in India and the West Indies, was probably not at his best at Balaclava – 'He was a very clever and agreeable man,' Temple Godman wrote, 'in fact very superior and had seen an immense deal of life.' William Inglis was the opposite – 'a very bad officer, does not care about [army life],' was Godman's comment. Charles Halford was photographed by Roger

Fenton the following spring, alongside the grey he rode in the charge. A man who clearly enjoyed his luxuries, he was forever writing to his agent, a Mr Grace, to provide Fortnum and Mason hampers for him.

Frederick Swinfen had been with the regiment for five years by the time of Balaclava. As he rode forward behind his troop, he took a lance thrust to the chest and a bad cut to his sword hand. He was lucky to survive. Robert Montgomery was ill by early December, but he came through the charge unscathed. Not so lucky was Grey Neville, whose letters we have come across already. Although his brother Henry, in the Grenadier Guards, was the more vocal of the two, we have a smattering of information from Grey himself. The younger brother seems to have had a presentiment of death on 25 October and found himself cut off from his troop. He believed he could ride through them and crashed into their centre. The concussion knocked Neville, his horse and a Russian over and he thought he had killed the man. Struggling on the ground, he was stabbed with lances. He heard the Cossacks wheeling away and tried to get up but a Russian dismounted and hacked at his head with his sword. His right ear was cut and the next minute horsemen rode over him. TSM Henry Franks saw what happened next. Private John Abbott dismounted and stood astride Neville's body. Still gripping his horse's bridle, he parried Cossack swords and killed three of them, before hauling the officer onto his back and carrying him off the field. Franks believed that Neville died within minutes, but in fact he clung on for days. Henry Neville wrote to his father two days later:

> I am sorry to say that poor Grey is severely wounded … the 'Heavies' made a most brilliant charge … Grey has four wounds in the back, besides scratches … one is very severe, being very deep, but as he has spat no blood I trust none of the internals are injured … His escape is miraculous and God grant that he may soon be restored to convalescence.

John Ferguson had had a rough time on board the *Himalaya*, shackling terrified horses in a storm along with Temple Godman. He had fallen ill at Varna in August as most men had but was fit for duty by the time of the charge. Thomas Hampton, from Beaumaris, Anglesey, commanded C troop on the left of the line at Balaclava. When the war was over, he realised that he was the only officer in the 5th never to have been off sick for the entire campaign. 'I have just heard from a wounded officer,' he wrote to his father four days after the battle, 'that ... our loss was 30 men killed and wounded.' Hampton's writing case has survived and he clearly helped himself to various spoils of war – a chair and a Bible from Sebastopol.

The initial problem the 5th had was negotiating the guy ropes of the 17th Lancers. Before he was hit with the lances, Grey Neville had fallen off his horse as a result of this. 'Poor Neville,' wrote Temple Godman, 'being a *bad* rider and too weak to use his sword well ...' Campbell's horse went down too.

Godman himself, typical of a fighting officer of his class, played down his own danger. In a letter to his father on 7 December, he wrote:

> I rode The Earl, an excellent mount for anything of the kind, he has such pluck he will go anywhere, while I can easily manage him with one hand. He is much faster than the Russian horses; two or three times I slacked my hand and in about three strides he ran alongside any of the followers going as hard as they could. I can't say I saw the man who hit me, we were all in a crowd cutting and hacking at each other, and I did not know till some time after that I was touched when my wrist got stiff, then I found the cut through my coat, it was only bruised for a few days. The Russians shot some of our men with pistols. I don't care about their swords, they use them so slowly and only cut [as opposed to thrusting] but I don't like their lances. The part where I was engaged were all the 12th Hussars [the

Ingermanland Regiment] in long grey coats … The wounds our long straight [*sic*] swords made were terrible, heads nearly cut off apparently at a stroke and a great number must have died who got away. Our corporal who was killed [James Taylor] was nearly cut to pieces, his left arm nearly severed in four places. I suppose there must have been a good many at him at once, as he was very strong and a good swordsman. All the Russians seem to cut at the left wrist, so many men lost fingers and got their hands cut.

Corporal Joseph Gough had a narrow escape:

I fell and got up again and was entangled in the saddle. My head and one leg were on the ground. I tried to gallop on but fell and managed to get loose. A Russian lancer was going to run me through, McNamara came up and nearly severed his head from his body, so thank god I did not get a scratch.

Gough grabbed a riderless horse, only to be confronted by another attacker. 'I had seen a pistol in the holster pipe, so I shot him in the arm; he dropped his sword. I immediately ran him through the body.' Private Michael McNamara received the Distinguished Conduct Medal for his action that day and achieved a kind of immortality on a second class postage stamp in 2008.

TSM Franks described what happened to Private Henry Herbert of his troop:

[He was] a fine dashing young fellow and was attacked by three Cossack lancers at the same time. He disabled one of them by a terrible cut across the back of the neck and the second one scampered off. Herbert made a point at the third man's breast, but his sword blade broke off about three inches from the hilt, yet Harry was not to be foiled by this mishap. He threw the heavy sword hilt at the Russian, which hit him in the face and the Cossack dropped to the ground. He was not dead but it spoiled his visage. Herbert also spoiled the appearance of two or three more of them after that and he escaped in the end with a nasty cut across his hand, but he was soon all right again.

Herbert won the Legion d'Honneur.

One of the mysteries of the Heavy Brigade is that of Corporal William Topham, born in Wicklow, who enlisted in the 7th Dragoon Guards in August 1851. His real name was William Dennis Lemmon. We know that he faked his date of birth too, so it may be that he wanted to avoid the disapproval of his family in 'going for a soldier'. He was one of fifteen volunteers from the 7th who joined the 5th on 1 April 1854.

Another man who was at least partially separated from his family was Private George Winterbourne. He originally intended to join the navy, cliché though it is, to see the world, but ended up joining the 5th Dragoon Guards at its Newbridge barracks, County Kildare – 'I know too well,' he wrote to his parents in June 1852, 'the severity of the stroke it will give you … I did not enter the army for want nor was I intoxicated when I enlisted.' Winterbourne was still writing on a variety of topics in 1898.

Kinglake reports that there were two regimental butchers in the melee that followed, conspicuous in their white shirt sleeves. And 'here and there a man of the Light Brigade'. The only two light cavalrymen involved were possibly John Vahey of the 17th Lancers and Henry Hope, 11th Hussars. Vahey had been in William Morris's troop in 1851. He was a married labourer from Wigan, perhaps 34 years old. Known for his heavy drinking, Vahey was in the guardhouse for drunkenness on the morning of the 25th and seeing the cavalry forming up, assuming there would be action, he thought he had better join them. TSM Pardoe witnessed what followed. 'Butcher Jack' appeared between the two squadrons of the Royals, sitting on Pardoe's right. Colonel Yorke, seeing a man in the grey overalls of the 17th, asked Pardoe who he was.

'I belong to the 17th Lancers, sir,' Vahey told him.

'I admire your spirit, man,' Yorke said, 'but you had better join your own regiment.'

'All right, sir.'

Vahey told a far more colourful version of the story to Archibald Forbes months later and was awarded the Distinguished Conduct Medal. Adjutant John Chadwick, who had been Vahey's RSM in 1851, bellowed at the man to get in line. Henry Hope we have met already, an epileptic Welshmen who rode behind the Scots Greys on a borrowed horse, having left his guard tent.

Henry Hope actually rode the charge. He survived and hurried over to the North Valley afterwards to join his own regiment, making him the only man known to have ridden *both* charges that day as far as the Russian guns. In his dark blue, yellow-braided jacket and crimson overalls, he must have stood out like a sore thumb in the Heavies.

Somewhere in the mass of Russians, Scarlett was hanging on for dear life, but he had the presence of mind to order his brigade major to fetch the other units in support. 'Blind as a bat,' as Temple Godman called him, he clearly had no idea where they were. Conolly had only to swerve his horse, however, to see the first squadron of the Inniskillings to his right, alongside the 5th. Major Shute commanded this unit, with Captain Hunt, Lieutenant Wheatcroft and, thin on officers as they were, Sergeant Major Shields.

Charles Shute was 38 at Balaclava, a gentleman from Hampshire. He was shortly to be appointed AAG to the Cavalry Division, but rode the charge that day, being recommended, as were several others, for the new medal, the Victoria Cross, two years later. Edmund d'Arcy Hunt had landed from the *Trent* on 1 October and 'led the squadron with great steadiness and gallantry'. Shute and Hunt were naturally most concerned about their regiment's squadron already committed under Dalrymple White, having seen it disappear into the Russian mass. Hunt had fought with the 9th Lancers in the second Sikh War 1848–9, and was a highly competent soldier. German Wheatcroft, by comparison, was a beginner. He had been shooting wild boar in September with Temple Godman of the 5th but hunting Russians was an altogether more daunting task. Alexander Shields had enlisted in the Inniskillings in April 1840. Experienced as he was, to command a troop in battle was not what was expected of an NCO and he acquitted himself well. The official description of the wounds he was about to receive was 'slight', but in fact a sabre had hacked the back of his head, another had hit his right arm and a lance had been rammed into his side. At least he got one of the queen's own handkerchiefs for his pains, when awards were handed out months later.

By the time Hunt's squadron hit the Russian line, at full gallop, the enemy had turned in on the Three Hundred so that they actually had their backs to the British; they can barely have known what hit them. A dead Russian fell across Conolly who had to stand in his stirrups and use all his strength to throw him off. And the Russians, improbably, were being driven back up the hill. Hodge and Forster were battling their way to the far side of the mass of enemy cavalry. The Russians began to pull back, riderless horses blocking an orderly retreat.

Scarlett, who had ridden into the melee at the head of the Scots Greys, now rode out at the head of the Inniskillings. So did Hodge, who bellowed to the two nearest trumpeters to sound the rally. Even so, a number of horsemen, their blood up, ignored the sound and drove the Russians to the foot of the Fedioukine Heights. The Horse Artillery with the Light Brigade blasted them too; so did the Royal Marine Artillery from a neighbouring hillside.

Captain McCreagh of the 4th Dragoon Guards summed up the charge in a rather bizarre way, which is perhaps why historians like Mark Adkins in *The Charge* have tended to belittle the action – 'it was just like a melee coming in or out of a crowded theatre, jostling horse against horse, violent language, hacking and pushing until suddenly the Russians gave way.' He must have attended some *very* strange West End productions!

Kinglake's figures, although open to conjecture, were 78 of the Heavy Brigade killed or wounded and 550 Russians. The last figure came from discussions after the war with General Todleben, who was happy to help the travelling gent with his history.

When the regiments reformed, most of the men were still seething. They had no idea of the losses involved, but saw a still vast horde of horsemen retreating. For the desperate sword-on-sword struggle that had just finished, it seemed as if they had achieved nothing at all. As became obvious later in the war, the Russian cavalry were so rattled by the charge of the Heavy Brigade that they dare not face British cavalry again.

The French were bowled over by the action. An unknown general told Colonel Beatson, 'It was truly magnificent … the victory of the Heavy Brigade was the most glorious thing I ever saw.' We have no clear idea where Beatson was. As a 'volunteer' from India, he had no specific role that day, but Scarlett praised him for his support. It is likely that he rode slightly behind his brigadier in front of the Three Hundred. One of the first to reach the Heavies lines was Colin Campbell, fresh from his triumph earlier in the day. 'Greys! Gallant Greys!' he shouted, tearing off his Highland bonnet. 'I am sixty-one years old and if I were young again I should be proud to be in your ranks.' Raglan, probably as astonished by the Brigade's success as anyone else, sent the message by galloper – 'Well done!'

The charge of the Heavy Brigade had lasted, perhaps, eight minutes.

Chapter 11

'A Mad-Brained Trick'

'Damn those Heavies, they have the laugh of us this day,' was Cardigan's verdict on what had just happened. Sitting, upright as ever, on his chestnut, Ronald, his pelisse was buttoned up because of the cold and he was furious that his Light Brigade had missed out on the action.

Slightly behind him, at the head of the 17th Lancers, the staff officer William Morris had already given orders to his field trumpeter, John Brown, to sound the advance. Morris should not have been with his regiment that day, but the illness of superior officer Lawrenson and the death of Willett meant that he, only a captain, was now commanding the regiment, rather as Burton was the 5th Dragoon Guards. Morris was the most experienced man in the Light Brigade. The 'man of the Sutlej' (as Kinglake called him) had fought three major battles in India; Cardigan, the 'man of the Serpentine' was about to face his first.

'What are you doing, Captain Morris?' Cardigan barked at him. 'Front your regiment.'

'Look there, my lord,' Morris pointed with his sword to where Rhyzov's cavalry were breaking up in disorder.

'Remain where you are, sir,' Cardigan snapped, 'until you get my orders.'

An exasperated Morris said, 'My Lord, are we not going to charge the flying enemy?'

'No,' Cardigan told him. 'We have orders to remain here.'

Nothing sums up the blinkered stupidity of the British high command better than this line, overheard by several men in the front line of the 17th. There was no room for initiative and experience, because Cardigan, 'the noble yachtsman', possessed neither. Lucan had told him to stay put and he had received no orders from Raglan, a tired old man over ten minutes ride away with a completely different physical view of the situation from anyone with the Light Brigade.

Morris would not let it go. He realised that this was the exact psychological moment for the rest of the British cavalry to strike.

'Do, my lord, allow me to charge them with the Lancers. See, my lord, they are in disorder!'

Private James Wightman of the 17th could hear every word of this conversation.

'We must not stir from here,' Cardigan said.

Morris was furious. 'Gentlemen,' he shouted to the 17th, 'you are witnesses of my request.' He pulled Old Treasurer back, slapping his leg with his sword. 'My God, my God, what a chance we are losing.'

Morris's adjutant, Robert White, muttered to him, 'If I were in command of the regiment, I would attack myself and risk a court martial. There is a C.B. [Commander of the Bath] staring you in the face as you cannot fail.'

But Morris was a good subordinate as well as an experienced fighter. To disobey Cardigan, Lucan and Raglan was the very stuff that destroyed cohesion and discipline in an army.

In the months ahead, when Cardigan came under scrutiny for his behaviour at Balaclava, he lied his way out of trouble:

> I entirely deny that Captain Morris ever pointed out to me my opportunity of charging the enemy or said anything to me of the kind; and it is quite untrue that I said I was placed in that particular spot, and should not move without orders, or anything to that effect. I further deny that Captain Morris ever begged me to be allowed to charge with his regiment alone, or that he gave me any advice, or uttered one word to me upon the subject of attacking the enemy. I remember upon one occasion during the engagement, after the Light Brigade had been ordered [by Lucan] to join the Heavy Brigade in the

valley, Captain Morris broke away from the column with his regiment without orders upon which I asked him, sharply, why he did so and desired him to fall again into column. That was all that occurred on the day in question, between myself and Captain Morris.

Morris stuck to his guns and wrote to the War Office, reiterating what really happened. This was backed up by a similar letter from Captain Godfrey Morgan of the 17th. Kinglake sums up the whole fiasco:

> The man of the Sutlej entreating that the [Light] Brigade might advance to the rescue, but rebuffed and over-ruled by the higher authority of the man from the banks of the Serpentine, who sits erect in his saddle and is fitfully damning the Heavies instead of taking part in their fight – these might be seen to be creatures of the brain evoked, perhaps, for some drama of the grossly humorous sort, but because of the sheer truth their place is historic.

Kinglake got it right when he wrote, 'Lord Cardigan had been charged to command; Captain Morris had to obey. The exaggerations men look for in satire were forestalled and outdone by the Horse Guards [the army high command].'

The passage of time softens the truth, so that by 1957 when Cecil Woodham-Smith wrote the seminal (but wrong) *The Reason Why*, she could say, 'Perhaps Cardigan's recollection was at fault.' Cardigan was no cavalry general, even though a gushing press at the time called him 'the English Murat'. What he was good at was, in the modern American phrase, 'covering his ass'.

Ironically, Lucan had sent another order to Cardigan via his own son, Lord Bingham, his ADC, urging exactly what Morris had already told his brigadier – 'My instructions to you are to attack anything and everything that shall come within reach of you.' He urged Cardigan to be careful of infantry, but implied that cavalry were fair game. That order, however, was superseded by Raglan's third of the day – 'Cavalry to advance and take advantage of any opportunity to recover the Heights. They will be supported by infantry which have been ordered to advance on two fronts.'

It was now twenty to ten in the morning and the Duke of Cambridge's Division and George Cathcart's were still on the march. Lucan and the cavalry could not see them at all. The Heights referred to in the order were the Causeway ridge, from which the Russians were now beginning to haul away the guns. Conscious that his great mentor, Wellington, had never lost a gun, Raglan was determined to stop this. Unaccountably, Lucan ordered the Light Brigade to change front and take up position at the end of the North Valley. The Heavies in the meantime stayed in the South Valley, waiting for the promised infantry support. All this took the best part of an hour, while the Heavies licked their wounds and no doubt, under Scarlett's watchful eye, straightened their jackets. Their work was not done. Lucan's explanation later was exactly the *opposite* of what Raglan's orders said. He thought he should wait for the infantry and support them, rather than the other way around.

Furious, Raglan fired off his fourth order to Richard Airey, his QMG, sitting alongside him on the Sapouné Heights. It was by now eleven o'clock: 'Lord Raglan wishes the cavalry to advance rapidly to the front – follow the enemy and try to prevent the enemy carrying away the guns – Troop Horse artillery may accompany – French cavalry is on your left.'

It was signed R. Airey and ended with the word 'immediate'. The order, scribbled in pencil on paper balanced on Airey's sabretache, has survived and is in the National Army Museum, Chelsea.

The next 'galloper' on duty was Captain Somerset Gough Calthorpe of the 8th Hussars. In Tony Richardson's *The Charge of the Light Brigade*, Louis Nolan butts in and insists that he take the message. In fact, he was Raglan's choice, probably because he knew the man was both a cavalry expert and a superb horseman. Kinglake builds up

Nolan's over-exuberance, citing examples from Blenheim to Salamanca when British cavalry had won the day. The writer of the official history had Nolan's journal in front of him when he wrote *The Invasion of the Crimea*; the last entry was made on 12 October. The staff officer, who had written books on cavalry, must have been delighted by the Heavies' performance; he was also furious at the inactivity of Lucan and Cardigan. Kinglake makes a great deal too of the slope down which Nolan rode the troop horse he had borrowed from the 13th Light Dragoons. Raglan was some 700 feet above the valley floor, but, having stood there, I can confirm that the ride was not that tricky for a man of Nolan's ability.

What was clear to Raglan – and should have been clear to Nolan – was that there were two valleys, North and South. The Russian cavalry had retreated to a mile and a half away, General Liprandi's men were roping up the guns from the Causeway redoubts and on the Fedioukine Heights, to Raglan's and the Right Brigade's left, General Jabrokritsky, with eight infantry battalions, four cavalry squadrons and fourteen guns, was firmly in position. Had the Light Brigade followed Raglan's orders, they would have rolled up Liprandi's men and driven them out of the redoubts, especially since those men had just seen what British cavalry could do. From where they stood, they could also see the infantry divisions creeping from the Chersonese.

What happened next is shrouded in confusion and controversy and historians still argue about it today. Taken alone, Raglan's fourth order is vague. 'Rapidly to the front' begged the question – which front? The Causeway Heights or the North Valley? 'Horse Artillery may accompany' – was that a serving suggestion? Had the Horse Artillery been given any orders? And what about the French cavalry? They may have been 'on [Lucan's] left' but d'Allonville's powder-blue-jacketed 1st and 4th Chasseurs d'Afrique were not visible to Lucan at all. In connection with Raglan's third order, however, the meaning was clear. The only Russian unit 'carrying away the guns' was Liprandi's on the Causeway Heights. How could Lucan not understand that?

Lucan said out loud that the order was meaningless. The job of a staff officer was to clarify anything not made clear in a written order and Nolan put Lucan straight.

'Lord Raglan's orders are that the cavalry should attack immediately.'

Lucan snapped back, 'Attack, sir! Attack what? What guns, sir?'

This was incomprehensible. Lucan, having sent his own ADC to Cardigan urging him to attack anything in sight, had first of all ignored Raglan's third order and was now querying his fourth in the most absurd way. Furious, Nolan then threw his arm behind him and yelled, 'There, my lord, is the enemy; there are your guns!'

According to Lucan, in the House of Lords inquiry that followed much later, Nolan was pointing down the wrong valley, the North, at the end of which sat Russian guns in position with a massive body of cavalry behind them. These men were a mile and a half away from the redoubts on the Causeway Heights and the only guns they were near were their own.

Kinglake is in no doubt that the guilty party was Lucan. A number of men, military as well as civilian, blamed the ADC for causing the disaster of the Light Brigade, but it is clear from all the evidence given that it was Lucan who was to blame. He demanded a court martial in the months ahead, in order to clear his name. He should have been granted it; and he should have been cashiered. In the North Valley, Lucan could have had Nolan arrested for insubordination. Instead, he let the man trot across to his old friend William Morris to ask permission to ride with the 17th (which an ADC had no right to do). 'Permission granted, dear friend,' Morris said and history was about to put a full stop to the recrimination arguments.

As for Lucan, he rode across to Cardigan at the head of the Light Brigade's front rank, the 13th Light Dragoons, and gave his version of Raglan's order. Cardigan may have been dim, but he was not a moron and calmly said, 'Certainly, sir, but allow me to point out to you that the Russians have a battery in the valley to our front and batteries and riflemen on each flank.'

'I know it,' Lucan said in a rare moment of civility to his brother-in-law, 'but Lord Raglan will have it. We have no choice but to obey.'

Cardigan pulled back his own regiment, the 11th Hussars, into the second line and Lucan told him to 'advance steadily and quietly' and to 'keep his men well in hand'. With a muttered comment to nobody but himself, Cardigan was heard to say, 'Well, here goes the last of the Brudenells.' He turned in the saddle. 'The Brigade will advance. Walk. March.' Trumpeter Britten sounded his bugle.

The charge of the Light Brigade has been told and retold countless times. Less well known is the support given to it by the Heavies. In what follows, I have concentrated on this rearguard action which, mercifully, Lucan called off as soon as he could. It was the only sensible move he made all day. The Scots Greys and the Royals were brought forward to form the first line of the Heavy Brigade and Lucan was determined to ride with them.

At the head of the Lights, Cardigan was astonished to see Nolan spurring his horse across his front, from the 17th Lancers' position on his left. He was shouting what sounded like 'Threes right!' having realised that the Brigade was turning into the wrong valley. Morris, for his part, had no idea about the confusion of orders and called out, 'That won't do, Nolan! We've a long way to go and must be steady.'

Riding ahead of the commander of a brigade was a court-martial offence. 'But a Russian shell,' Kinglake wrote, 'threw out a fragment which met Nolan full on the chest and tore a way into his heart. The sword leapt from his hand; but the arm with which he was waving it the moment before still remained high uplifted in the air and ... there burst forth a cry so strange and appalling that the hearer who rode the nearest to him has always called it "unearthly".'

The one man who could have turned the Brigade and saved it from disaster was dead.

As the brigades gained momentum, from the walk to the march to the trot, the canter and the gallop, the Russians on both sides of the North Valley and the scattered watchers on the hills, could not believe it. General Liprandi was afterwards to ask captured survivors if they were drunk and who was the officer with the horse with white socks who had led them.

'Faster and faster they rode, wrote Fanny Duberly, 'How we watched them! They are out of sight …'

The Odessa Regiment, with the redoubts, began to recoil, assuming that the Brigade would turn on them. It did not, but swept on past, in William Russell's words, 'glittering in the morning sun in all the pride and splendour of war. We could scarcely believe the evidence of our senses. Surely that handful of men are not going to charge an enemy in position?'

Kinglake tried to reconstruct the *sounds* of battle as the Light Brigade charged – the 'ping' of the bullet, the 'sighing', the 'humming' and the 'whang' of round shot, the 'harsh whirr' of iron fragments from a bursting shell, ripping horse and man indiscriminately. Grimmest of all was the 'slosh' as a man was hit. It seems likely that he heard these words from survivors.

The Heavy Brigade, vaguely under Lucan, but actually still under Scarlett at their head, followed Lord George Paget's 4th Light Dragoons down the North Valley, soon to be immortalised by Tennyson as the 'valley of Death'. As they rode past No 4 redoubt, still probably at the trot, shot and shell reached them. It had already decimated the Light Brigade, especially the front ranks of the Lancers and the 13th Lights and now the Heavies were within range. Walter Charteris, Lucan's ADC, had been sent off by his boss with an order, but it is still not clear where he went or why. He may have galloped to General Cathcart to tell him to hurry up, or to Captain Shakespeare of the Horse Artillery to open up his guns in support of the cavalry. Neither officer seems to have done much; Cathcart stayed where he was in front of No 4 redoubt; Shakespeare did not fire a shot because he had no clear line of fire. Barely had Charteris got back to Lucan than a shell killed him, his presentiment of death confirmed. Within minutes, AAG William Paulet had his plumed hat blown off. Thomas McMahon, the AQMG, a 'very gentlemanly person' according to Temple Godman, had his leg punctured by grapeshot and his horse was hit twice. At more or less the same time, Lucan's horse was hit too and a musket ball smashed into the general's leg. Lucan barely flinched.

The distance between the two brigades was increasing. The natural instinct of men under galling fire, as the Light Brigade was, was to gallop like hell, reach the guns and get out of trouble. The Heavies, no doubt exhausted after their own fight, were slower and not yet quite in the same lethal position. What was happening, however, was that the Greys and Royals in particular were being hit by the crossfire from the Fedioukine Heights and men breaking into a gallop with swords drawn had no opportunity to fire back.

Leading the Royals, Colonel Yorke wrote:

The very large shot (32lbs) that overcrowned the heights naturally bowled like cricket balls into our ranks. We should have been equally useful if we had been just a few paces clear of the line of fire, but as it was not so, the large shot came down upon us. The officers could easily escape, we had only to move our horses a few yards to let the shot … which movement I affected frequently, but when a shot came opposite the closely packed squadron, it generally took a front and rear rank horse and sometimes a man. In this foolish manner, we lost 7 horses and two men … The regiment were beautifully steady; I never had a better line in a field day, the only swerving was to let through the ranks the wounded and dead men and horses of the Light Brigade which were even then scattered over the plain. It was a fearful sight … and the appearance of all who retired was as if they had passed through a heavy shower of blood, positively dripping and saturated and shattered arms blowing back like empty sleeves, as the poor fellows ran to the rear. During all this time there was a constant squelching noise around me … another moment my horse was shot in the right flank.

He wrote to his wife two days after the battle:

> More bad luck but do not make yourself unduly uneasy …
> A grape or canister shot caught one on the left thigh bone and
> smashed my leg badly, but I continued to ride down nearly
> 4 miles with my leg swinging about. I suffered considerable
> pain but did not faint.

He later had the leg amputated.

Riding behind Yorke, 19-year-old Private James Aslett had his right arm smashed by round shot. It was amputated later that day and he received the Distinguished Conduct Medal for his trouble. Captain George Campbell was badly hit and his life may have been saved weeks later when a medical student friend came out to Balaclava to tend him and take him home. He had been shot through the shoulder and the friend found him 'in some straits' before his removal to Scutari. Orderly Room Clerk George Clements kept a diary throughout the Crimean campaign. He was Lucan's orderly at Balaclava and may well have ridden behind the man in this part of the battle. His account, however, focuses on the charge of the Heavy Brigade and not the follow-up. Riding Master George Cruse left a very detailed account of Balaclava in a letter to his father on 2 November. He had joined the Royals at the age of 18, at Frome, Somerset, and wrote sixty-three letters from the Crimea. He was not technically Riding Master at Balaclava, but he was TSM:

> Nothing could be more bold and daring than the advance of
> the Light Brigade who darted forward at a tremendous speed
> … We had been halted just between the fires of the cross
> batteries, which were also filled with riflemen and it was just
> at this spot that our officers [Campbell, Elmsall and Hartopp]
> and men were cut down. We retreated in a very orderly manner
> and our men did not bob their heads as they did in the morning

but it was the opinion of all the old officers present that in no previous battle on record was a body of cavalry exposed to such a murderous fire. How we escaped (a single man of us) God alone knows …

At that point, Cruse had not had his boots off for nine days.

Lieutenant Gilbert Robertson got off lightly with his horse shot from under him. Somebody else who lost his mount was Sergeant John Hill, but in his case, he was able to grab a Russian pony and retake his place in the lines.

Private Charles Howell made a speech later in life and it was taken down verbatim. He claimed to be Orderly to Scarlett, which we know was the post held by James Shegog of the 5th Dragoon Guards, but there is no reason to doubt the rest:

> The heavy cavalry followed the light in support some distance down. When we had got some four or five hundred yards down the valley a ball from a Russian cannon struck the horse I was on in the chest and killed him on the spot. In falling he pitched me on my head and the peak of my helmet left a mark here I shall carry about with me as long as I live. I thought when I saw the blood on my face that I had been hit as well as the horse … I pulled myself together … and soon got another horse belonging to some poor fellow that was less fortunate than I was.

The next day, Howell was with Scarlett when a roll call was taken. 'It was a sad sight to witness …'

Private George Taylor was hit twice with Minié balls, giving him a flesh wound in the arm but a more serious wound in his stomach. He was taken to Scutari but died of his wounds.

Among the Greys, the casualties were no less. Surgeon John Brush, who had dragged Colonel Darby Griffith and his horse out of trouble in the Heavy Charge, was dismayed to find the man, bandage on his head and the wound still bleeding, back in the saddle ready to support Cardigan. The other surgeon, Robert Chapple, had his horse wounded, but the animal kept upright almost by instinct as the bullets whipped around them both.

TSM James Dearden, who had joined the Greys from the 8th Hussars in 1848, was a veteran by the time of Balaclava. He got off lightly in the battle, his left thumb shattered by grapeshot. Private William Donaldson did not fare so well. He was only 18 at Balaclava and his horse was hit, his own leg being shattered. He was pinned to the ground in the North Valley and seeing the amount of blood, assumed that he was dying. He was helped up by a group of soldiers. He may have been delirious because he remembered seeing the Duke of Cambridge (who was about a mile away at the time) and saying to him, 'If no one is coming to help me, will your Royal Highness shoot me in the head?' The soldiers who *did* come for him were ordered back to their lines and it is by no means clear who these were. Some Turks eventually found him and he lost consciousness.

Private Alexander Gardiner was the son of a troop sergeant major in the Greys. He enlisted in the regiment at Athlone in April 1848, but was often in trouble, landing himself with a three-month prison sentence in 1851. Private Henry Ramage, who was cited for the Victoria Cross that day, saved his life. Gardiner's leg was smashed with round shot and his horse was down. Ramage hauled his animal across the ranks, driving a knot of Russians back and dragged the injured man across his saddle. The indomitable Ramage had already saved the life of James McPherson during the first charge. McPherson was surrounded by seven Russians until Ramage chased them off. Not content with that, he had managed to grab a Russian cavalryman and bring him back to the British lines as a prisoner.

'The round shot poured on us,' Captain Robert Hunter wrote to his sister, 'shells bursting before, behind and above us and anything like the balls from cannister and rifles you can't imagine but by the awful results. A grapeshot struck my cloak and bounded off, it was just 2 inches above my knee.' Hunter was almost certainly carrying his cloak rolled in front of his saddle and this saved his life. 'It was an awful time and the men were falling, and horses on all sides. The din deafening and the poor fellows who were struck groaned awfully. A man riding beside me had his leg shattered just below the knee with grapeshot, a fellow of the one I have no doubt hit my cloak.' Grapeshot was so called because it was a cluster of iron balls fired together in a canister that exploded rather like the pellets of a shotgun.

Sergeant John Louden was probably building up his part when he spoke to a Canadian journalist in St Pancras Workhouse in 1892:

> Until the Lights disappeared into a gulf of smoke from the Russian cannon, I was alongside General Scarlett when he gave the order 'The Heavy Brigade will support the Lights'. These were, I believe, his exact words. The Lights had broken into a gallop and were close to the 'Valley of Death'. I sounded [clearly, Louden was the Greys' bugler] and soon myself and General Scarlett were some 30 yards in front of the advancing squadrons.

Major William Forrest with the 4th Dragoon Guards wrote two days after the battle:

> We, the Heavies, were taken down the valley as a support to the Light Brigade and we had batteries playing upon us upon both flanks. We ... escaped in a most providential manner; the round shot were flying over us and both in front and rear and occasionally through the ranks ... I saw the Greys drop to the number of about 12 or 15 but I think they were principally the horses that suffered. I got a crack on the head ... but the Brass pot [helmet] stood well and my head is only slightly bruised. I got a rap on the shoulder but the edge must have been badly delivered for it has only cut my coat and bruised my shoulder.

TSM William Stewart of the 5th Dragoon Guards probably holds something of a record. He had three horses killed under him that day, as Henry Franks remembered:

> The first one was by a rifle bullet. Stewart caught another horse belonging to the 4th Dragoon Guards and he had hardly got mounted when a shell burst under him and blew him up. Stewart escaped without a scratch and managed to catch another loose horse which he rode for a while until a cannonball broke one of the horse's legs. Stewart, who was still without a scratch, took pity on the poor dumb brute and shot him. He then procured yet another horse which made the fourth he had ridden that day. Very few men, I should say, have had such an experience as this and all within hours …

Franks himself had a narrow 'shave' as he put it years later. He was riding knee to knee with TSM James Russell and Trumpeter Edward Baker when a shell exploded under Russell's horse, literally blowing the animal to pieces. The sergeant major was catapulted over the horse's head but was on his feet again in seconds, unhurt. Franks' horse and Baker's were lifted off the ground by the force of the explosion and Russell grabbed Franks' stirrup leather and clung on until he could catch a riderless horse. Another shell bursting nearby hit six horses, two of which died at once. Private Moses Plumpton, a lad from Lancashire, was pinned under the tangle of animals but he clawed himself free. Astonishingly, nobody was hurt. Three of those were the Kelly brothers, Luke, Thomas and Martin.

Halfway down the valley, Lucan had had enough. He raised his hand for the halt and said to Paulet by his side, 'They have sacrificed the Light Brigade; they shall not have the Heavy if I can help it.' He was already deflecting any blame from himself with the use of the word 'they'. Scarlett's battered Brigade pulled back to be out of firing range.

Scarlett himself had no idea that Lucan had ordered the halt. Riding well ahead, as he had in the first charge, this time with William Beatson alongside him, he glanced back and saw his Brigade slowing and preparing to retire. Astounded, he shouted at trumpeter John Louden, riding at his shoulder, 'Have you sounded retire?' 'No, General,' Louden assured him and Scarlett wheeled his horse to ride back to Lucan.

TSM Franks remembered:

> I can almost fancy I see the grand old soldier, cool, collected and erect in his saddle, when he took us into action. He had a stern and determined look that no one could misunderstand. He led his Brigade through the shower of shot and shell until he was convinced that some horrible blunder had been made; and only in time to save us. He gave the order "Troops, Right Wheel!" and thus took us out of the direct line of fire.

In the relative quiet that followed twenty minutes of the gallop, of shot and shell, Fanny Duberly, with others on the hillside, saw riderless horses cantering out of the smoke of the valley and straggling riders, on foot, shell-shocked and bleeding.

'What can those skirmishers be doing?' someone asked.

'Good God! It's the Light Brigade.'

There was a half-hearted attempt by a squadron of Russian lancers from the Causeway Heights to hit the pulverised and exhausted Brigade, but Colonel Shewell and little more than a troop of the 8th Hussars charged through them and they scattered. The guns on the Fedioukine Heights were silent now; d'Allonville's Chasseurs d'Afrique had knocked them out, sabring the gunners with the usual cavalry panache that had once been used against the British. Fanny rode among the dead – a Turkish soldier in the vineyard, a Russian next to her horse's hoofs. Most of the horses she saw were dead and already unsaddled. 'One poor cream-colour, with a bullet through his flank, lay dying, so patiently.'

Of Henry Duberly's regiment, the only horse unscathed belonged to Colonel Shewell. John, Viscount Fitzgibbon was dead, two bullets hitting him shortly after Nolan went down, although his body was never found. Neither was that of George Lockwood, who had looked out for Fanny during the past weeks. He was last seen in the smoke, looking for Lord Cardigan. Daniel Clutterbuck had had his right foot shattered with grapeshot; Edward Seager, the adjutant, had been hit in the hand. Edward Tompkinson's horse had been killed under him, Rodolph de Salis's animal, Drummer Boy, was wounded. Cornet William Mussenden showed Fanny the lead shot that had killed his mare. George Clowes's horse had gone down too and he had been hit with grapeshot. At the time she wrote, he was still a prisoner of the Russians.

'Ah,' wrote Fanny, 'what a catalogue!'

The shattered Light Brigade came back in little knots of men and horses. Cardigan, who had reached the guns first, said to a group of them, 'Men, it is a mad-brained trick, but it is no fault of mine.' Someone called out, 'Never mind, my lord. We are ready to go again.' 'No, no,' Cardigan said. 'You have done enough.'

The numbers at the muster of the Light Brigade were shocking, but of course did not include those missing in action at that stage. Six hundred and seventy-eight men had ridden down the valley and only 195 answered the roll call. Of the 13th Light Dragoons, which had been in the front rank, only ten men still sat in their saddles. Of the officers in the front line, the 13th and 17th Lancers, only two escaped injury.

The accusations began at once. Raglan rode down to the Light Brigade camp an hour or two later and snapped at Cardigan, 'What did you mean, sir, by attacking a battery in front, contrary to all the usages of warfare and the customs of the service?'

'My lord,' an outraged Cardigan blustered back, 'I hope you will not blame me, for I received the order to attack from my superior officer in front of the troops.'

So Raglan turned on Lucan. 'You have lost the Light Brigade!'

Lucan, literally smarting from a slight leg wound, said that he had obeyed Raglan's written order as given to him by Captain Nolan. Raglan was not having any of that. 'Lord Lucan, you were a Lieutenant-General and should therefore have exercised your discretion, and, not approving of the charge, should not have caused it to be made.'

The buck should have stopped there. Raglan was absolutely right. Allowing for the vagueness of his fourth order (which was less vague when coupled with the third); allowing for Nolan's impetuous rudeness to Lucan, it *was* the cavalry commander's job to interpret the situation. That was, in effect, what they paid him for. For the rest of his life, Lord Lucan was happy to point the finger in every direction other than at himself.

Chapter 12

Winter

From the time it happened, Lord Raglan knew how news of Balaclava would be greeted at home. In Kinglake's words: 'he used to lament the perverseness with which he believed that his fellow-countrymen would turn from the brilliant and successful achievement of Scarlett's brigade to dwell, and still dwell [Kinglake was writing four years later] upon the heroic, self-destructive exploit of Lord Cardigan's squadrons ...'

General Pierre Bosquet's famous quotation is rarely given in full – 'C'est magnifique,' he said, 'mais ce n'est pas la guerre; c'est de la folie.' (It's magnificent, but it's not war; it's madness) – and this, from a man who had climbed the heights of the Alma with only a few companies in the weeks before.

But Raglan was proved right. The 18 November issue of *Punch* showed Cardigan reaching the guns. A week later, under the caption 'Enthusiasm of Paterfamilias, On Reading the Report of the Grand Charge of British Cavalry on the 25th' an excited father is reading Russell's account (which in itself was heavily slanted towards the Light Brigade) while waving a stick around. The women in his hearing are weeping; the children cheering ecstatically. We cannot help thinking that the family is focusing on the 'noble 600' and Alfred, Lord Tennyson, reading the same account, was already dipping his pen into the inkwell.

Neither side could claim a victory at Balaclava. The Russians moved back to the Causeway Heights, narrowing the Allies' hold on the ground around the harbour. Psychologically, however, the Russians were seriously demoralised.

Years later, Cardigan remembered that he had been seething about Nolan's behaviour all the way down the North Valley. On his return, his thigh bleeding from a Cossack lance, he hailed James Scarlett. 'What do you think, General, of the aide-de-camp, after such an order being brought to us which has destroyed the Light Brigade, riding to the rear and screaming like a woman?'

'Do not say any more,' Scarlett said, 'for I have just ridden over his body.'

In the immediate aftermath of the charges, Scarlett wrote to Lucan extolling the heroism of Conolly, Elliot and Beatson who had ridden close to him during the action. He also recommended Elliot for the Victoria Cross in the months ahead, but Lucan turned him down on the plea that 'to charge and fight hand to hand was nothing more than the duty of a cavalry officer'. Typically of the nepotistic Lucan, he was perfectly happy to commend his own son, Captain Charles Bingham, for the award instead. Roy Dutton in his *Forgotten Heroes* book assumes that Bingham rode with the Heavies behind his father in support of the Lights, but Kinglake makes it clear that he did not.

For Lucan, things were about to get nasty. He reiterated to Raglan on 30 November that he was, in effect, just following orders. Raglan wrote to the Duke of Newcastle, the Secretary for War, on 8 January 1855, as a vicious Russian winter was destroying his army, an extremely clear and fair summary of the facts, that Lucan in effect ignored the third order of the day, made no attempt to liaise with either the Horse Artillery or d'Allonville's Chasseurs d'Afrique and, to cap it all, sent the Light Brigade the wrong way. Newcastle, General Hardinge, the commander-in-chief, and the queen all agreed that Lucan should be recalled.

Beside himself with fury, Lucan left the Crimea and was back in London by 2 March. He then demanded a court martial to clear his name. This was denied, but in the scheme of things, the whole messy business did not do Lucan much harm. In a typical Victorian whitewash, he was exonerated and went on to become a field marshal in June 1887 and a respected 'elder' of the House of Lords. The anti-Lucan lobby could at least take satisfaction in the fact that he never held a field command again.

Some years ago, it was fashionable to write counter-factual history – the 'what ifs' of the past – and one of the more fascinating books that emerged from this was John Harris's *The Court Martial of Lord Lucan* (Severn House, 1987). In this fictional account, Harris discusses the events of 25 October as though various participants are being interrogated. Scarlett is mentioned in evidence, but the only 'active' officer included is Hodge, who speaks in Lucan's defence. The outcome is a victory for Lucan. Fanny Duberly's evidence is dismissed because she is a woman; that of Kinglake and Russell because they are civilians. Nolan is loaded with guilt because he was an outspoken, flashy staff officer and because – although Lucan and Cardigan would never have admitted it – he was dead. The 'court martial' of Lord Lucan ends up being a whitewash, which, I suspect, is what would actually have happened if 'Lord Look-On' had really been given his day in court.

In another book on the subject, Mark Adkin's *The Charge*, the author describes Raglan, Lucan, Cardigan and Nolan as 'the four horsemen of calamity' and blames them all for the loss of the Light Brigade. While there is undoubtedly some truth in this, in terms of rank order of culpability, Lord Lucan must be at the head of the column.

In the real world, in the Crimea at the end of October, things were a little different, although the carping continued. John Harris might imagine that Colonel Hodge would speak in Lucan's defence at his virtual court martial, but in reality, he wrote to his mother on 6 December, 'I do think that Lord Lucan might as well have given me the credit of our flank charge and not have told such a falsehood about it in saying that he ordered it, when he never gave any orders at all.'

The battered Heavy Brigade and the shattered remnants of the Light remained in the saddle until eight o'clock, by which time it was dark. They were pulled back to their camp, 2 miles from the scene of the action and both Hodge's servants got drunk, lying on the ground.

The colonel himself put up a temporary bed in Forrest's tent, loathe the man though he did. 'The light cavalry were murdered in their work,' Hodge wrote in his diary, 'when infantry should have first been engaged and artillery were indispensable.' He noted one death in the 4th Dragoon Guards, Private Thomas Ryan, hit in the head several times and skewered with a Cossack lance. William Scanlan was badly hurt and he died hours later. Bearing in mind the bloody clash of arms, the regiment had got off lightly.

Temple Godman gave his father a clear account of both charges. 'Our brigade came in also just then for a heavy fire and the Greys alone lost forty killed and wounded, all for nothing.' He had not undressed or washed for two days. The weather was lovely.

Henry Franks could not understand why the Russians did not attack again and drive the British back to the sea – they certainly had the numbers. Dismounting for the first time in fourteen hours, Franks and his boys gratefully accepted the grog doled out by the commissary department. Then it was all hands-to as the camp was struck and moved. The skirmish the next day, as Liprandi re-established the ground the Russians had temporarily lost, did not involve the cavalry.

As a result of Balaclava, Allied attitudes towards the Turks worsened. They had abandoned the forts and left Colin Campbell's Highlanders to it in the battle's early stages. Franks, writing years later, was almost apologetic when he said 'from my experience of them I am reluctantly compelled to say that I believe them to be "born cowards".' The French, however, the enemy of a thousand years, could do no wrong. The Chasseurs d'Afrique had saved cavalry lives by knocking out the five guns on the Fedioukine Heights. '"Vive la France", I say,' wrote Franks.

In the meantime, Hodge sank into his usual gripes. Difficult man though he was, it may be that in the days after Balaclava, a real depression set in. It may well have been worse among the Russians but arguably it was the French who were the only ones to come out of the battle with a sense of achievement, and even that was limited. Hodge had lost his tent, his drunken servants had robbed the officers' stores and he was unwell again. At least he had got himself a Russian sword as a souvenir. On the 28th, there was a scare and Captain Webb galloped into the camp with his piquet claiming that a large body of Russian cavalry was approaching. It turned out to be a false alarm and another black mark against Webb. The Heavy Brigade camp moved again, even further from food and water and the tents were on an exposed and windy headland. By the end of the month, 'the weather is killing our horses'.

Hodge would not let Webb's behaviour go. There was a court of inquiry which acquitted him of wrongdoing, but neither Hodge nor Lucan agreed with that. Webb had to watch his back. Hodge had his revenge on one of his servants, Private John Bucknell, who was dismissed. John Little took his place. At the end of the month, too, there was an auction for the belongings of dead officers, as there had been after the Alma. A pair of gloves sold for 33 shillings.

Hodge was eating tolerably well as November came, but he was green with envy when he saw the French camp. They had wooden sheds, as opposed to tents, with mats on the floor. The men had bread three times a week, baked in their regiments' ovens. Lucan was still, in Hodge's phrase, 'an obstinate mule'. The colonel recommended TSM Edward Harran to be promoted to cornet without purchase with a view to replacing Webb, who was, predictably, ill. Webb eventually retired in September 1855 and Harran took over as adjutant. His promotion came on 4 November, the day that Hodge heard that the Russians were being reinforced with huge numbers from the north, led by the Grand Duke Michael, son of the tsar.

Temple Godman wrote to his brother on the previous day. It was bitterly cold by now and the day's routine began with picking lice out of clothes. He had got himself a Russian fur coat which he found essential. By that time, the cavalry's wounded had been sent to Scutari, arriving at more or less the same time as Florence Nightingale. The rumours from home, always, by definition, weeks behind events, were that the 5th Dragoon Guards were decimated (hence the need to amalgamate with the 4th). Godman was anxious to put his mother straight and Scarlett had promised to write to *The Times*.

Three days later, that paper's own correspondent wrote: 'Then commenced the bloodiest struggle ever witnessed since war cursed the earth' – the battle of Inkerman. Like the Alma, this was an infantry slog, in part because the British cavalry at least was so undermanned (and, especially, underhorsed). TSM Franks was aware of a heavier bombardment than usual from Sebastopol on the night of 4 November and when dawn came on the 5th, a thick fog made visibility difficult. 'The two Brigades of Cavalry were called out early in the morning and we remained on the Field the whole day; but for all the use they were, we might as well have stayed in our tents.'

Inkerman was a far bloodier encounter than the Alma. 'How,' wondered Fanny Duberly, 'can I describe the horrors and glories of that day?' A thick fog filled the rocky ravines and slopes of the battlefield, fought below Sebastopol. The Russians had been reinforced – Fanny heard – with 20,000 extra men and General Osten-Sacken. Somerset Gough Calthorpe, on Raglan's staff, believed they were pumped up by the arrival of the Grand Duke Michael and being blessed for battle by their Orthodox priests. It seemed as though a new order was given to the Russians, because the casualty rate among senior officers was abnormally high. Their plumed hats (like Elliot's in the Heavy Brigade charge) were an easy target, even for the clumsy and unreliable muskets of the Russians. General Torrens went down, a bullet in his side. Moments later, George Cathcart, calling on his division to attack, was killed instantly, a musket ball through his head. His AAG, Colonel Seymour of the Guards, was hit trying to recover the general's body, as was *his* assistant, Major Maitland. The Duke of Cambridge's horse was shot from under him and General Henry Bentinck was hit in the arm.

The cavalry had been ordered to stand-to early in the morning, the two brigades amalgamated now, but they saw almost nothing because of the fog. They had perhaps 350 mounted men and from time to time during the day, men and horses were hit by random shells. It was impossible to retaliate.

General Strangways of the Royal Artillery had a leg taken off by round shot. With the same calm shown by the Earl of Uxbridge at Waterloo, he asked officers nearby to help him off his horse. Canrobert's horse was killed and he himself wounded. Raglan's own staff were going down like ninepins, but the commander remained unruffled as shot whizzed around him. Someone observed later that 'my lord rather likes being under fire than otherwise'.

Fanny Duberly, anxious as ever to see the action, heard a rumour (yet again!) that the cavalry had been wiped out – 'but I had learned experience and this did not trouble me much'. On her way up to the front, she saw Sir George Brown, bleeding from an arm wound, in a steady stream of ambulances (actually, carts) winding down towards Balaclava. The Brigade of Guards had been badly hit – 'Ah, me! How ruthless is the sword!'

Colonel Hodge's regiment was turned out without breakfast (again) and he sat in his saddle with the 4th until half past twelve. Then Lucan ordered him with a squadron of his own men, as well as one from the Greys and Royals, to support the Horse Artillery as the bombardment died away. He sent the troops back afterwards and rode with Captain Forster over the Inkerman Valley. 'The ground was covered with dead and wounded Russians' and when his horse and Forster's were inexplicably led away by an infantryman, they had to trudge back to the Light Brigade camp on foot to borrow two more. When the horses were found, Hodge's water canteen and pistol were missing. Never a man to let an insult pass, Hodge found the guilty party but he does not record what happened to him.

Temple Godman heard that the enemy had lost 10,000 men. In the British lines, Henry Neville, the elder brother of Grey in Godman's regiment, was among the dead. Grey died at Scutari days later. On the 10th, he wrote to his mother to say that he had a bad cough, which, the doctors told him, would soon go away. Four days later, James Orr, Neville's servant, wrote to Neville's father, Lord Braybrooke:

> He died on Saturday morning, about eight o'clock, from wounds he received at the fated engagement we had at Balaclava ... He was two days on board [a troopship] attended by a head doctor, who waited on him as a parent; and since he arrived in hospital, no person could be better attended ... My Lord, so gently did he – so calmly did he – breathe his last, that a casual observer would consider him sleeping ... Doubtless your Lordship will receive letters from the officers of the regiment, relative to the sad affair; to them, and with them, he was a brother; to the men of his troop, he was indulgent, kind and courteous ... I enclose a lock of his hair ... it is all I could send.

Neville's broken rib had pierced his lung and this caused his death. His dying wish was that Private John Abbott, who had done his best to save his life, should be taken care of. Lord Braybrooke gave the man a grant of £20 a year for the rest of his life.

Temple Godman rode over the Inkerman battlefield too. Russian wounded still lay on the field and the 'bodies lie so thickly one can hardly walk'. The Allied troops were tending to them as best they could, giving them rum and biscuits from their own rations. One captured Russian officer said, 'What a pity two such nations as England and Russia should fight over such brutes as these Turks.'

It was possible to get hams, soup and potted meat from the ships in Balaclava harbour, but the *Himalaya*, newest and best of them, had run aground and had to be sent back home for repairs. 'They say,' Godman wrote to his father, 'we are to winter here.'

Inkerman made that inevitable. A council of war had been called by the Allied High Command for 7 November but the scale and ferocity of the Russian attack two days earlier threw those plans into confusion.

If the Russians had lost 10,000 men, they could afford it. The British losses amounted to 2,000, including some of the best officers in the army. Godman was quietly seething over the despatches sent by Lord Lucan concerning the events of 25 October. The 4th and 5th had *not* charged together and Hodge was nowhere near them – 'it was fortunate that Scarlett was there to put us straight when the moment came.'

By 12 November, a trickle of reinforcements was arriving, at least in the 5th Dragoon Guards. They had 450 men, 75 per troop, and 372 horses which rather modifies the general picture of a cavalry utterly destroyed at Balaclava and useless throughout the winter months. Officers were trying it on by going on sick leave to Constantinople. In Godman's regiment, Adolphus Burton, the commanding officer, and William Inglis both wanted out but were not keen to lose the price of their commission; no one was anxious to exchange into a battered regiment suffering a Russian winter. Godman consoled himself with a tot of rum and arrowroot before he went to bed, but he was up before daybreak every day and the horses were cold and wet. It narked Godman that the French were so cheerful, but they were not as obsessed with routine spit and polish as the British – 'lace and white belts and polished brass and steel'. Their uniforms – the famous French '*confort*' – never looked dirty and Godman could not understand how Wellington could have driven such men out of the Peninsula. Lucan, obsessive over appearance and protocol, upbraided the cavalry colonels in his tent two days after Inkerman. He ordered oil and pipeclay for cleaning belts and spurs, even though there was no time to apply them. The cavalry were turned out every afternoon for two hours, rushing to saddle their horses when Boots and Saddles sounded. By the time the horses were watered, it was dark. The ground was a foot deep in mud and slush. Some of the men got drunk, but Hodge was lenient with them – 'How man or horse can stand this work much longer I know not.' Like Inglis and Burton, the colonel was longing for 'a good lodging in foggy, murky London' and did some rough calculations of his finances in early January 1855 – 'The absolute loss ... will be reduced to £4,445 which I shall have paid the country for graciously allowing me to serve her.'

Then came the hurricane. All accounts agree, it was horrendous. Temple Godman spoke of huts being levelled, cooking pots and air-beds flying in all directions. The wind was followed by rain and snow. Hodge's tent pole snapped and the horses, knee-deep in mud, had nothing to eat all day – 'I think I have never passed a more miserable day in all my life'. William Russell wrote that the air was filled with coats, blankets, hats, tables and chairs. Tents whirled like leaves in the gale. The arabis were turned over, men and horses knocked down; the ambulance wagons were upside down. Half the cavalry horses broke loose, terrified by the noise and power of the wind. Commissariat stores were all over the place; men 'in the guardhouse' for some misdemeanour stood dutifully in little clumps, the guardhouse having gone. Cardigan was throwing up on board the *Dryad*, one of many boats being battered into potential matchwood by the storm. George Brown was nursing his wound on the *Agamemnon*; de Lacy Evans on the *Sans Pareil*. The *Star of the South*, with Fanny Duberly on board, was grinding, stern to stern, with the *Medway*. She heard of five ships that had gone down. Grimmest of all was the *Wild Wave*, sinking in Fanny's sight, together with three small cabin boys on board. Captain George Chetwode, 8th Hussars, spent half an hour chasing a favourite cap of his, blown in all directions by the wind, only to discover on catching it that it belonged to one of his sergeants! TSM Franks, however, was impressed with the behaviour of his own officers:

> Their tents were the same material as ours, and, as the sun shines on the just and the unjust, also rain and sleet wet all alike, but I can testify that all the Officers of the 5th Dragoon Guards without exception grasped the nettle like true Britons ... But winter was coming on.

It occurred to William Filder, the commissary general responsible for supplies, that 'in this crowded little harbour [Balaclava] we can do little more than land sufficient supplies to keep pace with daily consumption … the road from the harbour to the camp, not being a made one, is impassable after heavy rains.'

What bothered Hodge most was not the coming winter, but the fact that Lord George Paget, moping about missing his wife, had gone home. The jury was out on officers doing this. Today, when such casual resignations do not happen and none of it is linked with the purchase and sale of commissions (abolished in 1871), to leave a theatre of war in this way would be widely attacked in the media. So was it in 1854–5, but many officers, disillusioned with the stalemate that had developed, saw nothing wrong with it. The Other Ranks, of course, had no choice but to stay.

Hodge read the final service for Private Frederick Burbidge of the 4th on 20 November by the light of a lamp. The man had died from cholera, although cases had almost disappeared – 'He was a terrible old drunkard.' The colonel was having to work hard by this time, supervising the Horse Board, preparing meals, even peeling onions. He cannot have expected to do this; he had nothing to spend his money on (Balaclava is still like that!) and sent his gold coin home every month. Lucan was doing nothing but scream at everybody and it was annoying to see the French and Turks in huts, while the British still shivered in their tents. The rain was incessant by the end of November, the men's accoutrements filthy and the horses suffering. Only the stoicism of officers and men kept things going. Scarlett, at least, had a hut by this time, built into an excavation in a hillside to keep out the weather. Even though he was losing his hair, Hodge sent a lock of it to his sister, Eleanor. He was horrified to come across a piquet of the Greys out on the road, drunk on rum they had found in a commissary cart. On 1 December, he recorded 100 men and 3 officers of the 4th on piquet duty 'all soaked'.

Major Forrest wrote of the illnesses that were beginning to take their toll. Coughs, colds, diarrhoea, rheumatism and numbness, much of it brought on by the weather. He acknowledged that things were even worse in the infantry. By 6 December, the cavalry camp had moved to a less exposed position, but the horses were still knee-deep in mud, some suffocating in it. 'The cavalry are quite *hors de combat*,' wrote Hodge. 'They are utterly done for.' At least, Cardigan was going home. A medical board had decided that because he had dysenteric diarrhoea and 'difficulty in voiding urine', it was time he left. His arrival in Britain was a sensation, people flocking to see him and helping themselves to hairs from Ronald's tail. He was on everybody's guest list and made dozens of speeches in London and the provinces criticising the high command, Raglan, Lucan, *anybody* but himself. By the summer of 1855, he was created KCB (Knight Commander of the Bath) and Inspector General of Cavalry. Everybody in the Crimea prayed that he would not return.

On 9 December, Hodge bought some luxuries at Balaclava, but the cost was prohibitive. Ham was 2s 2d a pound, butter 2 shillings. Brandy was 5 shillings a bottle and North Wiltshire cheese an astonishing 15 shillings. The next day, Lucan grandly announced that huts were to be built for the cavalry; Hodge could not see, in the absence of fit men, timber and tools, how this could be done.

In the 5th Dragoon Guards, Temple Godman was not impressed by their new surgeon, who had exchanged from the Life Guards – 'much too great a swell for me ... I don't like such chicken-hearted men.' Another storm had washed the doctor's tent away and Godman asked the man, who was shouting for his servant, whether this was 'as pleasant as Knightsbridge Barracks. He seemed to think I was joking and did not half like it.' Godman's two horses were doing well, the brown (The Earl) an easier ride than the chestnut (Chance). He needed new leather for his overalls and more quinine. His bottle was broken and he had given most of it to his servant, Kilbourne, who had not been well. Godman was often in bed by five o'clock as the only place to keep warm and his days were spent on the lookout for Cossack patrols. He was determined to get himself a Russian lance and send it home as a souvenir. Elliot was back in action despite his Balaclava head wounds and Edward Fisher's request to sell out and go home was refused – 'he is not much of a soldier'. Godman wrote to his sister Caroline, asking her for waterproof clothing, potted meat and 'those floating cork wicks'. All this could be sent via Messrs Oppenheim who had a depot at Constantinople. Halford, as usual, had already placed his order.

The cavalry horses were skin and bone, officially described by Lucan as unfit for service. Godman saw two troop horses eating a dead one early in December. Everybody was moaning about the absence of Lord Raglan, who rarely visited the camps and when he did, it was very low key, with him in mufti. On more than one occasion he was taken for a T.G. (Travelling Gentleman) on a tour. Godman was feeling sorry for himself – 'Never I suppose in any war were cavalry treated as we have been.'

He wrote to his mother, thanking her for the woollen jersey and the cholera belt (which was actually useless against cholera). In general – and unsurprisingly, his letters to her are more cheerful than to his father and siblings – he did not want her to worry. He was happy to rant against Lucan, however, who lived in a house and was abusive to everyone. In a very un-politically correct moment, he wrote re the Scutari nurses:

> I think ladies are very much out of place as hospital nurses, however kind their intentions might be; it is better left in other hands. I must say I should not like a lady to attend me if I knew it. I look upon it as a sort of fanaticism …

On 21 December, Florence Nightingale wrote to Sidney Herbert that, on her arrival at the Scutari barracks hospital there were 'no mops – no plates, no wooden trays – no slippers … no knives and forks, no spoons, no scissors … no basins, no towelling.' The stench was unbearable, both from festering wounds and the blocked drains. The place was like a tomb, silent except for the occasional moan of the wounded. Drinking water was in short supply and the nurses had to share cramped, unhygienic accommodation. Window panes were broken and there were no fires. The place was crawling with rats and lice (called 'heavy dragoons') and fleas ('light cavalry'). The beds were eighteen inches apart with no separation of surgical and medical patients. Nurse Sarah Terrot, who looked after several cavalrymen at Scutari, wrote that the men 'lay in places such as no gentleman would allow any horse he cared for to be stabled'. The death rate was horrendous.

With frightening efficiency, Florence set up a little army of wives, left behind at Constantinople when the army moved east, to clean, cook and wash. Some of these were local Greeks. Moslem Turkish women refused to be hired, even though the rate, at 10 to 14s a week was good money, more, in some cases, than the troops earned.

Even here, however, where Florence brought hope and optimism, there was acrimonious dissention. The French Sisters of Mercy were a race apart, responsible for their own system, but English Catholic nurses under Reverend Mother Bridgeman and Mary Stanley's team from Bermondsey were cold-shouldered by the 'lady with the lamp' which proved that she was just as difficult and proprietorial as the army doctors themselves. To Florence, Mother Bridgeman was 'Mother Brickbat'; Florence herself was the 'Goddess of Humbug' and 'Priestess Miss N. Magnetic'.

To minimise the bitchiness, Miss Stanley's ladies were sent to the hospital at Koulali, 5 miles from Scutari, converted from a barracks in January 1855. The river ran nearby, so that sick men could be unloaded direct from the steamers rather than being jolted around on bullock carts. Most of the patients here were medical cases, suffering from dysentery, diarrhoea and, an increasing problem as the winter worsened, frostbite. In February, the mortality rate was 52 per cent.

Despite appalling difficulties, in the two main base hospitals, improvements were seen quickly. The chaplain-general, George Gleig, who spent most of his time delivering the last rites, wrote glowingly at the end of December that new wards had been constructed with sturdy flooring to replace the mud. There were large, efficient boilers for hot water and the stoves burned all day and night. Large tin baths were available and every man had a decent wooden bed and clean bedding. Virtually all of this, at least until the spring, was paid for by private fundraising back home and Florence's hammering away at prominent individuals for much-needed cash.

Back in the Crimea, Filder of the Commissariat had joined the self-preservation society, claiming that if the cavalry horses did not have enough fodder, it was because the 5th Dragoon Guards had sold it for profit, exactly as they had done in the Peninsula. Temple Godman was livid. He pointed out in a letter that when that had happened, General Thomas Picton had threatened hangings. The same threat, Godman believed, should be made against Filder! To add insult to injury, the troopship *Jason* keeled over while landing baggage at Constantinople, tipping a considerable amount of materiel for the 5th into the sea.

Shortly before Christmas, Godman's 'hut' was just a hole in the ground, dug by him and Kilbourne, rapidly filling with water when it rained. There was no timber to be had. Large siege guns were being dragged up from the ships and there were constant 'alarums and excursions' with rumours of Russian attacks; nothing major happened.

The photographs that Roger Fenton and James Robertson would take in the spring show some of the men as Temple Godman described them in December – 'The Heavy Dragoon and smart Hussar, what if some of our lady friends could see us now … with uniforms torn and hardly to be recognised, legs bound up with hay and straw bands, some without shoes or socks.' Everybody took it out on the Turks, who were cowardly or lazy or both. When shells burst over the infantry trenches, the sailors in particular took delight in throwing stones at the Turks, just to make a point.

The battlefield of Inkerman was a forlorn sight by Christmastime. Horses' flesh had been ripped from bones by eagles, and cannonballs, still black with powder, lay everywhere. 'There are several graves here.'

Promotions were happening among the officers. Major Forrest, of the 5th, was now brevet lieutenant colonel; Hodge was a full colonel. Scarlett became a major general in January and lost his purchase money as a result. Since he had a rich wife, Hodge sneered, he would not feel the pinch.

The curmudgeonly Hodge made no reference to Christmas, but others did. Forrest wrote to his wife before the woman came out, especially, as Hodge saw it, to make life difficult for him. 'Our camp is beginning to present a quite Christmas appearance as far as eating is concerned. Paddy Webb has got a turkey tied by the leg to his tent. Briggy [Captain George Brigstocke] has got a couple of geese fastened up in the same fashion.' Temple Godman had got a plum pudding off a ship.

Quartermaster John Drake of the 4th, who would give evidence to the commission of enquiry set up in March, explained that the salt pork rations were preferable to beef because the beef was of such poor quality. Chilley Pine, the regimental surgeon, agreed that, in terms of the men's health, pork was preferable. Two ounces of rice a day, as well as onions, potatoes and peas were only available sporadically. The monotony of coffee was broken by the arrival of tea by December. Fresh meat was served on Christmas Day and was given out seven times in January. Where possible, the troops bought soft bread (as opposed to hard tack) from local bakers, but 1½lb cost between 1s 6d and 2 shillings.

Forrest found it amusing that Hodge was so miserable, talking to himself as he often did in the hut they eventually shared. He found the condition of the wounded and sick trying to reach Balaclava far less funny:

Many of these poor fellows were scarcely able to sit on their horses, but were leaning down with their heads resting upon the horses' necks. The road was like a sheet of ice and though our men led the horses of the most helpless, yet occasionally a horse would slip and fall. One poor creature's foot caught in the stirrup and he would have been dragged, but that I caught hold of his horse's head.

The cavalry were doing all the legwork carrying supplies on this dangerous road. They were losing 120 horses a week and neither Raglan nor the Quartermaster General Richard Airey had any clue what to do about it. Hodge waxed lyrical about the French. They were 'good fellows' helping with supplies and the wounded. 'I hope the two nations will never again go to war.' But he was in a philosophical mood as the year ended – 'I have begun war too late in life. I prefer my comforts. As to honor [sic] and glory, they are empty bubbles.'

The casualty lists were beginning to get to Temple Godman. When the 5th left Cork they had nineteen officers. Of these, only ten were left; five were dead and four had gone home ill. An officer of the Greys had fallen ill after Balaclava and had gone to Scutari. While dying there, an order for his arrest was sent to him because he had absented himself without leave. The shock of this killed him, Temple Godman believed. He does not name the officer, but he may have been Cornet Francis Maconachie, wounded in the Heavies' charge. He had originally enlisted in the ranks as Francis Campbell for reasons that are unclear and he died on 29 November.

The new year brought little change. There was talk of a railway linking the harbour to the camps, but no sign of one nor the navvies to build it. Horses continued to die in large numbers and increasingly bold eagles and vultures hopped onto their corpses, enjoying the fine dining. January brought the snow, drifting in the icy wind. The tents were 'stiff as boards', as were Temple Godman's boots, overalls, breakfast pork and ink. They sold off William Campbell's things, his horses going for £20 whereas they had cost £150. There was a scare in the middle of the bidding, random firing and a skirmish by Cossacks, but they were soon chased away.

William Russell was vitriolic in his attack on the commissary department, hidebound by red tape and tradition. Stoves sent out from Constantinople gave off lethal fumes and could not be used. Supplies carried (mostly by the cavalry) from the harbour were regularly raided by the Zouaves who helped themselves to virtually anything. At Christmas, there had been 3,500 sick men in the camps, apart from those who had gone to Scutari and the other base hospitals. Russell painted a grim picture of a water-logged tent, the permanent home of twelve or fourteen men. They huddled for warmth under wet blankets in their saturated uniforms; in the case of the infantry, having been twelve hours in the trenches. On 7 January, the 65th Foot had only seven men fit for duty; the Scots Fusilier Guards 210 out of the 1,562 they had started out with.

There were dead and decaying horses everywhere and no one had the time or the energy to bury them, especially by January when the ground was frozen hard. The thermometer in Russell's tent read 20 degrees Fahrenheit (minus 7 Celsius) and men dared not take off their boots for fear of not being able to put them on again; some of them hopped around barefoot in the snow. The horses that had been killed at Balaclava were skinned by the French and the Turks to make their tents. The royal presents sent by Napoleon III, including tobacco and brandy, had all reached the French lines. Similar gifts from Victoria and Albert mysteriously vanished; only the Guards and the Rifles got their tins of Cavendish tobacco.

Russell was astonished to realise how the personnel had changed. The familiar senior officers of Gallipoli, Scutari and Varna had largely gone. Raglan was still there, but rarely seen, and the only two divisional commanders left were Lucan and Richard England. *The Times'* man tried to find a little humour in the misery:

It was inexplicably odd to see Captain Smith of the – Foot, with a pair of red Russian leather boots up to his middle, a cap probably made out of the tops of his holsters and a white skin coat tastefully embroidered all down the back with flowers of many-coloured silk [the Afghan] topped by a head dress à la dustmen of London, stalking gravely through the mud of Balaklava, intent on the capture of a pot of jam or marmalade.

Oh, and by the way, the man was suffering from frostbite, chilblains, severe rheumatism and a 'touch of scurvy'.

On 15 January, Forrest wrote home of a clash between the rarely seen Raglan and surgeon Chilley Pine. The doctor had been promoted by this time and transferred to the 3rd Infantry Division. 'How are you getting on with your sick, Mr Pine?' the commander had asked.

'Nothing can possibly be worse, my lord,' the doctor told him. 'It is merely a question of time as to the existence of this Division.' The hospitals were not coping with the sick; the medicines were inadequate.

Raglan asked him who was responsible for those shortcomings.

'Everybody, my lord,' Pine told him. 'I have reported all these deficiencies … and have received no answer; in no case, any help.'

Raglan was now on the defensive, demanding to know how long Pine had been in his post and where he had come from – 'I rather think you are an old dragoon surgeon?'

Pine told the commander that that was the case. Sniffy he may have been, but the next day, Raglan came back and asked Pine for details. The doctor had written to Richard England, his divisional commander, outlining the lack of shelter, the lack of provisions and the impossible amount of work expected of the army doctors.

Less than two months later, Pine was dead. Hodge wrote: 'At 2 p.m. we marched down to Balaklava and buried Pine with proper military honours. We laid him in the cemetery of the hospital in a nice spot, facing the harbor.'

It would be weeks before Pine's demands were met and in the meantime, men already dead were being carried in carts and on packhorses along the road to the harbour. And when Russell was able to get a clear view of Sebastopol, it was obvious that General Todleben was throwing up new defences. Russell was feeling defensive. He had been criticised, as had his editor, Delane, for publishing the truth, instead of 'babbling of green fields, of present abundance and of prospects of victory'.

This was not the way to make war.

Chapter 13

Reinforcements

In January 1855, things at last began to happen. Aberdeen, the prime minister, had not wanted a war in the first place and by now, he was widely criticised for the mishandling of it. Lord John Russell resigned from the Foreign Office and the radical MP for Sheffield, John Roebuck, put forward a motion of censure. Aberdeen had to go, despite the objections behind the scenes by Albert and Victoria, neither of whom had a genuinely constitutional say in such matters and both of whom were out of touch with public opinion. The country wanted Lord Palmerston, 'Lord Cupid', who was the darling of London society. Notorious for his womanising and his bullying of foreign ambassadors, 'this terrible Milord' was the very man to kick Tsar Nicholas's backside. He became prime minister on 6 February.

The Roebuck commission was looking into the mismanagement of the armed forces in the Crimea, and Palmerston, with Lord Panmure at the War Office, kick-started a drive for men, money and, above all, efficiency. Benjamin Disraeli was almost alone among politicians who were unimpressed, but Disraeli was unimpressed by anyone who was not Benjamin Disraeli and would find himself, in the years ahead, hopelessly entangled in the ongoing Eastern Question himself.

To be fair to Aberdeen, some of the reforms that came into being were already underway. Uniforms were already known to be inadequate both for hot colonial climates and freezing Russian winters, yet it took the Crimea to turn the short 'bum-freezer' jackets of cavalry and infantry into the more sensible tunics of 1856. Firearms had already improved – the use of rifles as opposed to smooth-bore muskets was already a reality. The 1853 pattern cavalry swords, which a couple of Light Brigade regiments carried at Balaclava, were actually no better than their predecessors, whatever the Whitehall Board of Ordnance maintained, but their arrival meant that the Horse Guards were, at least, *thinking* about such problems. The *really* important changes, to the commissariat, the purchase system and the training of officers, all developed as a result of the collective Crimean experience. And nothing summed up better the change of government and the arrival of spring than the Grand Crimea Railway. Somerset Gough Calthorpe was not impressed by the slowness of all this. The previous Secretary for War, the Duke of Newcastle, had promised navvies by 20 December and six weeks later there was no sign of them. By early February, however, the tracks were laid. A stationary engine had replaced horses in dragging equipment and supplies up the slopes from the harbour. Going back down was left to gravity! Raglan inspected it on 20 March, noting that it saved the cavalry and other transports nearly 3 miles of back-breaking work. Several of Roger Fenton's photographs show the railway in operation. His photograph of the Old Post Office, for example, taken on 15 March, shows a trackway in the foreground as well as rubble from buildings demolished to build it.

The railway was a private venture undertaken by Samuel Peto and the engineer was James Bentley; it was one of the first series of photographs taken by Fenton who arrived on 8 March. Roger Fenton was not the first war photographer – John McCosh had taken photographs of soldiers in India in the 1840s – but he was the first to make an impact. His visual images, coupled with Russell's despatches, brought the war to the public in a way not possible before. The Manchester-based publishers Agnew and Sons had commissioned Fenton, actually a lawyer, to photograph officers, Other Ranks and places as working projects for paintings and lithographs. Because photography was still relatively new (the first recorded photo was taken in 1826) it was too expensive for use in newspapers, so etchings and line-drawings had to suffice.

Fenton was criticised in some circles for taking part in a government-backed whitewash. Nine years later, Matthew Brady would take 'warts-and-all' photographs of battlefields of the American Civil War, complete with corpses. It was not Fenton's intention to shock and of course he arrived in the war zone when most of the fighting was over; he also left before it ended.

The Heavy Brigade photographs taken by Fenton include one in April of James Scarlett sitting on a grey pony, in conversation with Captain Alexander Low of the 4th Lights. Low appears to be wearing a French cap and jacket. Captain Halford of the 5th Dragoon Guards appears twice, once in frock coat and forage cap riding a shaggy pony and the second time in full dress as he probably appeared at Balaclava. Lieutenant George Burnand of the same regiment was also 'snapped' sitting a rough-coated horse in the cavalry camp. This is probably the best likeness of an officer's appearance in the charge, even though, ironically, Burnand did not ride it. He is referred to several times by Temple Godman, but he was usually off sick. Captain Inglis was photographed on horseback, a civilian overcoat over his jacket. Colonel Clarke of the Scots Greys is a subject rarely seen in modern editions of Fenton's work. He is sitting on a chair outside what may be his hut, with the now ubiquitous overcoat, the regimental peaked forage cap, his sword in his hand. A second photograph, complete with servant, shows Clarke with Sultan, the skittish horse he rode at Balaclava.

There are two versions of the 4th Dragoon Guards camp, with a hut and a relaxed, convivial group outside. There is a sheep in one – presumably next Sunday's roast – and pipe smoking. Pipes feature in the other photograph too and this includes Mrs Rogers, one of the rare images of women in this war, as well as visiting Zouaves. What is infuriating in the group portraits is that Fenton does not appear to have noted who was in them, so we cannot identify individuals. That poses a problem in the next photograph, that taken outside Captain Webb's hut in the 4th's camp. Webb himself is lounging in the doorway, looking every bit the louche officer his comrades knew him to be. Mrs Rogers got in the act again, but some recent books containing this photograph claim that the central figure, talking to Webb, is Colonel Hodge. But the figure is far too tall for him; it is actually Captain Forster of the 4th, who appears in a separate photograph alongside his grey. Hodge is the squatter figure to Forster's left, legs apart, facing the camera. Equally frustrating is the group of 5th Dragoon Guard officers. Major Burton, as he was by this time, is on the right, but we have no idea who the others are. All sorts of dress, military and civilian, appear in this one. Burton appears again, on his own, mounted à la the charge. Temple Godman appears, alongside The Earl, looking very much as he did at Balaclava. Private Kilbourne, however, hugely bearded by this time, is in a very unmilitary get-up. Most of Fenton's photographs show men with huge beards. They were allowed to grow these in the mistaken belief that a beard keeps a man warm. In the Crimea, beards froze and were very uncomfortable.

Apart from numerous landscape views of the Crimean countryside from a variety of angles, including the cavalry camp, Fenton did not overlook the civilians involved. He has the railway construction team, Turkish labourers, Croat locals, as well as the more colourful French and Turkish troops. Noticeably, he has three photographs of the same rather attractive French *cantinière*!

The arrival of supplies from home brought a sense of relief. Major Forrest of the 4th was tickled to see his colonel in a new overcoat. 'I came out and saw the little man array himself in an immense great big long coat … He has also got a pair of sailor's boots and a high fur cap … I thought of "Puss in Boots".' Everyone, at least by May when they probably no longer needed them, had drawers, socks, gloves, jerseys and woollen neck comforters. By that time, Hodge not only had a hut for himself but another for his three remaining horses. Cornet Fisher had built himself 'a little kennel' too, papering the cracks with matting.

As long as the bad weather continued, however, and before reinforcements arrived, the daily routine of the cavalry was grim. Each man had to clean his horse as best he could and polish his belts, sword and scabbard and carbine. The horses of men on camp duties – hospital orderlies, cooks, guards and butchers – had to be attended to as well. Horses had to be watered twice a day. Dung had to be cleaned up and carried from the piquet lines. Tents had to be patched and re-patched and horseshoes had continually to be replaced. Wood and water had to be collected. Funerals must be attended, horses buried (although, from Russell's account in the last chapter, this was not happening). Several of the horses of the 4th were suffering from glanders, swelling of the glands in the lower jaw. When Darby Griffith of the Greys suggested to Lucan that wooden shelters be built for the sick horses, Lucan threatened to put him under arrest. It would be months before this kind of petulant mismanagement became public.

Then there was the obstinacy of the colonels. At the end of January, Hodge objected to the arrival of 5,000 revolvers on the grounds that they would be 'more dangerous to our officers, men and horses, than to the enemy'. And he clearly had no faith in British workmanship – 'besides, they would constantly be out of repair'. The American experience in all this was very telling – as early as 1840, the Texas Rangers had been equipped with revolvers, which saved lives against outlaws and Native Americans. I doubt that Hodge had ever considered the problem.

The monthly returns provided by the cavalry regiments are interesting. Between November 1854 and March 1855, the 4th Dragoon Guards had lost 126 animals; the 5th had lost 121; the Royals 90; the Scots Greys 101; and 84 for the Inniskillings. Hodge's claim in his diary that his was the strongest cavalry regiment in the Crimea was simply not true.

At home, the Royal Patriotic Fund had been set up to raise money for the wounded, widows and orphans and by July, the figure had reached £1,171,270 (£1,257 million today – compare this with a recent Children in Need total of £37 million). In May, a grand auction was held, including paintings by the royal family. When the Princess Royal, then 15, was asked what price she would put on one of her paintings, she said 'Would a guinea be too much?' It sold for 250 guineas!

Hodge was impressed with mules imported as pack animals from Spain but criticised General Airey, 'that conceited coxcomb', for not obtaining good pack-saddles and mule chairs for the wounded. The colonel was pleased with Mrs Rogers, however. She 'is a hard-working good person. She cooks for the Captain of her Troop.' Forrest, as ever, has a more cynical point of view – 'Little Ben [Hodge] has presented a pair of his flannels [underpants] to poor Mrs Rogers.'

Presents were arriving by the boat-load by February and with typical bad grace, the troops were soon complaining of over-indulgence. 'It is kind of the senders,' Hodge conceded, but Robert Portal, of the 4th Light Dragoons, wrote home, 'Pray don't send another box of any kind. I hear of seven more coming out. What in life I shall do with them I don't know.' Aunt Jane had sent similar boxes to Temple Godman and he in turn had sent the Cossack lance he had acquired back home to his father as a souvenir.

Meanwhile, *The Times* was still spouting rubbish which Godman was happy to correct. The paper claimed that the French lost no horses, whereas the 6th *Dragons* had lost over seventy the previous week. The cavalry were turned out at dawn every day as there were constant rumours of a renewed attack. There were said to be 90,000 men in Sebastopol. The 5th had a new vet to replace Thomas Gudgin who had exchanged into the Scots Greys. Consequently, the horses were improving, with about sixty fit for duty in the middle of February.

Everybody was glad to see the back of Admiral James Dundas, known in the army as 'Damn'd Ass', who was too old and too tired to be of much use. As he sailed out of Balaclava harbour, he hoisted a flag signal to his successor, the popular and capable Edmund Lyons, 'May success attend you'. Lyons' flag officer *intended* to reply 'May happiness attend you', but it fluttered from the mastheads as 'May hanging await you'. Temple Godman swore to his family that this was true! In the 5th, preserved cabbage was improving the men's health. They had over seventy sick at Scutari and had lost sixty since the start of the campaign.

The buzz in the cavalry camp at the middle of the month was the removal of Lucan – he had 'resigned in great wrath,' wrote Godman, 'and declares he will show Lord Raglan up when he gets home.' Hodge was a little more circumspect about this, as might be expected from a man who hoped for Lucan's job. Lucan spoke to Hodge and John Douglas, colonel of the 11th Hussars, as the most senior men in the two cavalry brigades. '[Lucan] has been uniformly kind and civil to me,' Hodge wrote, 'and though I think he is not the man to command, being obstinate and headstrong, he will be better than Lord Cardigan ...' which really was not saying very much. The junior officers saw things more clearly. 'It is quite a relief to get rid of Lord Lucan,' Cornet Fisher of the 4th wrote. 'Poor old man [he was 54] he was a horrid old fellow.'

Scarlett's appointment to replace Lucan was welcomed by everyone and Forrest wondered, with some trepidation, whether Hodge would command the Heavy Brigade. With Cardigan and Lucan gone, eyes swivelled in other directions to lay blame for the army's stagnation. The most popular were Richard Airey and the adjutant general, James Estcourt. Estcourt, photographed by Fenton and looking exhausted in a chair, by Fenton, died of cholera in June.

Hodge liked Scarlett, even though, like his entire Brigade then and since, his name rarely appeared in the papers. He looked after the Heavies well and the colonel was writing home full of praise for his regimental cooks. One particular man (unnamed) made excellent scones, 'very fair' soup and 'can make a rice pudding'. Hodge got through cooks at a rate of knots. In October, the colonel replaced Private Elijah Clipsham with 'a youth named Munro, a clean sort of lad, but utterly ignorant of cooking'. The new bug coped well with roast chicken and boiled ham, whereas Clipsham, 'our late beast', was found guilty of leaving camp by court martial – 'This is the effect of drink.' Hodge was hoping for command of the Heavies, or a CB at least, but he was not happy with *The Times* publishing officers' letters (lucky that they did, or this book would not exist!).

By early March, William Russell was waxing lyrical on the improvements that were appearing everywhere. Raglan was out and about, so (contrary to what most people thought) were Airey and Estcourt. There was a new railway in the Crimea and new roads built between Sebastopol, Kamiesch and Balaclava, all of which the tsar would be grateful for in the years ahead. There were huts everywhere, for men and horses, flatlands were drained and water-courses dammed. Sickness was lessening and there was a cheery atmosphere in the camps. An electric telegraph had been set up between army headquarters and Kadikoi. And, in the middle of it all, Tsar Nicholas died.

Alexander II has gone down in history as the tsar liberator, freeing the serfs in 1861 and instituting reforms across the board in Russia. None of this happened because Alexander was a liberal. He had the typical Romanov aversion to change and loss of power, but one thing that influenced him was the abject failure of his army and navy to make much of a dent against the Allies in the Crimea. With a superiority of numbers and internal lines of communication, the Russians should have made short work of the invasion. Had they struck at Kalamita Bay back in September 1854, there would have been no Crimean War.

Despite the appearance of nothing happening, there was a series of short, bloody attacks as the Russians built and fortified the Malakoff, a new fortress in Sebastopol. Russell walked over scores of dead bodies and noted, rather embarrassed, that while the French turned out *en grande tenue* (full dress), British troops looked like unmade beds, dressed à la 'Balaklava'. On 9 April, Easter Monday, the heaviest Allied bombardment of the war hurled iron balls, up to 68lb in weight, into the Russian masonry. Firing went on sporadically for a week, Raglan urging a direct assault on the town, the French having second thoughts.

In the meantime, the British officer class were trying to recapture normality with horse racing. Fanny Duberly rode out to the 'First Spring Meeting' on Monday, 4 March. Men who had been half drowned in mud and snow over the winter were now 'as eager and fresh for the rare old English sport, as if they were in the ring at Newmarket'. But the meeting was broken up with an alarm of a Russian attack. They took to feral dog hunting instead, although Fanny, happy to see foxes torn apart at home, could not join in – 'so unsportsmanlike, so cruel, so contrary to all good feeling …' The Duberlys' hut now had a sheet-glass window, thanks to the good offices of Captain Franklyn of the *Columba*, but Fanny herself stayed on board *The Star of the South* in the harbour.

On 29 March, however, she moved in to the hut and the Duberlys dined with Major Edward Peel and Captain Edwin Cook of the 11th Hussars. The next day, she and Henry went shopping near Kamiesch, picking up chickens, carrots and peas. Lord George Paget, back from England with his wife (though Fanny does not mention her) promised Mrs Duberly a terrier. She had never been without a dog before and was delighted by this. Fanny wrote pages in her diary about the increasingly frequent races in which the British and the French competed in good humour.

She accompanied General England towards the Malakoff the day after the great bombardment began and was alarmed to note how much more formidable the Russian defences looked. By the 17th, however, she was consoling herself that the Duberlys now had a large tent outside their hut, to serve as a drawing room and dining room. But that day, there was great excitement because the 10th Hussars had arrived from India. Their commanding officer was Lieutenant Colonel William Parlby and the regiment was said to be 680 strong, more men than had ridden the charge of the Light Brigade. They were mounted on Arabs and there was an immediate dichotomy in the cavalry – from the stance that such horses could withstand anything to they would not survive the first storm. Fanny thought they looked beautiful, their groomed glossy coats such a contrast to the animals that had survived a Crimean winter. With astonishing foresight, Parlby had ordered, as soon as the 10th got the nod from Panmure at the War Office, that his men should abolish the use of pipeclay for their belts and ditch their razors. The horses were magnificent, but the men looked like old campaigners and would blend right in.

With the 10th was Captain Valentine Baker, who would go on to replace Louis Nolan as *the* cavalry expert in the 1860s and 1870s. He wrote: 'No-one, who was not present, can form any conception of the British cavalry in the Crimea during the summer of 1855. Young, weakly, half-drilled recruits were sent out, who could barely sit on, much less manage, a horse properly.'

Two squadrons of the 12th Lancers left Mysore, India, soon after the 10th. The heat was so intense that they had to rest by day and travel at night, their supplies carried by camels. They arrived at Balaclava on board the *Etna*, everybody pleasantly surprised how easy it was to transport the horses.

At the end of May, a reconnaissance led by Omar Pasha, the Turkish general, moved over the battlefield of Balaclava. Russell wrote:

> The Scots Greys and Inniskillings, the 4th and 5th Dragoon Guards, all had been there and the survivors might well feel proud when they thought of that day. The 10th Hussars were conspicuous for the soldierly and efficient look of their men and the condition of their light, sinewy and showy horses.

Back in March, the cavalry, still at that stage without reinforcements, felt brave enough to try a field day. Paget led it and even Hodge was impressed by him. Even so, he could not let his personal animus go – 'he is a goose' he wrote on 18 March. The colonel had made a fool of himself by writing to *The Times*, claiming that *his* regiment was the best in the cavalry. Forrest, of course, could not resist gossiping to his wife about it in a letter home. The Greys and Inniskillings were having a picture painted of *their* charge, as though only the Three Hundred took part, so Forrest could not see what they had to grumble about. Hodge had dinner with Darby Griffith of the Greys – 'soufflé made to perfection and some good mutton'. But the cook could not compare with Scarlett's.

The end of March saw the disappearance of the brigadier. Mrs Scarlett was ill and the general had to go home. Paget, therefore, was to command the division in his absence and Colonel Shewell, 8th Hussars, got the Lights. There was no mention of Hodge in any of this.

Forrest left much unsaid when he told his wife in April that he and the colonel shared a hut – 'He occupies one end … and I the other.' They had a garden and a hen house, but no one could imagine the pair as anything other than 'an odd couple' since they detested each other. Sir John MacNeil had arrived by this time, sent out by Lord Panmure to investigate first hand the shambles of the commissariat. Hodge spent two and a half hours with him, talking about provisions and forage.

The colonel explained the lack of hay for the horses, but a proficiency of barley. He admitted that no records were kept in November or December, but that had been corrected in the new year. The commissariat had given no help to the transporting of goods, all of which had been carried out by the cavalry. Even when discussing something positive, however, Hodge moaned. The new blue 'pilot coats' (referred to as 'cloaks' in later officers' dress regulations) were 'the best outer covering for a cavalry soldier' but when the piquets of the 4th were taken prisoner because they were 'enveloped' in these garments, they were discontinued. Veterinary provisions, Hodge noted, were non-existent; the Heavies were still relying on supplies brought out from England when the war began.

On the 13th, new overalls arrived for the cavalry and Hodge gave out seven medals for distinguished service. Hospital Sergeant Major Joseph Drake was given a £20 annuity along with his medal; he sent £5 of it to his wife, Jane. Sergeant Patrick Fleming got a medal, as did: Sergeant John Gilligan (who already had five good conduct awards); Sergeant William Perry (wounded in the charge and the only man in the regiment to receive both the DCM and the Legion d'Honneur); Sergeant Frederick Wallace; Corporal Henry Preece (wounded in the charge); Private Benjamin Courd (sometimes, unfortunately, spelt 'Coward' in army records) and Private Thomas Marks (who was promoted to corporal).

The arrival of the 10th Hussars and the 12th Lancers was greeted with delight by the cavalry. Cornet Fisher wrote: 'This will make the work much lighter than it was.' On 10 May, however, word arrived that both regiments were to be reduced in size from their maximum Indian strength. Hodge was, for once, right to be annoyed – 'Here we are in the field. We want every man and horse we can get … Now was ever such folly heard of …' Not for the first or last time, idiotic decisions were being made by pen-pushers and 'feather-bed soldiers' in Whitehall who had no idea of the realities of a war zone.

For some time, Hodge had been at daggers drawn with Raglan over the use of the cavalry as general dogsbodies. He had pointed out that the surgeons of the Royals (Alexander Forteath) and the 17th Lancers (probably Hampden Massey) had warned of serious sickness among the men if this continued.

Since April, the eccentric, reclusive Duke of Portland had been using his extensive fortune to send treats to the Crimea. On 22 April, Hodge himself enjoyed the strong, dark ale of the Welbeck company supplied by his lordship but two days later had to punish two men for breaking open a keg of the stuff. With the warmer weather, of course, came the pests. Bluebottles swarmed everywhere and every hut was alive with ants. With them came an army of travelling gentlemen and their ladies. Foremost among them was 'the belle of the Crimea', Agnes Paget. Fanny Duberly was put out to find a prettier magnet for young officers flitting about the place and Hodge was appalled at the attention that Lord George paid to her when he should have been attending to his brigade. Lord Stratford de Redcliffe was there too with most of his family. Although Hodge does not say so, the man, as British ambassador to Constantinople, had done more than his share to start the Crimean War in the first place.

It was now that Hodge had several photographs taken by 'the daguerreotype man'. One was of Hodge's quite palatial hut and the tents of the 4th Dragoon Guards. Another showed him with Captain Forrest and his grey outside just such a tent and yet another, showing him with the horse he rode at Balaclava, has not survived.

Early in May, Hodge was given command of the Heavy Brigade in Scarlett's absence. Edward Fisher approved – 'he is in every way fit for it' – but he may have been in a minority of two. About the only other contemporary who spoke for the colonel was TSM Franks – he was

> one of the most kindly and genial of men and he took every pains to show us that we had his sympathy. He always had a word of encouragement for us and his example in this respect seemed to be followed by every Officer and soldier in the 4th Dragoon Guards.

Since Colonel William Parlby of the 10th Hussars outranked everybody, Hodge was destined to slip down the chain of command again. He was perfectly happy, however, that Florence Nightingale had arrived in the Crimea. It was one of three visits that she made and with her was Alexis Benoit Soyer, chef of the London Reform Club and all-round cooking guru. His portable stoves and sumptuous meals were designed to improve the diet of the men and relieve the monotony of army food.

In the meantime, Hodge had found another woman to moan about. While Florence was some kind of saint – 'I wish I could be of any service to her. She is worthy of all honor [*sic*]' – Fanny Duberly was 'out grazing' with Henry and Paulet Somerset (Raglan's ADC). Hodge found the publicity that surrounded the woman disgusting. The troops called Fanny 'Mrs Jubilee' and the French had named a Polka – 'L'Amazone' – after her. Two days later, Hodge learned that Mrs Forrest was on her way and his world came to an end!

Temple Godman managed to drop his adjutant duties on 1 May, for which he was very grateful. Rumours abounded that Prince Menshikov, who had by now left Sebastopol, was dead, as of course was the tsar. There was excitement early in the month, which came to nothing, as fifty hand-picked men of the 5th went with Godman to Kertsch, the most easterly point of the Crimea. The venture was top secret (which is, of course, why junior officers like Godman wrote home about it) under the overall command of Omar Pasha. As far as the 5th were concerned, there was no action and they were towed back to Balaclava by the *Valorous*. A furious Godman wanted to see William Russell so that yet another debacle could be reported in *The Times*.

By 18 May, the temperatures were in the nineties and a new batch of heroes was on its way from England. Thomas McMahon, who had served on Lucan's staff since the outbreak of war, now became lieutenant colonel of the 5th. He was a 'sharp fellow' according to Godman, who liked him, but after his illness (he had been sent home) he had aged ten years and his hair had turned grey. The ex-adjutant, soon to be promoted to captain, found the Sardinian troops who had arrived rather amazing, with their plumed wide-awake hats. Everybody called them 'sardines'.

Godman's younger brother Fred arrived as a T.G. at the end of the month and the brothers took every opportunity to see the sights, Fred hoping to be able to watch a real life bombardment. A downpour flooded Godman's hut, but the brothers baled out, as best they could. Fred was put up with Lieutenant Hampton and Godman himself with Robert Montgomery who was a particular friend. The pair of them (or perhaps all three) had hoped to get leave to visit Constantinople, especially as Montgomery knew Stratford de Redcliffe. Fred was delighted with the cavalry review on the queen's birthday (24 May) and Godman saw General Pelissier for the first time, Canrobert's replacement as commander of the French – 'He is a very fat, coarse, vulgar-looking man, more like an old coalheaver than a General …'

Fanny Duberly, who was there too, was dazzled by the mercurial Omar Pasha, the hilt of his sword blazing with diamonds, but was not impressed by the new cavalry regiments – 'The remains of our Heavy Cavalry looked to my eyes far more soldierlike, more English, more solid.'

The next day, the ground lost at Balaclava – largely the Causeway and Fedioukine Heights – was retaken by the Sardinians under General La Marmora and the French. There was very little opposition. Hodge helped himself to war souvenirs from the captured village of Tchorgaum and intended to send them home via Tom Tower, one of the (civilian) agents of the Crimean Fund, who was bound for England. The colonel was not impressed with the new recruits sent out from home. Their clothes were too tight for constant remounting and dismounting – always the dichotomy between cavalry 'spit and polish' and reality. The second assault on Kertsch had worked well and the navy was sinking dozens of Russian merchantmen in what, until now, had been regarded as a Russian lake.

Between June and August, two more regiments of cavalry arrived. The 6th Dragoon Guards, the Carabiniers, caused something of a stir in the camps because they wore dark blue jackets, the colour of the Light Cavalry. The plan had been to convert the regiment to Light Dragoons or Hussars and several officers had jumped the gun and kitted themselves in the new uniform. The change never happened, but the Carabiniers kept their dark blue. The other regiment was the 1st, the King's Dragoon Guards, so that there was a preponderance of Dragoon Guards over Dragoons, something which passed most civilians by but which raised a few eyebrows in army circles. It was almost as if mere Dragoons were not up to the job, despite the heroism of the Greys and the Inniskillings. In July, the Crimean cavalry was divided into three – the 'Heavies', the 'Bashis' (the Light Brigade) and the 'Dirties' (a Hussar Brigade). It was all rather messy and pointless because all cavalry was used in the same way by the British.

A new assault on the Mamelon, another new fortress in Sebastopol's defences, took place on 6 and 7 June. British losses, according to Hodge, reached 670, but the Russians suffered 5,000. It was high summer by now and Hodge was appalled by the sight of Zouave corpses, bloated and blistered in the sun. On the 17th, the bombardment began at three in the morning. 'God be merciful to us,' wrote Hodge. 'How dreadful is this war. By this time tomorrow, how many fine fellows will be struck down?'

But back at home, a different kind of war was raging.

Chapter 14

The Whitewashing Board

Military historians used to think of the American Civil War (1861–5) as the first modern war, with its trenches, *chevaux de frise* (barbed wire) and slaughter on a massive scale. More Americans died in that war than in all their other wars over two and a half centuries. This has now been reconsidered. To begin with, the casualties in the Crimea were higher – between 485,000 and 640,000 dead, depending on the rather dubious accuracy of the Russian figures. The British army lost 22,000. Although the charges of both cavalry brigades can be viewed as war in the old style – the historian Corelli Barnett once wrote that the Crimean army was 'simply the Peninsular army [1808–14] brought out of its cupboard and dusted down' – the days of bombardment by heavy artillery, infantry in the trenches, the use of technology; all this adds up to the Crimean being regarded as the first of the modern wars.

What is most glaring of all is the sheer scale of publicity that covered it. As far as Britain was concerned, the Falklands War of 1982 was the first televised conflict, with saturation coverage morning, noon and night. Daily bulletins by the Ministry of Defence would make Raglan turn in his grave. The Americans had already had this with the Vietnam fiasco and in the late twentieth century, one thing is certain – a literate, educated public is not going to take incompetence lying down.

By 1854, increasing numbers of the British public were able to read. There was still no compulsory education, but among the middle classes, those with money and opinions, there were plenty of people who watched events 'in the east' very closely. Genuinely cheap newspapers and the 'new journalism' of the gutter press lay in the future, but technological improvements meant that papers were being read on a regular basis. John Delane at *The Times* was, arguably, the first to capitalise on this. *The Times* became the arbiter of news and debate, *the* paper to which retired colonels wrote, usually in high dudgeon over something or other, because it was, in Delane's phrase, 'a Tory island in a sea of Liberalism'. The Liberal Party itself would not be formed until 1859 but there were already two armed camps in politics – reactionaries versus progressives. If a reactionary newspaper like *The Times* criticised institutions like the army, it was time for everyone to listen. The queen, more of a High Tory than ever Wellington had been, was outraged at Delane and Russell's attacks on 'her' army, taking her role as commander-in-chief very seriously. Albert, as ever, backed her – 'the pen and ink of one miserable scribbler [Russell] is despoiling the country'. The War Office had been about to ban journalists from the front until John Roebuck's demands for an inquiry 'into the condition of our Army before Sebastopol' effectively stopped the feathered hats in their tracks. There were 305 votes for such an enquiry; 148 against. Aberdeen fell and Palmerston took over.

It is an interesting indictment on past times and our own, that Russell's uncensored despatches took nineteen days to arrive in Fleet Street; in 1982, newsreel coverage of the Falklands took three days longer – and they were censored.

Although it was Russell's breathless – and breath-taking – accounts of the Crimea that gripped the public's attention, so did the photographs of Roger Fenton and James Robertson and the artwork of William Simpson. Names like Balaclava, Inkerman, Raglan, Cardigan, Alma and the Redan became standard names for streets, squares and pubs up and down the country and war memorials of the dead appeared for the first time, rather than individual gravestones weathering in some country churchyard.

The British people, of all classes, embraced this war as their own; and the army was not Victoria's – it was theirs. Small wonder, then, that probing questions should be asked. For the nation that had beaten Napoleon and was carving itself a vast empire around the globe, to be bogged down in a frozen slum somewhere few people (before 1854) could find on a map, was simply appalling.

The blatant jingoism and Russophobia of the spring and summer of 1854 had seen a simplistic 'us versus them', which is inevitable in any conflict, but is a distortion nonetheless. 'We are not now engaged in the Eastern Question', said Lord Clarendon, Aberdeen's Foreign Secretary, 'but in the battle of civilisation against barbarism, for the independence of Europe.' Similar tripe was being spoken in 1914–18 (the word 'civilisation' even appears on war medals) and it is simply not true.

What is noticeable is that Palmerston's new government, which promised so much in terms of efficiency, the removal of dead wood and a brave new world, was nothing of the sort. When Lord Cardigan rode Ronald in the streets of London, thronged by an admiring crowd, no one spoke against him as a talentless idiot who had carried out a pointless and robotic command. Instead. Palmerston himself gave Cardigan as an example of the shining success of aristocratic leadership!

While Colonel Hodge disapproved of officers writing to *The Times*, his own diaries confirm that he agreed with most of them. At the end of December 1854, he wrote: 'Lord Raglan deserves no credit for the conduct of the campaign, and as to his staff, they are abominable.' Someone described them as 'a nest of noodles'.

An anonymous officer summed up the Crimea admirably when he said;

> The fact is that a grave and inexcusable fault lies with the English people in ignoring as they virtually do, in time of peace, the existence of a standing army, reducing every department to the lowest possible state and yet engaging in a Continental war on a gigantic scale.

The same would be true of every British war, before the Crimea and since.

Ironically, a commission had already looked into the problem of an army led by an ageing aristocracy, but since the commission itself was largely made up of elderly generals, little headway was made. William Thackeray, the novelist, invented a gouty old general, Sir George Granby Tufto – he is 'a greater ass at sixty-eight than he was when he first entered the army at fifteen. He is selfish, brutal, passionate and a glutton … He swears considerably in his talk and tells filthy garrison stories after dinner.'

Readers at the time – and historians since – have sidelined Thackeray because he is writing fiction, but novelists from Chaucer to Iturbe have routinely based their fictional characters on the factual. No one knew that, after Balaclava, Cardigan slept in a tent, cradling the head of the trumpeter of the 17th Lancers, Billy Britten, who had been fatally wounded in the charge; all people knew was that 'the noble yachtsman' dined on board the *Dryad* every night.

How did the soul-searching enquiries affect the cavalry? Young officers like Robert Portal of the 4th Lights had written home for months on cavalry incompetence – Cardigan was

> one of the greatest old women in the British army … He has as much brains as my boot. He is only equalled in want of intellect by his relation, the Earl of Lucan … Without mincing matters, two such fools could not be picked out of the British Army to take command …

Among the handful of cavalry officers who spoke to the McNeill-Tulloch Committee (no Other Ranks were questioned), Surgeon Robert Cooper of the 4th Dragoon Guards was the most detailed and outspoken. He had joined his regiment six days after Balaclava and, almost unheard of in the British army, had lived in Canada and the United States for five years. As such, the Crimean weather did not faze him. For British soldiers unused to it, winter had been grim, but, as Russian winters go, it was nothing out of the ordinary and Cooper found it less cold than Nova Scotia and Cape Breton.

Lack of fresh vegetables, he reported, had caused scurvy, diarrhoea and even some chest complaints. Inadequate clothing, poor accommodation and lack of sleep had all taken their toll. Turning out the cavalry in the early hours of the morning in case of an attack may have been a sensible military precaution, but it caused havoc to the health of men and horses. Cooper had complained to Hodge who had eventually done something to improve matters. Bell tents were useless, the doctor contended – stiflingly hot in the summer, wet and miserable in the autumn, cold and wretched in the winter and unserviceable in storms.

The recruits drafted in from January were inadequate – 'lads scarcely beyond the age of boyhood. An army on active service needs other support than that derived from undeveloped youth.'

Much neglected were the medicine dispensers and regimental orderlies, men like John Drake of the 4th, Dennis Lees of the Royals, William Todd of the Greys and William Sutcliffe of the Inniskillings. Such men must be qualified, be able to write with a clear hand and, a radical concept in 1855, not under the thumb of the regimental commander.

Back home, Victoria was appalled by the return of her cousin, the Duke of Cambridge, whose nerves were shattered after Inkerman; as royalty, he ought to have stayed to the bitter end. It was unfortunate that Raglan's official despatches continued Wellington's habit of referring to generals and their staff, as though no one else was involved in the War Office. All five of the commander's nephews received promotion.

'Tear-'Em' Roebuck had, like everyone else, banged the patriotic drum at the start of the war. Now, he turned his sharp legal brain and natural gift of eloquence, to attack the high command and the War Office in the Commons. As always, there were men who backed both Lucan and Cardigan. Lieutenant Colonel George Mayow, on Cardigan's staff at Balaclava, said that his boss 'not only thought of his cavalry by day, but he dreamt of them at night'. But this was still the man who had refused William Morris's request to join the Heavy Brigade charge and who had done so much damage to two regiments once under his command – the 15th and the 11th Hussars – that the Horse Guards had, at one time, been on the point of cashiering him. Most of the cavalry officers, Heavy and Light, had more time for Lucan than Cardigan, even though he was guiltiest of all of stupidity and pig-headedness at Balaclava; his nonsensical interpretation of Raglan's orders had led directly to the destruction of the Light Brigade.

Lucan, back in England in early March, had kept all his correspondence relating to his cavalry command – either the work of an extremely competent man or a guilty one – and he sent his son and former ADC, Charles Bingham, to Lord Hardinge, the commander-in-chief, to demand a court martial. He was turned down. He then used his peerage to demand the same from the House of Lords, as the highest court in the land, and was again refused. Lord Panmure, Secretary for War, did not want the full glare of publicity. As is usual in matters military, civil and sometimes criminal, the man at the top carries the can; that meant Raglan. So, lesser fry, equally, if not more, guilty of incompetence and mismanagement, like Lucan and Cardigan, got away with it. For Balaclava, by all means, said the whitewashers, blame the commander on the Sapouné Heights; blame the dead galloper who brought the message; but as far as two generals of cavalry, responsible for making things work, just promote them somewhere out of harm's way. It had happened before and it has happened since.

Historian John Harris believes that Lucan was unlucky. In fact, it was his own unpleasantness to virtually everybody he met, from his commander-in-chief to his fellow officers and members of the House of Lords, to his tenants at Laleham and County Mayo, which makes this feeling that he was more sinned against than sinning particularly unpalatable. Typically, when he was criticised in a letter to *The Times* from Anthony Brown, a former colonel of Lucan's previous regiment, the 17th Lancers, 'Lord Look-On' engaged in a vitriolic personal debate which lost him even more popularity.

Even Russell, who should have known better, later wrote, 'He was an indefatigable officer … and had as little to do with the "glorious" Balaclava bungle as I had.' And this, from the man who had seen the events happen and clearly, for all his glittering rhetoric, did not understand a word of it. By the mid-1860s, no one was surprised by any of this. In covering the American Civil War, as he had the Crimea, Russell unwisely allied himself with the doomed South, at a time when British sensibilities lay with the North and anti-slavery; *The Times* lost a large number of readers.

Lord Raglan's death in the Crimea – 'I shall never return home. I should be stoned to death' – made criticism of him the job of the historians who came after. Lucan and Cardigan were still very much alive. As we have seen, Cardigan became KCB in July 1855 and Inspector General of Cavalry, a post he held until 1860. That year, no doubt to the regiment's horror, he was made full colonel of the 11th Hussars. The following year he became a lieutenant general and wrote *Cavalry Brigade Movements* at the same time. Louis Nolan and Valentine Baker he was not – the book is one of the dullest ever written. Typical of the colourful flashpoints of his life, however, Cardigan went to law in 1863 over a libel by Somerset Gough Calthorpe, now a colonel, who had served on Raglan's staff. He too had written a book, *Letters from Headquarters*, exposing Cardigan's high-handed contempt for everybody around him. The ridiculous part of this was that Calthorpe accused Cardigan of never having ridden the charge of the Light Brigade at all, owing to confusion between him and a lieutenant in the 11th, who also rode a chestnut horse. Cardigan won the case, but the facts that came out ruined his reputation for ever. It was precisely what *should* have been made public by the commission of enquiry eight years earlier. Lucan's promotions followed a similar pattern – full colonel of the 8th Hussars in November 1855 and lieutenant general just before Christmas three years later. He was a full general by August 1865 and, rather belatedly, field marshal in June 1887.

At the end of May 1855, there were still horse carcases littering the 'valley of Death', now ablaze with forget-me-nots, mignonette, larkspur and dwarf roses. Fanny Duberly counted five with 8.H (8th Hussars) stamped on their hoofs. 'We gathered handsful of flowers and thought – oh, how sadly – of the flowers of English chivalry that had there been reaped and mown away!' She watched a bloody French assault on the Mamelon early in June and bemoaned the deaths, later in the month, of infantry officers of the Guards and the Highlanders. General Estcourt died from cholera on Sunday, 24 June and Raglan followed him five days later – 'It seems as though some pulse in this vast body had ceased to beat, the army is so quiet.' But Scarlett was back to command the Cavalry Division; everyone who had expected Cardigan's return breathing a sigh of relief. Lawrenson of the 17th Lancers got the Light Brigade.

On 3 July, as regimental bands played the Dead March from *Saul*, Raglan's body was escorted by several squadrons of cavalry down to the harbour to be taken on board the *Caradoc* and home to England. Temple Godman's comment on the commander-in-chief's passing was typical of most officers – 'he was kind and willing to do his best, but was not fit for the post he held.' General Pennefather, one of the most energetic of the divisional commanders, had gone home and George Brown was ill on board ship. The 8½ miles of Raglan's funeral procession was lined by British, French, Sardinian and Turkish troops. During the whole process, the Russians did not fire a shot.

Hodge, of course, found something to whinge about. Even though his regiment formed part of the escort, he had to remain in camp, as did everybody not actually part of the ceremony. All four of Raglan's ADCs went home with him, including Gough Calthorpe, whose regiment was still in the field. 'He ought to be ashamed of himself … He has lived on the fat of the land all the winter, and now runs away just when something is likely to be done.'

By that summer, Mary Seacole had arrived in the Crimea and had set up her British Hotel. In her own words, she was 'doctress, nurse and "Mother"' to the officers who turned up. Most of her time was spent coping with civilians – Greek, Turkish, Croat and Jewish – many of whom were 'incorrigible rogues', to use the contemporary term for re-offending criminals; theft for them was a way of life. In her book, with what is supposed to be due modesty, she records testimonials and letters of thanks from patients who had benefited from her care. Sergeant William Knollys of the Land Transport Corps wrote: 'I certify that I was severely attacked by diarrhoea after landing in the Crimea. I took a great deal of medicine, but nothing served me until I called on Mrs Seacole. She gave me her medicine but once and I was cured effectually.' John Hall, the Inspector General of Hospitals, supported letters like this. William Paulet, AAG on what had been Lucan's staff, was a fan, describing Mary as 'most praiseworthy ... even in positions of great danger'. *Punch* even took to (excruciatingly bad) poetry about her:

> No store she set by the epaulette.
> Be it worsted or gold lace;
> For K.C.B. or plain Private Smith,
> She had still one pleasant face.

Mary had called in to see Raglan several times in the weeks before his death. They had let her pay her last respects and she touched the Union Jack draped over his coffin. Agnes Paget was there too, the 'belle of the Crimea', keeping a vigil at his death-bed – 'a curious event it was, a lady by the bedside of a dying commander-in-chief in the field'.

And, of course, the war went on. Raglan's replacement was General James Simpson, who had been in the Crimea since February as chief of staff, but was actually there to keep an eye on Raglan. As was to be expected, perhaps, Simpson did his own whitewashing – 'I must say I never served with an army where a higher feeling and sense of duty exists than I remark in the General Staff officers of this army. It pervades all ranks, except among the low and grovelling correspondents of *The Times*.'

Hodge had resigned himself, in the officer reshuffle in the cavalry with Scarlett's return, not to be a brigadier any more. In fact, it gave him time to whinge about the quality of the new recruits for the 4th. Two had died of cholera, which was returning with a vengeance with the hot weather and eleven were sick in hospital. By 11 July, the figure had risen to forty-nine, including an old sweat, William Neeson of F Troop. Hodge visited the imposing monastery of St George, high on its rocky promontory. He was not impressed – 'All was truly Greek to me'. The colonel noted that people at home were far more affected by Raglan's death that they were at the front. As for Simpson – 'He is a quiet looking old gentleman, cleanly shaven and looks healthy; but what capacity he has for the command of an army, I know not.'

In the 5th, too, it was the new men who were suffering most. Temple Godman wrote of Captain George Sidebottom, who had recently arrived, with four trunks, champagne and Fortnum's boxes. He could not take the heat and the flies and died at the beginning of August. Godman did not like the sound of some of the new officers coming out – 'Travers, I am told, is a regular *Irish savage* [Godman's italics].' And still, the old problems with troopships continued – the *Oneida* bringing the new men caught fire three or four times on the journey, but there were, amazingly, no casualties.

By 9 July, Godman had command of a troop without purchase, complete with seventy-four men and forty-seven horses. 'Many are quite children,' he wrote to his sister, 'and none of them half-drilled.' Perhaps it was just as well that the cavalry were not needed at the Tchernaya, the last full-blown conflict of the war, on 16 August. Hodge summed up the day brilliantly in a letter home; the Russian plan was to have driven the French back from the walls of Sebastopol, taken Balaclava, 'eaten up the English cavalry' and sixty guns, burned the Allied ships and taken Kamiesch. This had, more or less, been the Russian plan since the previous October and it got nowhere. 'Poor misguided people,' wrote Hodge, 'they never even got beyond the first line of our defences ...'

At home, the whitewashing went on. Lewis Dillwyn, MP for Swansea, raised the issue in the House that he hoped the good service pension granted to Lord George Paget was not merely because of his 'high birth and connexions'. Palmerston defended Paget, on the rather flimsy grounds that the award had been made by the commander-in-chief (Raglan) and that he should know best. The fact that the commander-in-chief's decision-making about everything was now widely called into question was ignored.

Hodge was busy catching mice using his mess-tin as a trap and was delighted to see the navvies of the Army Works Corps, which Mary Seacole praised so highly, arrive on 21 August. The next day, however, most of them lay blind drunk by the roadside – 'I blushed for my country.' In the meantime, he was doling out punishments; one man who received the lash had been drunk six times since May. His thoughts, like those of many, turned to a second winter in the Crimea and Hodge planned to build with brick this time, rather than the timber of his leaking hut.

Being Hodge, he still had time to sneer at one of his officers who had gone home. On 11 August, he wrote: 'A sale in the camp of Brigstocke's things. He has deserted and has sent in his papers … I do not approve of officers doing this.' It was not actual desertion, of course, merely a continuation of what had been going on since the previous December. Hodge would have been even more annoyed to hear of the lavish street party put on for Brigstocke by his doting mother in their home town of Ryde, Isle of Wight.

Temple Godman was eating well, with mutton, goose, turkey or chicken on the menu. The cavalry turned out at three o'clock every morning and took up positions in case of attack, exactly what Surgeon Cooper had complained about three months earlier to the McNeill-Tulloch enquiry. Over 3,000 Russians had been buried after the Tchernaya, the Allies helping with grave-digging under a flag of truce. Even so, as the world would find out in two wars in the twentieth century, it was the Russian way to send thousands as fodder under the guns; they could not win wars without this tactic. The Heavy Brigade was 1,500 strong by the end of August, but the new men, officers and Other Ranks alike, were suffering with the heat and the cholera.

Temple Godman shot quail with Thomas Hampton and they ate them for breakfast. As Godman was now a captain, he had a second servant (which was not strictly allowed) and his pay was 17 shillings a day. He told his father how hopeless the new officers were (something that would be echoed in the trenches of the First World War) and that the new mess provided excellent Black Sea turbot, preserved tarts and rice pudding.

By 10 September, the Russians were planning to pull out of Sebastopol. Exactly as they had done in Moscow in 1812, when Napoleon's army had arrived, they set fire to the south side of Sebastopol. Hodge took out four squadrons, Heavies and Lights, to hold a hill overlooking the town. The French attack on the Malakoff went off perfectly, with virtually no resistance, but the simultaneous assault on the Redan by the British was driven back by an overwhelming force. Hodge was furious – the British attack was superfluous once the Malakoff had fallen.

The next day, the colonel was among the first to ride into Sebastopol. The dockyard buildings were ruined by months of Allied bombardment and as Hodge watched, the locals were firing Fort Paul and their own houses. He was amazed to be posted as glorified policemen with his cavalry to prevent looting, but he saw plenty of it as men came away with coats, helmets, anything they could get their hands on. The Russian retreat had been handled superbly. They crept away under cover of darkness exactly as the British would do at Gallipoli sixty years later. But the dead were left to rot and the stench in some parts of the town was unbearable. 'I cannot help thinking,' Hodge wrote, 'that the war is over.'

Temple Godman knew he was writing history when he sent a letter to brother Fred on 10 September. He was appalled at the behaviour of the infantry recruits who had not supported their officers in the Redan.

Like Hodge, he rode into the burned out areas of Sebastopol, aware that the Russians had left mines wired up to electric batteries. The houses were riddled with shot and the French were helping themselves to valuables. The ditches were piled with Allied dead, five feet high. Pieces of flesh and smoke-blackened uniform lay among the debris. There were rumours that the cavalry were to be sent to the Bosphorus or Egypt. Godman told his father that the Crimean medals had arrived; he would send his home and keep the ribbon for his jacket.

Inevitably, Hodge was disgusted with them – 'vulgar-looking things, with clasps like gin labels. How odd it is, we cannot do things like people of taste.' One hundred and eighty-five of them reached the 4th Dragoon Guards and Hodge made a speech while giving them out. 'These medals,' he wrote in his diary, 'given to all the world are of no value. They are *too* common.' Today, Chargers' medals not in museums sell for thousands.

Hodge was busy digging up crocus bulbs to take home while the French helped themselves to bas-reliefs and church ornaments from ruined Sebastopol. To the victors, the spoils. True to form, the colonel was still suspicious of the new-fangled technology creeping in as the war ended – 'Sent a party to assist the Electric Telegraph in conveying messages. It is found to be done quicker by heavy dragoons.' The 4th's personnel had changed so much, what with casualties and officers selling out, that Hodge was losing interest in the regiment – '*All* my old friends are gone' – although, arguably, he only had two, Edward Fisher and TSM Franks. Perhaps because of this, the colonel was being as much of a martinet as ever. He ordered a wild dog being noisy at night shot, broke his orderly to private and had a man flogged. He railed against newspapermen, especially Russell, who had to be protected by cavalry piquets at all times.

By the end of October, the *Himalaya* arrived in Balaclava harbour to transport the Heavy Brigade to Scutari. Three hundred and forty horses went along with sick and injured men. Interestingly, in the context of a debate that is still raging, Hodge had breakfast with Scarlett on 23 October and they discussed the charge. 'His account and mine do not quite agree. I am sure that in an affair of that sort, we only know what is taking place immediately about us.'

Two days later, to commemorate the charge a year before, Scarlett organised a field day. Hodge was still moaning – 'I fear that Scarlett cannot handle a large body of troops … Much singing in the men's huts and of course much drunkenness.' For the regiments involved, this would become an annual event. Temple Godman's brigade (the Heavies) were 1,300 strong that day, the Hussar Brigade (the Dirties) 1,000 and the Light Brigade (the Bashis) the same. Godman was convinced, of course, that his unit was 'by far the finest in appearance'. 'My dear father,' he wrote, 'we sailed from Balaklava about 11 a.m. the 19th [November].'

Hodge was gloomily totting up his regiment's losses. Of the 295 who had arrived in the Crimea, 62 were dead, 2 had deserted, 43 had been invalided home, 12 were currently absent through illness and 8 were in a field hospital. The colonel noted the difference between the camps of a year ago. All was railway track, stone houses, stacks of timber and corn. The vultures that circled over the dead had gone. Kadikoi bazaar was booming, Turkish barbers 'shaving the head of the faithful', kebab shops, French cafés, fish and vegetable markets. Scarlett left on 29 November on board *The Earl of Aberdeen* with the Inniskillings. Hodge, needless to say, fumed about this. Scarlett, he maintained, had always had a down on the 4th. He finally left the Crimea on 8 December.

Fanny Duberly's last diary entry was made on 27 September when nothing had been decided on embarkation or where the cavalry would be sent. It no doubt made William Russell smile when he read, in her journal published the following year:

Our best general, our most unflinching leader, has been the Press. To the columns of *The Times* the army owes a 'National Debt'; and so long as every incident of this war is laid before the public at home, so long as every man is familiarised, as it were, with the life of the soldier, so long will this be a popular war and so long will the sympathies of all England be enlisted on our side.

Mary Seacole was one of the last to leave. Her British Hotel was dismantled and she said her goodbyes – 'But I had other friends in the Crimea – friends who could never thank me. Some of them lay in their last sleep, beneath indistinguishable mounds of earth; some in half-filled trenches.' She planted flowers where she could – 'And by the clasped hand and moistened eye, I knew that from many a heart sped upward a grateful prayer to Providence which had thought fit in his judgement to take some, and in his mercy to spare the rest.'

Russell of *The Times* was there until the end too – 'The war had drifted to an end. For nearly three months scarcely a shot had been fired by either side. Now it seemed too late for rejoicing. A feeling of anti-climax had blunted the edge of expectation. It was time to begin counting the cost.'

Reviews and Reunions

I n May 1855, long before the Crimean War came to an end, the country welcomed home some of its heroes. The queen and Prince Albert had already visited the wounded, on 3 March, at Fort Pitt, Chatham and the Brompton barracks. In her journal, she described the little darkened rooms where they lay and, a keen watercolourist, she sketched some of the men she saw there, including one-armed Sergeant John Breese of the 11th Hussars. In a painting made from contemporary sketches by Jerry Barret, Private John McCabe of the 5th Dragoon Guards was shown in the shadows on the extreme left of the canvas, in the shapeless hospital slops of the time. He had received ten lance wounds and three sword cuts during the Heavy Brigade charge and had had two horses shot from under him.

Another of the men the queen acknowledged was Trumpeter William Heywood of the Scots Greys, who had lost three fingers of his left hand at Balaclava. Each patient had a card on which the nature of his wounds was written. The queen was very concerned about the Crimean wounded. In February 1856, the palace replied to a request from TSM Gardiner of the North Shropshire Yeomanry, whose son Alexander had lost a leg at Balaclava, his life saved by Sergeant Ramage. Gardiner senior had ridden the Waterloo charge of the Greys, so there was a strong family tradition in the regiment. The letter read:

> I have received Her Majesty's commands to desire that Douglas A. Gardiner may be supplied with a cork leg and that you will send me the account of the expenses incurred … It will give the Queen much pleasure thus to be able to alleviate the privations of a wounded soldier.

The 18 May presentation, of the new Crimean medal which Hodge hated, was a more positive follow-up to the queen's visit to the first unwounded troops to arrive, at Woolwich on 13 March. A painting of this glittering occasion was the work of William Simpson, who had made dozens of sketches in the Crimea itself. Perhaps to show the modernity of the army, the artist portrayed the troops in the new tunics issued in 1856. A whole series of photographs by Cundall and Howlett was commissioned by the queen in that year and the Heavy Brigade was represented by Corporal Robert Swash and Sergeant Robert Bailey of the Royals. Both men sport their Crimean beards as well as medals. Bailey's citation for his Medaille Militaire reads 'Never missed a day's duty and was always a valuable man on pickets'. Swash had been presented to the queen at Aldershot on 17 June, when Victoria walked through the stables there and spoke to the wounded and medal-winners. The 5th were represented by Michael MacNamara, given the DCM for saving the life of Joseph Gough of his regiment, and William Stewart, who had three horses killed under him in the charge.

Wearing his full dress uniform of a British field marshal (to which some people said he was not entitled), Albert stood beside the queen as she handed out the medals at the Horse Guards. The royal princes wore Highland uniforms and a number of Heavy heroes queued up to receive their awards.

Captain William de Cardonel Elmsall, badly wounded in the charge, received the clutch of the Crimean medal, the Medaille Militaire and the Turkish Order of the Medjidie. He would go on three years later to become a magistrate in Yorkshire and a major in the West Yorkshire Militia. He died around 1880. Riding Master George Cruse, who left a detailed account of the charge, did not get his medals until September, with clasps for Balaclava, Inkerman and Sebastopol. He remained in the regiment as a lieutenant without purchase until 1871, when he became a captain and went on to half pay, the traditional semi-retirement for ex-officers. He died in Bristol in February 1878.

Lieutenant William Wrey Hartopp had had his leg smashed at Balaclava and soon after receiving his medal, he was back in the Crimea with the newly arrived Royal Horse Guards. He died in July 1874, leaving his estate of less than £2,000 to his wife, Lina. The only ranker from the Royals to be presented in May was Private Samuel Woodward, wounded in the charge. He retired from the army in Dublin in February 1859.

Captain Francis Sutherland of the Scots Greys may have got his purchaseless promotion as a result of his performance at Balaclava. He left the regiment in 1856 and settled in Malvern, very much an elite retirement area for ex-army officers. Lennox Prendergast, whose foot had been smashed at Balaclava, became a captain in June 1856 and a major three years later. He retired as an honorary colonel in 1881, living in Hanover Square with his wife and four children. He died in January 1907, one of the last survivors of the Heavy Brigade. Alexander Turner was a private at Balaclava, where his horse was killed and he was shot in the head. It is unknown what became of him later.

Private Charles Adam is equally anonymous, except that he was discharged from the army in 1857. Robert Hunter, on the other hand (no relation to the officer in the Greys) was discharged in 1866 but was still sprightly enough to attend a parade of Crimean veterans in Edinburgh in May 1903.

The 4th were represented by Captain Arthur Robertson who was to go on to a rather scandalous future. He was the officer involved in a very public dispute with Colonel Dickson in 1862 that led to his being cashiered. Perhaps because she had met him in person, the queen overturned the sentence of the court. Nevertheless, it was effectively the end of his career. Next came Robert Gunter, the 'nobby pieman' son of the chocolatier, whose table manners had so disgusted Hodge. And Farrier John Innes, of whom nothing is known after 1855. There is a similar silence over the subsequent career of Private James Parke. And over Henry Scholefield, slightly wounded at Balaclava.

In the 5th, the most prestigious recipient of the May medals was Captain Alexander James Hardy Elliot, badly cut up riding alongside Scarlett in the charge. An article in the *New York Times* in May 1882 carries the story soon after the battle – 'his brother officers went into his tent and found him standing before a looking glass. "Haloa, Elliot, beautifying, are you?" "Yes," was the answer, "I am sticking on my nose".' It had been slashed nearly off his face in the melee. He was a major by July 1856, colonel by 1871. He became a major general ten years later and retired as a colonel of the 21st Lancers in 1902. He died at his home in Ennismore Gardens, London, in July 1909. Frederick Hay Swinfen had been wounded in the charge with a lance thrust to the chest. There are two paintings of him in his full dress uniform, mounted on different chargers and a carte de visite photograph in civilian dress. He remained with the 5th throughout his career, ending up as commanding officer from 1869–71. A military Knight of Windsor, he died in the castle in June 1914, just before the guns of another war opened up.

Edward Malone was still a private by May 1855 and had lance and sabre cuts all over his body. He was promoted to corporal in the following year and died at Crewe in April 1901. A local newspaper carried his obituary:

> The deceased was 75 years of age and came to Crewe to enter the L&N.W. [London and North Western] Railway Co. thirty years ago ... Mr Malone was one of Her Majesty's soldiers for 24 years and for nine years before leaving the service was a Corporal in the 5th Dragoon Guards ... where he took part in the famous Balaclava Charge, receiving no less than 17 wounds ...

His three children were all dead by this time and his wife Anne outlived him by twelve years. Nothing is known of Private Michael Carney but John Wilkins holds something of a record. He probably rode the charge because he was orderly to Lord Lucan and would have been with the general in the Heavies' support of the Lights. In the same role, however, he was the *only* heavy cavalryman to be present at the Alma, at the general's side. Accordingly, his is the only Crimean medal to the Heavy Brigade with a clasp for what was a purely infantry battle.

We have heard of TSM Alexander Shields of the Inniskillings before. He had been badly cut in the charge, but the survival of a random letter from his comrade TSM Joseph Insole, proves that Shields had returned to his wife and children and that they were all well. Insole was writing from Canterbury on 3 September, looking forward to an opportunity to meet up. Captain Conyers Tower had taken over command of B Troop and Insole had volunteered for the 'Grand affair of the 18th of June', the failure at the Redan. Insole claimed to have recovered from 'what you very properly call horrors of field pestilence, filth and famine'. Even so, he shot himself on 17 October 1856. John Brown was discharged from the regiment in March 1857. Private Michael Rourke, with his sandy hair and pock-marked face, had been saved in the sinking of the *Europa*. He was discharged from the Inniskillings in July 1855, his left arm useless from the musket wound he got in the charge.

Private Alexander Robinson was presented to the queen at Aldershot, along with the mare, Jenny, that he had ridden at Balaclava. She patted them both on the shoulder, congratulating them on being 'a clever pair'.

What happened to the men who stayed in the cavalry? In the 4th Dragoon Guards, Paymaster John Biggs exchanged into the Osmanli Irregular Cavalry in the spring of 1856, perhaps under the auspices of Major General Beatson, whose own career, in defence of his irregulars, led to accusations and lawsuits throughout the late 1850s. Beatson himself, Scarlett's indispensable staff officer, commanded troops in India until 1872 when he came home on leave. He died in the vicarage, New Swindon, Wiltshire, in February of that year. Private William Hancox, who had enlisted at Coventry in 1851, was promoted to corporal in August 1855 and sergeant two years later. He re-engaged in the 4th at Dublin in 1863 and became TSM four years later. He seems to have been the perfect soldier, with no entries in the regimental defaulter's book, no courts martial. When he retired in 1873, he was 41, too old to continue in the ranks and by this time, although the purchase system had been abolished two years earlier, applying for a commission was clearly not an option. Instead, he did what many Victorian ex-soldiers did and joined the Dorsetshire Yeomanry as instructor on their permanent staff. The yeomanry had been raised in the 1790s to protect hearths and homes from invasion by Revolutionary France and Napoleon. By 1899, they were professional enough to be sent to war zones in South Africa, and Hancox must have played his small part in that. Again, his service was exemplary and he finally left the cavalry in April 1889.

From the ranks of the 5th, Farrier John Addy was commissioned into the Land Transport Corps in September 1855. The following year, he exchanged into the 5th Royal Irish Lancers as quartermaster. The next year, his commanding officer was George Sulivan of the Scots Greys and the senior major, Robert Portal of the 4th Lights. Addy went on to half pay the following year and became a recruiting officer at Limerick, reaching the rank of lieutenant colonel by 1879. He died in Brighton twenty years later. Private William Blood, with five good conduct medals to his name, had no interest in promotion. In March 1871, aged 37, he fell down stairs when on leave with his officer-master, Captain Bourne. His left ankle refused to heal and he was discharged from the service. Ten years later, in the category of pensioner, he was living, appropriately, at Alma Terrace in York with his wife and their 18-year-old son.

George Harker of the Royals transferred to the 7th Dragoon Guards in September 1857 and was almost immediately shipped out to India. Sections of the Bengal army of the East India Company had gone on the rampage at Meerut, the largest barracks in India, in May and had killed several British officers. What came to be known as the Indian mutiny spread fast and a number of home-based regiments were sent out to put it down. The 7th saw no action as it happened and Hawker left the army at Canterbury in 1863. Sergeant Maillard Noake, who had been nursed by Sarah Terrot at Scutari, had hoped for a commission after the charge, but found himself with a DCM and no job by 1857. Accordingly, he joined first the Dumfries Militia, then the 15th Hussars as Riding Master. He exchanged into the Colonial Defence Force as a sub-inspector in 1863, settling in New Zealand. Eventually, he became a lieutenant colonel in the First Regiment (North Island) Cavalry in 1886, dying in 1914, the year before his adopted countrymen were sent down their own 'valley of Death' in Gallipoli.

Private Charles Glancy of the Greys continued with the regiment until 1866 when he was discharged at Newbridge. Clearly, he was suffering – as no doubt many men did – with physical and psychological problems, because the reason for his discharge was 'in consequence of his being unfit for further military service, as a result of disease contracted from wounds received at Balaclava'. A lance had been rammed into his head, followed by a sword cut across his face and a third wound to his left shoulder. He had served in the army for 22 years and 170 days. Quartermaster Thomas McBean was one of those who went on to achieve minor fame. He was still with the Greys in March 1863 when a bomb went off at their Birmingham barracks. McBean had gone to the regiment's magazine to get blank cartridges used in the training of troop horses. No sooner was he inside the building than an explosion ripped through it and might have been followed by others given the quantity of black powder on the premises. McBean was dragged out unconscious and when he came to, had no idea what had happened. A used box of matches was found but since he did not smoke, they were unlikely to have belonged to the quartermaster.

Quartermasters seem to have had a rather tough time after the Crimea. *The Times* for September 1869 carried the tragic story of QM Samuel Seggie, who had served as a private in the war. By this time, he was quartermaster to the 9th Lancers, based at Hounslow. He had been 'in very low spirits' for some time and was found in the barracks toilets with his throat cut. The weapon used – and the wound was clearly self-inflicted – was a small pocket knife with a two-inch blade.

Similar pen-knives were made by the Sheffield firm of Westenholm and presented to officers and men of the 4th. The surgeon who dashed to help Seggie could do nothing for him, but the verdict by the coroner was unsatisfactory – 'He had been confined to his room lately with a bad ankle [there is no mention of an old Crimean wound] which might have induced temporary insanity.'

Various men of the Inniskillings were inevitably caught up in the toxic 'Crawley affair' at Mhow in 1862 (see page 21). One of those was Sergeant James Gibson, who had no direct involvement in the clash between officers at all. Gibson's wife, with the regiment in India, spoke to RSM Lilley, a 'conspirator' who was under arrest at the time. Private Little, the duty guard, was arrested for allowing this to happen. When his troop commander, Captain Swindley, a Crimean veteran himself, tore up the charge sheet against Little for such a non-offence, Colonel Crawley was furious. Mhow was a classic example of the petulant, schoolboy behaviour of some officers in the school of Lucan, Cardigan and Le Marchant of the 5th. One soldier in even hotter water was William Madgwick. He had joined the Inniskillings in November 1846 at the age of 20 and remained a private all his army career. At the end of 1857, he was court-martialled for 'disgraceful conduct' (precisely what is unrecorded). He already had five entries in the defaulters' book. So, despite the fact that he almost died on board the *Europa* and survived the charge of the Heavy Brigade, he got neither the long service nor the good conduct medal.

Many men left the army soon after the war and disappeared into the melting pot of Victorian history. Some became grooms because of their cavalry experience; others continued to wear uniform as coachmen, liveried servants, policemen and prison officers. One dazzling example was Private Walter Fawke of the Scots Greys, a former barber who, by 1871, styled himself 'Professor of Athletics' and gave strong-man demonstrations, cutting a sheep carcase in half with his sword and slicing an apple neatly with the same weapon. Clearly, the wound he received at Balaclava had not slowed him up at all! And, most tantalisingly of all, in the autumn of terror in 1888, when 'Jack the Ripper' was butchering women in Whitechapel, was the witness with the 'soldierly bearing' who saw Mary Kelly talking to her killer, the same George Hutchinson who had ridden the charge with the 5th Dragoon Guards?

The Heavy Brigade came home in fits and starts in the spring and summer of 1856. The Royals, on the *Orinoco*, reached Spithead on 28 May. They mustered 411 men and 241 horses. William Russell listed the officers under Lieutenant Colonel Wardlaw; the old hands who had ridden the charge along with the new men who had not. Badly wounded individuals, like Colonel Yorke, had already got home a year earlier. There was no room on board the Cunard line's *Alps*, so the captain gave Yorke his own cabin. He put up at the George Hotel, Portsmouth, at the end of March 1855.

It was a time for rewards, flags and bands. For all the horrors of the war itself, it was over now and the country was in a mood to celebrate. Cornetcies were given out to deserving NCOs in the cavalry, free of charge. The Victoria Cross, made from the melted bronze of captured Russian cannon, became the highest award for gallantry in the field. Despite the much-trumpeted list of eleven VCs awarded in 1879 for the defence of Rorke's Drift by the 24th Foot, nearly twice that number was awarded for Inkerman, backdated to November 1854. If, today, that is largely forgotten, it is because no one has made a movie about Inkerman! In the Heavy Brigade, three VCs were awarded and we have noted the stories behind them already. The accolade went to the Scots Greys where both RSM John Grieve and Sergeant Henry Ramage won the award. Charles Dickens said of Grieve:

> What John Grieve did, then, was an act of the purest and most unselfish heroism; but I daresay, when the Queen pinned the Cross to his breast in Hyde Park that day, he felt he was more than rewarded for what to him was a very ordinary matter-of-fact bit of duty.

Grieve went on to become lieutenant and adjutant of his regiment and when he died was buried in Inveresk, Lothian. Ramage received his VC at Portsmouth in August 1858 when twelve recipients lined up to have the medal presented. A year later, he was dead at 32 and was buried in an unmarked grave in the cemetery of Newbridge barracks, County Kildare. James Mouat of the Inniskillings got his medal at the same time as Ramage, on Portsmouth Common, for saving the life of William Morris of the 17th Lancers. The following year, he was promoted surgeon major and a CB in 1859. He served in the Maori wars in New Zealand in the 1860s and was given special thanks for his 'valuable services to the Colony'. He retired in 1876 and was appointed an honorary surgeon to the queen in 1888. He died in his London home in Kensington in January 1899. According to his obituary, he was 'held in deserved respect by all branches of the service; and in private life was an attached and sincere friend to those who won his esteem'.

The Crimean was the first war in which heroism was recognised among the rank and file. Even though every soldier who fought at Waterloo was given a medal, there were none for the Other Ranks before that. The fact that neither John Grieve nor Henry Ramage were officers speaks volumes for a new approach to war and how it was perceived by the public. Allied rulers also lavished decorations on the British; the Medaille Militaire was in the gift of the Emperor Napoleon III; the Medjidie bestowed by the Sultan; the king of Sardinia added to the glitter with the Al Valore Militare medal. And, of course, it was a two-way street – recipients from Allied armies won British Crimean medals too.

There were parties everywhere, in London, Dublin, Edinburgh and Sheffield. At one 'bash' in Sheffield, in honour of Hodge's 4th Dragoon Guards, John Roebuck MP said '[soldiers] are the protectors of our glory, they are the protectors of our freedom ... We are not afraid of soldiers. We love you as brethren and we know that you will protect us as such'. The queen made a similar speech at Aldershot in August 1856 – 'I thank God that your dangers are over, whilst the glory of your deeds remains.'

For the regiments that formed the Heavy Brigade, regular dinners became the norm. There may not have been a T.H. Roberts fund (see page xvi) but the regiments themselves remembered. Balaclava banquets were held by officers of both cavalry brigades and it is intriguing to note the promotions of the men involved. By 1883, for example, with virtually all of them retired, we have *Generals* Hodge, Clarke, McMahon, Godman and Mouat. A number of distinguished colonels were there too; Duberly, Ferguson, Swinfen and Prendergast. Among the majors were McCreagh and Manley, possibly lording it just a little over their old comrades, Captains Halford and Fisher.

Army reforms followed as a direct result of the Crimean experience. The Land Transport Corps became the Royal Military Train, and in time the Army Service Corps, responsible for supplies and ammunition. The antiquated Board of Ordnance was scrapped, to be replaced with far better provision of equipment and weapons. The Medical Staff Corps replaced the lottery of over-worked and sometimes badly trained regimental surgeons. Widows' pensions were increased. For the men who continued to serve with their regiments, an extra 6d a day was awarded. Abuses, however, continued. The purchase system, based entirely on money, lingered on for another fifteen years, until the reforms of Edward Cardwell in William Gladstone's first ministry swept it all away and reduced the length of service for the common soldier. From then on, officers had to pass written examinations and attendance at Sandhurst (or Woolwich for the Artillery) became de rigeur. It would be another sixty years before a further European war was fought and by 1914, the soldiers of the Crimea were almost all dead. The rest of the nineteenth century witnessed the growth of the British empire and a rash of small wars, each with its own challenges, against an array of opponents around the globe.

As so often happens in international politics, what had been won by men's blood was thrown away by politicians. The Treaty of Paris which was supposed to lay down lasting rules and keep the Russian bear in check for ever, was ignored. By 1871, Sebastopol, which had been burned by the Russians and dynamited by the Allies, had been rebuilt and Russian warships once again threatened Turkey. The Eastern Question still had no answers and the Congress of Berlin was called into being to try (again) to sort things out. No doubt there were many Crimean veterans, including survivors of the Heavy Brigade, who sat together, over their port or their pints and asked 'What was it all for?'

What happened to the men and women we have heard from in this book, those who charted the ups and downs of a campaign through their diaries and letters? In the 4th Dragoon Guards, Trumpeter John Nichol was superintendent of Durham County Lunatic Asylum for eighteen years. He died on 3 November 1893 – 'With that memorable day at Balaclava has been severed by the death of Mr John Nichol for many years Trumpet-Major … and the last remaining trumpeter who rode in the famous and daring charge of the Heavy Brigade. He was the youngest boy in the regiment at that time.' Private Timothy O'Neil left the army as a sergeant in 1868 and continued to wear his uniform until his death in 1908, replacing the arm badge of the Barrack Department with the harp and crown of the 4th. He attended a regimental dinner in London six months before he died, at which he was the guest of honour.

The annoying and bitchy Colonel Hodge lost three horses on his way home. His sarcastic sense of humour never left him. He wrote to a friend – 'I shall take the earliest opportunity of running up to see you, so if your servants see a ragged looking ruffian in a red jacket trying to get in to No. 19, beg them not to call the police.' By 1862, Hodge commanded the cavalry brigade at Aldershot. Nine years later he was a lieutenant general and was given a knighthood in 1873. A full general fifteen years later, Hodge died in his London home in South Kensington in December 1894. He was 84 years old.

Dr William Cattell of the 5th Dragoon Guards went on to see service with the 10th Hussars in 1872, taking his wife and three children to India with him. He fought in the Afghan War of 1878–9 and retired in December 1889 as deputy surgeon general. Dying in March 1919, he may have been the last survivor of the charge of the Heavy Brigade.

Captain William Inglis, who never impressed Temple Godman, became a JP for the North Riding of Yorkshire and an inspector for reformatory schools. He died at the age of 70 in June 1900. Private Patrick Keating earned a kind of immortality as being a prisoner on the last convict ship bound for Fremantle, Australia. He and two others of the regiment were found guilty of conspiracy by joining the Irish Fenian movement which had developed in the 1860s as a precursor to Irish Home Rule. Sergeant James Shegog who had ridden the charge directly behind Scarlett, missed out for the rest of his life. Colonel Yorke put him forward for the VC, but it was turned down. He applied to become a Yeoman Warder at the Tower of London but was too old. Even the military funeral suggested after his death in Tasmania in 1896 was not granted. TSM Henry Franks, one of the very few ordinary soldiers to write a book on the Crimea, in 1904, went on to a new life in Canada in 1862 as a cavalry instructor. He lived for a time with relatives in New York and Chicago before retiring to Dalton, Yorkshire, where he died in 1909. 'I have nothing to say,' he wrote, 'with regard to the War, whether it was right or not. That is not my business …' At the end of his book, he wrote:

> I am led sometimes when in company of a friendly neighbour or two, to look back to some of the scenes I have passed through and, as it were, to fight my battles over again, and I am consoled by the thought that any little service I have been able to render to my country has been duly appreciated and rewarded.

Temple Godman never wrote a book, but his letters were collected by Philip Warner in 1977 as *The Fields of War*. The last letter he wrote to his father was on 25 June 1856 from the George Hotel, Portsmouth. Six horses had died on the rough journey home, but his were all right and the regiment was due to be posted to Edinburgh, according to the rumours that had swirled around him throughout the campaign. He was a major by 1870 and a major general by the time of his death in 1912.

One of the most famous of Roger Fenton's photographs shows him with his soldier-servant Kilbourne and his horse, The Earl. There is a much later one, taken at Highden in Sussex, when a white-haired general is still in the saddle, along with his four sons, all mounted on grey horses.

Shegog may not have been given a military funeral but Sergeant Henry Pavey of the Inniskillings was. He joined the Ellesmere Troop of the North Shropshire Yeomanry as instructor and died in Ellesmere in May 1871. At his funeral, his two brothers led a black horse with a black shabraque with Pavey's boots reversed in the stirrups and a volley of shots was fired as his coffin was laid to rest. The Inniskillings, under Colonel White, were presented to the queen at the VC ceremony and described by the Duke of Cambridge as 'a model to the British cavalry'. Even Lord Cardigan, never an easy man to please, said, 'I have the honour to add that I consider the Inniskilling Dragoons to be one of the finest and most perfect regiments in the Queen's service.'

What of the women of the Crimea? When the bronze memorial to the Crimean War was erected in London in 1915 – while men were dying again 'in the east', this time against the Turkish allies of 1854–6 – there had only been one woman's name carved on it; Florence Nightingale. The subject of countless articles in the press, her 'soothing voice, sleepless care and heroic zeal' became synonymous with nursing, a career which, nevertheless, has remained undervalued and underpaid up to the present time. In 1860, St Thomas's Hospital in London set up the first British nursing school that we would recognise today. Not everybody approved; even women themselves shared Temple Godman's view that nursing was not for women. The poet Elizabeth Barrett Browning was among them – 'Every man is on his knees before ladies carrying lint, calling them "angelic".' Nightingale and her angels were given no medals. Two hundred and twenty-nine had served in the theatre of war and eleven had died there. Contrast that with the French *cantinières*, every one of whom received an award. Even so, Florence lived on until 1910, stoically resisting change in medical practice as the older generation invariably do.

Mary Seacole *did* get medals – and she wore them in public – but these were presents from her officer admirers and technically, she had no right to them. Funds were raised for her in 1857 and 1867 and she received a letter of 'approbation' from the queen. She died in 1881.

Fanny Duberly wanted a medal too – and Colonel Hodge was determined that she should not get one. She turned up at various royal presentations in the months after the war ended, smiling hopefully at the queen who ignored her. Her husband Henry eventually became a colonel and no doubt, she had to be content to bask in the glory – and the diminishing royalties – that her *Crimean Journal* brought her. She rode behind her husband across India in the year of the Mutiny, as enthusiastic as ever, but when a journalist asked her about the Crimea, she said, 'Those days are best forgotten.' She lived on until 1902.

At the end of his report into the assistance given to wives, widows and children of serving soldiers (the Heavy Brigade among them), Charles Bracebridge wrote: 'Let not the wife and child of the soldier be forgotten.' But, in the scheme of things, and certainly by the public outside the army, they were.

There is a clutch of gravestones on Cathcart's Hill in the Crimea, where a cohort of senior officers, most of them killed at Inkerman, lie buried. There are also dozens more in the hills and valleys around Sebastopol, those that have not been bulldozed by progress and Russian indifference. Perhaps the saddest was a wooden marker, now long gone, which had carved into it, perhaps with the bayonet of her semi-literate husband, 'Woman. English'.

But there is another grave, nearer to home, that seems to sum up the Heavy Brigade perfectly. In a corner of Ryde Cemetery in the Isle of Wight stands the tomb of Captain George Campbell Henville Player Brigstocke, late 4th Dragoon Guards. The last lines on the stone read:

> In the midst of life we are in death
> Not lost, but gone forever

Appendix

A list of officers and men of the Heavy Brigade, with their ranks at the time of their charge, 25 October 1854

Key: Wounded, *Killed*

Staff

Scarlett, Brigadier-General James
Beatson, Lieutenant Colonel William
Conolly, Major James
Elliot, Lieutenant Alexander
Shegog, Sergeant James
Monks, Trumpeter Thomas

4th Royal Irish Dragoon Guards

Hodge, Lieutenant Colonel Edward
Forrest, Major William

Captains
Brigstocke, George
Forster, Francis,
McCreagh, Michael
Robertson, Arthur
Webb, John

Lieutenants
Gunter, Robert
McDonnel, Christopher

Cornets
Deane, the Honourable M. Fitzmaurice
Fisher, Edward

Paymaster
Biggs, John

Quartermaster
Drake, John

Surgeons
Pine, Chilley
Armstrong, William (Assistant)

Veterinary Surgeon
Rainsford, James

RSM
Joice, William
Price, George

TSM
Barker, Charles
Evans, John
Harran, Edward
Talbot, William
Williams, Soloman

Sergeants
Armstrong, Guy
Blake, Joseph
Cooke, Michael
Costello, Walter

Cox, William

Dooley, John

Drake, Hospital Sergeant Joseph

Fletcher, Saddler Sergeant Robert

Harrington, Farrier Major Jackson

Mitchell, Henry,

Pedley, Armourer Sergeant Henry

Percy, William

Shamburg, Bernard

Walford, Thomas

Corporals

Abbot, George

Brady, Thomas

Cantell, William

Carleton, Thomas

Cartwright, William

Chadwick, Thomas

Crofts, George

Dooley, Martin

Finucane, Edward

Flemming, Patrick

Goldstone, James

Harran, James

Marks, Timothy

O'Keefe, Joseph

Rothwell, Thomas

St Aubert, Henri

Talbot, Edward

Wallace, Frederick

Watson, Richard

Privates

Adams, John

Allen, Thomas

Anchinclass, James

Anderson, Thomas

Arkell, William

Bagnall, James

Barker, William

Bartram, John

Bell, John

Benison, John

Bennett, John

Beverlin, Samuel

Blackie, Jasper

Bott, Thomas

Bracken, Michael

Bratty, James

Brown, Josiah

Brown, William

Bryant, William

Bucknell, George

Bucknell, John

Burbridge, Frederick

Burke, Thomas

Burrows, William

Byrne, Patrick

Campbell, Michael

Campbell, Farrier William

Carroll, Charles

Carswell, James

Chadwick, Thomas

Chambers, Charles

Chatten, Walter

Clarke, Timothy

Clipsham, Elijah

Coffey, John

Courd, Benjamin

Cowhig, Patrick

Crawley, James

Croshaw, Thomas

Crossley, John

Curren, Henry

Dalton, John

Daniels, John

Delaney, David

Delaney, Nicholas

Donovan, John

Dooley, Maurice

Drury, Michael

Dunne, Robert

Dunne, Thomas

Dunne, Thomas

Egan, Denis

Enright, Patrick

Field, Denis

Field, Patrick

Fisher, William

Fitzgerald, Michael

Fitzpatrick, John

Fletcher, William

Flynn, Bernard

Flynn, James

Flynn, Lawrence

Fox, Samuel

Fullerton, Robert

Gallagher, Michael

Gallagher, Michael

Gannan, Martin

Gannan, Patrick

Gaskin, Johnson

Gill, Thomas

Gillett, William

Gilligan, John

Gilligan, Mark

Good, William

Gordon, Robert

Grant, John

Griffiths, Simon
Hackett, Patrick
Hackforth, John
Hall, Thomas
Hall, Thomas
Hancox, William
Harper, William
Harrison, George
Harrold, William
Hartley, John
Healy, James
Healy, William
Heely, John
Higginbotham, Samuel
Hoagan, Connor
Hogan, Patrick
Horgan, James
Houlton, Thomas
Hyland, Richard
Illston, Charles
Inglam, Farrier Joseph
Innes, Farrier John
Irving, William
Jackson, James
Jackson, Robert
Jacques, Joseph
James, Trumpeter John
Jennings, John
Johnson, John
Johnstone, Francis
Jones, Benjamin
Jones, James
Jones, Thomas
Jones, Thomas
Keating, Jeremiah
Keegan, John
Kelly, William

Langton, John
Lawder, John
Leary, John
Little, John
Lotty, William
Lynch, Michael
Madden, John
Madden, Thomas
Magwick, John
Marks, Thomas
Marlow, James
Marshall, Edward
Mason, Charles
McGuire, John
McKee, James
McKenna, Garrett
McTrustry, John
Meade, Robert
Meares, Lewis
Mervyn, Trumpeter
   Henry
Mervyn, Robert
Moloney, James
Moore, Daniel
Moore, John
Moran, Trumpeter
   Francis
Morris, Edward
Morris, Edward
Morrison, James
Mossop, Charles
Murray, John
Neeson, Daniel
Newman, John
Nichol, Trumpeter John
O'Brien, Edward
O'Brien, James

O'Connor, John
O'Donnell, Henry
O'Donnell, William
O'Hara, John
O'Leary, Timothy
O'Neil, Timothy
Orson, John
Parke, James
Potter, George
Pratt, John
Preece, Henry
Proudfoot, Adam
Purcell, James
Rae, John
Ransome, Farrier David
Reid, Alexander
Ritchie, William
Robertson, Thomas
Rogers, John
Rutledge, Robert,
Ryan, Thomas
Savage, James
Scanlan, William
Scholefield, Henry
Sellick, John
Shawe, Michael
Shea, James
Sherlock, James
Shine, Denis
Short, Bartholomew
Smith, Thomas
Smith, William
Smith, William
Stables, James
Stephenson, Isaac
Stewart, James
Stone, Thomas

Suff, Francis
Taylor, Farrier James
Taylor, James
Taylor, John
Thompson, Henry
Thompson, James
Toole, Arthur

Turke, Thomas
Vaughan, Thomas
Wallace, Frederick
Wangford, Richard
Wardrop, Henry
Watson, William
Webb, Samuel

Whelan, Michael
Whiteman, Farrier John
Wilkie, Duncan
Wilmot, Farrier Jeremiah
Wilson, George
Winterbourne, Frederick
Wykes, Charles

5th Princess Charlotte of Wales's Dragoon Guards

Captains
Burton, Adolphus
Campbell, William
Inglis, William
Swinfen, Frederick
Thompson, Richard
Lieutenants
Burnand, George
Montgomery, Robert
Cornets
Ferguson, John
Godman, Adjutant
    Temple
Halford, Charles
Hampton, Thomas
Neville, Grey W
Quartermaster
Bewley, George
Surgeons
McCullough, George
Cattell, William
    (Assistant)
Veterinary Surgeons
Constant, Stephen
Gudgin, Thomas
RSM
Fitzgerald, Hobart

TSM
Franks, Henry,
Green, Erasmus
Griffiths, George
Russell, James
Stewart, William
Sergeants
Addy, Farrier Major John
Aldwell, William
Baker, William
Blevins, William
Boyle, Richard
Calvert, Edward
Ellison, Paymaster Clerk
    William
Elston, William
Fisher, James
Fisher, John
Hartnell, Thomas
McGregor, James
McLusky, William
Partridge, Samuel
Plant, Edward
Windram, William
Corporals
Allen, John
Carroll, John

Cleaver, John
Darrell, Mark
Davidson, Maxwell
Donahue, Matthew
Gough, Joseph
Haveron, John
McKeegan, Charles
Mulholland, Samuel
Perry, William
Reyner, Henry
Taylor, James
Topham, William
Walsh, David
Walsh, Thomas
Privates
Abbott, Charles
Abbott, John
Allsop, Henry
Anderson, Isaac
Armstrong, Henry
Babbington, Charles
Baker, Trumpeter Edward
Barrett, John
Barrington, Richard
Birch, Thomas
Bird, William
Birmingham, Francis

Blackburn, John
Blood, William
Bolton, Robert
Bonwell, James
Breakwell, Farrier Andrew
Brownrigg, William
Buckley, James
Bunting, Thomas
Burton, Thomas
Callery, Bernard
Campbell, James
Carney, Michael
Carrington, Trumpeter
   Charles
Clare, Thomas
Clarkson, George
Clay, David,
Collett, Daniel
Conway, Francis
Cowie, John
Cowie, William
Crofts, John
Dallison, Mark
Daveron, Michael
Dawson, John
Degunan, Patrick,
Delaney, Peter
Dempsey, Martin
Dickson, George
Doherty, Thomas
Donegan, William
Donnelly, Malachy
Donnelly, Michael
Donnelly, Thomas
Dugdale, Henry
Egan, Patrick
Evans, William

Failam, Thomas
Falls, James
Farrell, John
Fisher, John
Fitzgerald, James
Flynn, James
Foster, James
Gamble, James
Geary, Daniel
Geary, John
Gilleese, John,
Glanville, Samuel
Gleeson, Thomas
Glyn, John
Greatholders, John
Green, Edward
Hanlon, Patrick
Harper, Joseph
Hart, William
Hawkes, William
Healy, Patrick
Herbert, Henry
Higginbottom, Joseph
Hindle, John
Horne, George
Howard, Charles
Hughes, John
Hughes, William
Hunter, James
Hutchinson, George
James, Robert
Jamieson, Alexander
Jenkins, Joseph
Jenkins, Thomas
Jenkinson, William
Jennings, Richard
Jennings, Robert

Johnson, John
Jones, John
Keating, Patrick
Kelly, Denis
Kelly, Luke
Kelly, Martin
Kelly, Thomas
Kempson, Thomas
Kendall, Charles
Kerr, Peter
Kilbourne, Joseph
Kirkwood, Edward
Lacey, William
Lamb, James
Lawrence, Robert
Leavers, George
Lee, John
Lee, Patrick
Liversidge, James
Magher, William
Malone, Edward
Martin, George
May, Samuel
McAneny, Philip
McCabe, John
McCabe, Mathew
McCree, Edward
McDonald, James
McGall, Trumpeter John
McIlroy, John
McLean, William
McNamara, Michael
Meakin, John
Mealiagh, John
Miller, William
Moodie, Walter
Moore, Farrier George

Moore, Farrier Joseph
Morley, Alfred
Morley, Thomas
Morris, William
Morton, Edward
Murphy, George
Murphy, Henry
Naylor, Joseph
Nickless, John
O'Leary, David
O'Toole, Peter
Orr, James
Owen, James
Penkeyman, William
Plumpton, Moses
Pole, John
Porter, Robert
Price, James
Prince, James
Ramsbottom, Thomas
Reazler, John
Reid, James
Reid, Mark

Reilly, Mathew
Richards, Hiram
Ringer, Benjamin
Roberts, George
Robertson, William
Rowan, Charles
Russell, James
Sandham, George
Sands, Richard
Scott, Arthur
Scott, William
Simpson, James
Skiffington, Hugh
Smith, William
Smout, Richard
Spirit, Isaac
Stather, Joel
Stead, Michael
Stephenson, John
Sterrett, Joseph
Stewart, William
Sykes, James
Tagg, Joseph

Thomas, David
Turnbull, John
Venton, John
Walch, Edward
Walch, William
Warden, William
Weymes, James
Wilkins, John
Williams, John
Williams, Joseph
Willis, Richard
Wilson, Robert
Wilson, William
Winterbourne, George
Wintle, Charles
Wixted, Trumpeter
   Joseph
Wood, David
Wood, Henry
Wood, William
Yates, Richard
Yorke, Farrier James

1st Royal Dragoons

Yorke, Lieutenant Colonel
   John
Wardlaw, Major Robert
Captains
Campbell, George
Elmsall, William de
   Cardonnel
Stocks, Michael
Lieutenants
Basset, Arthur
Charlton, St John

Coney, Walter
Cornets
Glyn, Richard
Hartopp, William
Pepys, Edmund
Robertson, Gilbert
Sandeman, John
Quartermaster
Scott, William
Surgeons
Forteath, Alexander

Gorringe, John (assistant)
Veterinary Surgeon
Poett, Matthew
RSMs
Lee, John
Matthews, William
TSMs
Bailey, Matthew
Cruse, Riding Master
   George
Norris, John

Tripp, George

Sergeants

Baker, Robert

Clements, Orderly Room
  Clerk, George

Clerk, George

Davis, Edmund

Emms, George

Forster, Trumpet Major
  William

Goodwin, John

Gordon, Walter

Hill, John

Hunter, Peter

Jewhurst, Edward

Keyte, William

Lambert, Charles

Lees, Hospital Sergeant
  Dennis

Moorhouse, John

Murray, Henry

Noake, Maillard

Pardoe, Joseph

Pole, Armourer Sergeant
  James

Remlance, Farrier Major
  Charles

Ridgeway, William

Corporals

Bald, William

Finn, Thomas

Hall, Edwin

James, John

Johnson, Thomas

Jones, John

Nicholls, William

Richardson, George

Shannon, Robert

Stafford, William

Swash, Robert

Wale, John

Young, John

Privates

Abbott, Charles

Adams, Farrier Alexander

Adams, George

Adamson, Henry

Alderson, Thomas

Aldridge, John

Aldridge, Thomas

Allen, Robert

Andrews, William

Appleby, John

Arnold, William

Aslett, James

Avery, William

Aves, Trumpeter Samuel

Bailey, James

Balcomb, James

Balshaw, John

Barber, Charles

Barnfield, William

Bates, Thomas

Bates, William

Batt, James

Benge, William

Bettles, Thomas

Bexcon, George

Bird, James

Blackshaw, Robert

Blake, James

Blount, Henry

Bowerman, Thomas

Bridge, Henry

Briggs, Richard

Britton, Richard

Brophy, Jeremiah

Bull, William

Carney, Edward

Challis, Robert

Clark, James

Clayden, William

Coates, James

Coombes, George

Cooper, Henry

Cooper, James

Cooper, Farrier William

Coup, Bernard

Crane, Farrier Evi

Dalton, Michael

Davidson, William

Davies, Thomas

Davis, William

Diprose, Henry

Drew, John

Dudley, John

Duke, Robert

Ellis, David

Falconbridge, Edward

Falconer, William

Fawell, John

Fitzmaurice, Lewis

Flitton, David

Franklin, Robert

French, Mark

Gee, John

Gibbs, Trumpeter John

Gill, Charles

Gray, William

Greenwood, Walter

Gribbin, Farrier Thomas

Hallett, Charles
Hare, Richard
Harkness, James
Harkness, David
Harlock, William
Hatch, William
Hawker, George
Hebb, William
Hegarty, Samuel
Henshaw, William
Hibbs, Joseph
Hill, Henry
Hill, William
Hoare, Thomas
Hodge, John
Holland, James
Holmes, William
Horner, William
Howell, Charles
Hulse, Joseph
Hunt, George
Hunt, George
Jackson, William
Jacob, Stephen
James, John
Jelly, John
Johnson, George
Johnstone, Thomas
Jones, John
Kennedy, Bryan
Kenward, Henry
Kinnaird, William
Laws, William
Lewis, William
Lincoln, William
Lock, Alfred
Lofts, Henry

Louch, George
Lucas, John
Lynskey, Farrier
    Patrick
Maguire, Thomas
Male, John
Mansell, William
Marchant, Henry
Marchant, Richard
Marshall, Edwin
Martin, William
Matthewman, Richard
May, Frederick
Maycock, Thomas
McMurray, Thomas
Meehan, Terence
Mercer, Joshua
Meredith, Hugh
Metcalf, Thomas
Middleton, Charles
Millen, Wilson
Mitchell, Robert
Moffatt, George
Nealon, William
Newall, John
Ogden, James
Oliver, Edward
Overton, William
Pack, Joseph
Palmer, Joseph
Portington, Charles
Paterson, William
Pattenden, George
Peters, James
Pollard, Abraham
Powell, Thomas
Ramsden, Thomas

Reading, William
Richardson, Thomas
Roberts, George
Robinson, George
Rogers. Robert
Root, John
Russell, George
Russell, Thomas
Sapwell, George
Savage, John
Sayer, William
Sewell, William
Sherry, Henry
Shore, Thomas
Shreeve, James
Slater, Henry
Smith, George
Smith, William
St Clair, Grant
Stacey, Trumpeter
    George
Stacey, Trumpeter
    William
Stainbridge, Stephen
Stonehill, Henry
Sumner, Thomas
Taylor, George
Taylor, Peter
Thomas, Charles
Thomas, John
Thomas, William
Thornback, James
Thornett, John
Tobin, Laurence
Tressler, Joseph
Tudor, John
Turner, Joseph

Wainwright, Joseph
Wales, Henry
Walsh, William
Wanlace, Lancelot
Ward, William
Warden, Edward
Wardrop, Thomas
Waters, Patrick

Weaver, Paymaster Clerk
   Edward
West, Daniel
Whelan, John
White, Henry
Whitmarsh, John
Whittaker, John
Wick, Charles

Wickham, William
Williams, Henry
Williams, Samuel
Wilson, William
Woodhall, William
Woodward, Samuel
Wright, Andrew

2nd Dragoons, the Scots Greys

Darby Griffith, Colonel
   Henry
Majors
Clarke, George
Sulivan, George
Captains
Boyd, William
Miller, William
Williams, Samuel
Lieutenants
Buchanan, George
Hunter, Robert
Sutherland, Francis
Cornets
Handley, Henry
Moodie, Adjutant Daniel
Nugent, Andrew
Prendergast, Lennox
Paymaster
Antrobus, Philip
Quartermaster
McBean, Thomas
Surgeons
Brush, John
Armstrong, James
   (Assistant)

Chapple, Robert (assistant)
Veterinary Surgeon
Jex, Thomas
RSM
Grieve, John
TSM
Brown, Matthew
Davidson, James
Dearden, James
Sturtevant, Richard
Tilsley, George
Wilson, John
Wood, Archibald
Sergeants
Angus, John
Beeston, Saddler Thomas
Blackwood, William
Ferguson, John
Flanagan, Armourer John
Flockhart, James
Gibson, David
Hardy, David
Hone, William
Irvine, Paymaster
   Sergeant Robert
Kneath, Thomas

Louden, John
McGregor, Charles
Ramage, Henry
Rant, William
Ruxton, William
Todd, Hospital Sergeant
   William
Corporals
Campbell, Francis
Clifford, Andrew
Davidson, Donald
Dawson, Thomas
Kirk, James
Lauder, John
Liddle, John
Lowdon, Charles
McEwing, John
Mitchell, Alexander
Scott, Thomas
Selkrig, John
Short, David
Simmonds, Thomas
Stevenson, Norman
Watt, George
White, William
Windor, Robert

Privates

Adam, Charles
Aitken, James
Alexander, George
Allen, James
Allen, Robert
Allis, William
Armour, James
Arneill, Matthew
Bain, James
Bain, James
Barnett, Robert
Barrie, William
Bell, James
Bell, James
Bennett, Charles
Bishop, Charles
Blackwood, William
Blair, Thomas
Blandford, George
Booth, James
Borland, John
Borthwick, James
Boswell, Peter
Boyd, James
Boyes, Richard
Brassington, Joseph
Brodie, James
Brodie, William
Broomfield, Thomas
Brown, John
Brown, Thomas
Brownlie, Robert
Bruce, Peter
Burley, Peter
Burns, George
Cairnes, William

Cameron, Archibald
Cameron, James
Campbell, James
Campbell, Henry
Campbell, William
Canning, James
Christie, James
Christie, James
Clapperton, James
Colter, James
Colvin, George
Comittie, Alexander
Connell, William
Cowan, George
Crawford, George
Cree, John
Culmer, George
Currie, Charles
Davis, William
Deardon, Trumpeter
    Robert
Deer, George
Dickson, David
Donaldson, William
Dorsett, Edward
Downie, Peter
Drysdale, John
Farrell, Trumpeter
    Edward
Fawke, Walter
Findlater, Gilbert
Fisher, Hugh
Flemming, James
Foster, John
Foster, Richard
Galbraith, McAdam
Gardiner, Alexander

Gaunt, Frederick
Gilmour, William
Glancey, Charles
Graham, Alexander
Gray, Farrier Major David
Gray, Francis
Grossett, John
Hackett, James
Hall, Elijah
Hamilton, James
Hamilton, Samuel
Hammond, William
Hawkins, John
Hector, James
Hepburn, Thomas
Hepburn, William
Heywood, Trumpeter
    William
Hill, George
Hislop, James
Hogg, Robert
Hood, William
Hunter, James
Hunter, John
Hunter, Robert
Huntingdon, John
Irvine, James
Jackson, John
Jackson, William
Johnstone, George
Johnstone, James
Johnstone, Thomas
Johnstone, William
Jones, Trumpeter David
Jones, Francis
Keall, Robert
Kelly, Nathan

Kennedy, Robert
Kerr, Robert
Kinlay, James
Kirk, George
Knevett, Henry
Knevett, John
Knevett, Thomas
Knowles, John
Lacey, James
Laidlaw, Robert
Laing, Andrew
Langdon, Thomas
Leishman, Archibald
Linnan, John
Lister, Thomas
Little, William
Livingstone, Richard
Lochrie, Henry
Lockhart, Robert
Love, Duncan
Manson, George
Marshall, William
McArthur, Henry
McComrie, Archibald
McConnell, Samuel
McCowan, Robert
McDonald, Alexander
McDonald, Henry
McDonald, Hugh
McDoughall, John
McFadyan, James
McKay, Daniel
McKay, Donald
McKechnie, Hugh
McKimnings, William
McKinnon, Donald
McLellan, John

McLeod, Donald
McLeod, John
McLuckie, Robert
McMillan, Alexander
McMillan, James
McMillan, John
McNee, Duncan
McNee, John
McPhedron, John
McPherson, James
McPherson, William
Meikle, John
Meldrum, William
Mills, William
Milne, William
Morrison, William
Mowat, Alexander
Muir, John
Neill, Thomas
Neilson, David
Neilson, William
Nesbett, Trumpeter
    Charles
Nesbitt, William
Nimmo, Thomas
Orchard, William
Paterson, Thomas
Patton, Alexander
Penman, James
Pirnie, John
Polson, George
Preece, William
Ramage, David
Ramage, George
Ramsay, James
Ravely, John
Robb, Charles

Robertson, Adam
Robertson, John
Rodgers, James
Rollo, Peter
Russ, James
Rutherford, Peter
Scurr, Robert
Seggie, William
Seggie, William
Shillinglaw, Walter
Sinclair, James
Sissons, George
Skinner, Thomas
Small, William
Smart, William
Smellie, George
Smith, Charles
Smith, David
Smith, Edwin
Smith, George
Smith, James
Smith, Joseph
Smith, Robert
Smith, Samuel
Smith, William
Softley, Thomas
Soutar, William
Stevens, George
Stevenson, Thomas
Stewart, John
Stewart, William
Stocks, James
Stockton, Charles
Streeter, James
Swanstone, William
Taylor, James
Thomson, David

Thomson, John
Thomson, Robert
Traill, Thomas
Turner, Alexander
Valence, Dixon
Ward, Owen
Warren, John

Watson, James
Watt, Peter
Watt, William
Weir, Alexander
White, Cornelius
Whitehead, Joseph
Whyte, Thomas

Wilson, Andrew
Wilson, James
Wilson, William
Wylie, Joseph
Young, David
Young, John

6th Inniskilling Dragoons

White, Lieutenant Colonel
    Henry
Shute, Major Charles
Captains
Hunt, Edward
Manley, George
Tower, Conyers
Lieutenants
Rawlinson, William
Weir, (adjutant) Archibald
Wheatcroft, German
Paymaster
Marshall, James
Surgeons
Mouat, James
Boate, Henry (assistant)
Grylls, William (assistant)
Veterinary Surgeon
Collins, James
RSM
Mountain, Quartermaster
    Sergeant John
TSM
Foster, George
Hall, William
Insole, Joseph
Rowe, Robert

Shields, Alexander
Wakefield, Thomas
Sergeants
Bolton, Frederick
Brackley, David
Bridges, Saddler Sergeant
    John
Dibble, William
Frost, Armourer Sergeant
    George
Groves, Jacob
Hickmott, Henry
James, Edward
Jeffreys, Richard
Morton, Andrew
Mountain, William
Nicol, John
Parker, Charles
Pavey, Henry
Pigott, Paymaster
    Sergeant Henry
Sherrin, James
Smith, William
Sutcliffe, Hospital
    Sergeant William
Corporals
Burkitt, Edward

Cook, Henry
De Carle, Benjamin
Gibson, James
Gibson, John
Gray, John
Kennard, John
Kidney, John
McNamara, John
Renton, Robert
Sandford, George
Single, William
Smallman, Henry
Privates
Ainsworth, William
Almond, John
Appleby, James
Archer, William
Atkin, John
Backler, James
Ballard, William
Barnett, Charles
Barr, James
Biggs, William
Blackwell, William
Botterill, Matthew
Boult, Charles
Brady, James

Breadon, William
Bridges, James
Brooks, Isaac
Brown, Alfred
Brown, Trumpeter
    Edward
Brown, John
Brown, William
Budd, John
Burke, Thomas
Burns, Charles
Burns, Thomas
Bush, Jeremiah
Butler, Peter
Campell, William
Carter, James
Caughie, Thomas
Clarke, Charles
Coates, John
Corps, William
Corrie, John
Corston, Edward
Cowan, James
Cridge, John
Dale, William
Daly, Charles
Davies, John
Delaney, Charles
Devenport, Henry
Dobson, John
Dones, Trumpeter Joseph
Dooby, John
Double, John
Doulan, Peter
Easey, Robert
Elliot, Robert
Elmes, Henry

Elmes, John
Fairburn, John
Fall, William
Farnes, Farrier Major
    Charles
Fellows, William
Ferguson, Andrew
Ferris, John
Flannery, John
Fletcher, Trumpeter
    Charles
Forsythe, Samuel
French, George
George, Charles
Gibb, William
Gibson, John
Gibson, William
Gillice, James
Goble, Charles
Goldingay, William
Gordon, Joseph
Grainge, George
Gray, Daniel
Green, Albert
Green, Farrier Henry
Grover, William
Haines, George
Hambrook, George
Hand, Charles
Hanson, William
Hardy, Trumpeter John
Harte, John
Hasler, Thomas
Herrin, George
Higgs, George
Hilson, Henry
Hughes, Richard

Hunter, Henry
Jackson, John
Jenkinson, Robert
Jennings, Robert
Johnston, Arthur
Johnston, James
Jones, Thomas
Keane, Robert
Kelly, James
Kelly, James
Kennedy, William
King, William
Kisbie, Trumpeter
    Franklin
Knight, David
Lahey, James
Lakin, Charles
Lattimer, Alexander
Lawrey, Thomas
Lees, Robert
Lemmon, Farrier George
Lewis, Frederick
Little, John
Littlewood, Daniel
Lowe, James
Lucas, William
Lyons, Alexander
Lyons, William
Lyons, William
Madgwick, William
Maguire, John
Maughan. George
Mawson, William
McCanna, John
McCarten, Arthur
McClean, Samuel
McConvill, Edward

McKee, William
McKeown, John
McKibbin, William
McManus, Patrick
McManus, Thomas
McVeigh, Patrick
Middleton, William
Miles, Trumpeter William
Millar, Joseph
Mills, Edward
Mitchell, Michael
Monaghan, Patrick
Monday, Henry
Morris, James
Morrison, Nathaniel
Morton, Peter
Muruss, Robert
Needham, Edward
Nevin, Robert
Nugent, George
Ovens, Francis
Paine, Farrier David
Parker, William
Patterson, Walter
Patton, John
Pepper, Thomas

Polkinghorn, Humphrey
Pooley, James
Porter, Farrier Henry
Price, Joshua
Pryke, William
Quinn, Edward
Renwick, George
Rhodes, Samuel
Richardson, Joseph
Roberts, John
Robinson, Alexander
Rourke, Michael
Russell, Alexander
Ryson, James
Salt, Farrier James
Saunders, Farrier William
Scollan, John
Seymour, George
Singleton, John
Smith, George
Smith, George
Smith, William
Snell, Abraham
Snelling, Henry
Stannard, John
Stocker, William

Stothort, William
Sugdon, Charles
Taaffe, John
Tarlton, William
Taylor, Orderly Room
    Clerk George
Taylor, Robert
Thompson, Archibald
Thompson. James
Tooth, John
Torrens, John
Tribe, John
Turner, Robert
Tuton, George
Vernon, Edward
Walker, William
Wallace, William
Walsh, Patrick
Warren, George
Whelan, Timothy
White, William
Whittaker, William
Whittle, James
Willis, George
Wilson, William
Wire, Thomas

Bibliography

Anglesey, Marquess of, (ed), *Little Hodge*, Leo Cooper, 1971

Anglesey, Marquess of, *A History of the British Cavalry, Vols 1 & 2*, Leo Cooper, 1973

Baker, Anne, *A Question of Honour*, Leo Cooper, 1996

Bamfield, Veronica, *On the Strength*, Charles Knight & Co, 1974

Beckett, I.F.W., *Victoria's Wars*, Shire Publications, 1974

Beckett, Ian, *The Victorians at War*, Hambledon and London, 2003

Bentley, Nicholas (ed), *Russell's Despatches from the Crimea*, Panther Books, 1970

Boston, Roy, *The Essential Fleet Street*, Blandford Press, 1990

Bowles, Peter, *Ask Me If I'm Happy*, Simon and Schuster, 2010

Brighton, Terry, *Hell Riders*, Viking (Penguin), 2004

Buttery, David, *Messenger of Death*, Pen and Sword, 2008

Carman, W.Y. (ed), *Dress Regulations 1846*, Arms and Armour Press, 1971

Connelly, Mark, *The Charge of the Light Brigade*, I.B. Tauris, 2003

David, Saul, *The Homicidal Earl*, Little Brown, 1997

de Gaury, Gerald, *Travelling Gent*, Routledge and Kegan Paul, 1972

Duberly, Mrs Henry, *Journal Kept During the Russian War*, Elibron Classics 2005 (Reprint of 1856)

Dutton, Roy, *Forgotten Heroes: The Charge of the Heavy Brigade*, Infodial 2008

Franks, TSM Henry, *Leaves from a Soldier's Note Book*, Unknown Publisher, 1979

Gough Calthorpe, Somerset, *Cadogan's Crimea*, Hamish Hamilton, 1979 (reprint of 1856)

Grey, Elizabeth, *The Noise of Drums and Trumpets*, Longman, 1971

Harris, John, *The Court Martial of Lord Lucan*, Severn House, 1987

Hawkey, Arthur, *Last Post at Mhow*, Jarrolds, 1969

Hibbert, Christopher, *The Destruction of Lord Raglan: A Tragedy of the Crimean War, 1854–55*, Viking, 1984

Hichberger, J.W.M., *Images of the Army*, Manchester University Press, 1988

James, Lawrence, *Crimea*, Van Nostrad Reinhold, 1981

Kinglake, A.W., *The Invasion of the Crimea (9 Vols)*, Naval and Military Press (reprint of the original, William Blackwood and Sons, 1885)

Lummis, W.M and Wynn K.G., *Honour the Light Brigade*, J.B. Haywood, 1973

Mollo, John and Mollo, Boris, *Into the Valley of Death*, Windrow and Greene, 1991

Moyse-Bartlett, H., *Louis Edward Nolan*, Leo Cooper, 1971

Neville, Henry and Neville, Grey, *Letters Written from Turkey and the Crimea*, Kessinger Rare Reprints, 2008 (reprint of original private publication, 1870)

Nolan, Capt. L.E., *Cavalry: Its History and Tactics*, London, 1854

Ryan, George, *Our Heroes of the Crimea*, George Routledge 1855 (reprinted 2017)

Seacole, Mary, *Wonderful Adventures of Mrs Seacole in Many Lands*, OUP 1988 (originally J. Blackwood, 1857)

Seaton, Albert, *The Russian Army of the Crimea*, Osprey, 1973

Somerville, Alexander, *The Autobiography of a Working Man*, Macgibbon and Kee 1967 (reprint of 1848 original)

Stocqueler, J.H., *A Familiar History of the British Army*, Edward Stanford, 1871

The Robertson Court Martial, Photocopy of the 1862 original

Thomas, Donald, *Charge! Hurrah! Hurrah!* Routledge and Kegan Paul, 1974

Thomson, George Malcolm, *The Prime Ministers*, Secker and Warburg, 1980

Trow, M.J., *The Pocket Hercules*, Pen and Sword, 2006

Tylden, Major G., *Horses and Saddlery*, J. Allen & Co, 1965

Warner, Philip (ed), *The Fields of War*, John Murray, 1977

Warner, Philip, *The British Cavalry*, J.M. Dent and Sons, 1984

Weinreb, Ben and Hibbert, Christopher (eds), *The London Encyclopaedia*, Macmillan, 1983

Wilson, Harold, *A Prime Minister on Prime Ministers*, BCA, 1977

Woodham-Smith, Cecil, *The Reason Why*, Constable, 1957

Index